Reiki and Other Ways

Updated & Practical for the Aquarian Age

M000275870

by Kathleen Ann Milner

Healing Arts Series

Copyright
Unpublished manuscript TXu © July 2009
Copyright November 25, 2009
United States Library of Congress
All right reserved under Pan American
and International Copyright Conventions
Photo on front cover by Tim Sayer - www.sayerphotography.com
Artwork, *Angel,* on back cover by Kathleen Ann Milner - www.kathleenmilner.com

Chapter Outline

Release

Kathleen Milner is not a medical specialist capable of diagnosing or prescribing. She works with symptoms and healing energies. She is a channel of healing energy, which facilitates self-healing. She is neither responsible for, nor is she able to guarantee the form the healing may or may not take. <u>Reiki and Other Ways of Healing</u> is not a substitute for conventional medical treatment.

Foreword

After my divorce, I prayed to God that all of the abilities that I had as a young child be returned to me. It wasn't my parents' fault that they feared and suppressed the Gifts of the Spirit that their daughter was born with. Only later in life did I discover that both of my parents were incredible psychics. If it was difficult for me to grow up with Otherworld talents, how much more so it must have been for them. When I began writing my first book on metaphysics, my ex-husband expressed extreme displeasure in that his family name would be used for such purposes. So, I simply took my maiden name back. My parents and ex-husband are not the only ones who are apprehensive or misunderstand these abilities, even though the Bible states that there are Gifts of the Spirit; it is how they are used that is important. Because of my books, many, many people approach me looking for answers to unexplainable experiences. As this world moves into the Aquarian Age, more and more people will have such experiences.

Passage from the Piscean Age into the Aquarian Age is a physical reality that astronomers are able to observe. Time is cyclical and change is predictable. Great prophets, such as, Nostradamus, Edgar Cayce, and even Jesus in his original teachings, predicted that the Age of Aquarius will be a golden age. They and notable astronomer/astrologers from Egyptian, Mayan and Aztec cultures, and Native American Shaman also foresaw the time of disruption prior to December 21, 2012, which would precede this New Era or Golden Age of the Return of the Angels. For those who would rather stick to the Bible, it is noteworthy to remember that by definition the Magi mentioned in the New Testament had to have been astronomers as well as astrologers. We are about to find out that God's Love and His Creation is much more dynamic than has been taught. For example, The Creator is also Feminine, and The Goddess aspect is manifesting on Earth and uniting with The Masculine aspect. This alone changes everything! This is not the first time that the ending of one era and the beginning of another has brought impactful and far-reaching change.

Since my first book, I have learned a great deal regarding healing. This is due in part to my wonderful students, some of whom are mentioned herein, and the healing work that I have done with my own horses, which has been applicable to people who come to me for healing. In my quest for answers, Spirit unexpectedly revealed Truths to me during my journeys. Results of all this being that my own healing abilities and the healing potentials for Tera Mai have expanded exponentially. It has been well worth the effort, time, sacrifice and expense.

This book contains material from my first book, <u>Reiki & Other Rays of Touch Healing</u>, which has been re-edited, condensed, clarified, or expanded upon. There is also brand new material, offering further explanations, new healing techniques, and additional information. The book transformed to the point that a new title was required. <u>Reiki and Other Ways of Healing</u> offers help in understanding the Otherworlds of Spirit, and changes that the New Era will bring.

Introduction

The subject of Reiki and its roots has been a controversial subject for many years. Power struggles happen in every modality, and Reiki is not without exception. No stranger to controversy, Kathleen graciously took on some of the issues that were unclear and unproven, and dared to speak her truth. That is why I admire her so much. What has resulted from this open minded debate (on some parts), is a rich diversity of Reiki modalities, new symbols and techniques. Most importantly, a proven lineage for Reiki, is not as important as the proper attunement, which allows healing energy or Reiki from The Creator to flow through the heart and soul of the practitioner

After a Reiki attunement, the mind begins opening to clear thought. Reiki brings forth paradox and; therefore, opens our minds to question things we once thought were true. At the same time, Reiki reveals the subtle textures of the unseen or supernatural world. As a culture we have been trained to follow and accept what others say, especially regarding the spiritual realm. Reiki helps answer questions, which tend to unfold on our journey. All we have to do is keep an open mind and keep practicing Reiki.

When I first met Kathleen in 1992, I was surprised at her ease with Spirit and her knowledge of healing. In Reiki 1 and 2 classes, Kathleen's confidence in herself and the energy inspired me. I opened up! A lifelong intuitive, my abilities to see spirit increased and my intuition grew as well. I integrated what I learned from Kathleen with the sixth sense that came naturally to me.

Years later, when I reconnected with Kathleen again, I was surprised to learn that what I had been shown by the Reiki energies, Kathleen was writing about in her books. There was so much more information for me to access. As Kathleen's path grew, new combinations and potential for the healing also taught me. This completely blew me away. Inspired, that the energy that had evolved through my teacher had evolved me. My healing ability and intuitive sense grew as well. We are so blessed to have a Reiki teacher who is a real human, who struggles with spirit, battles the darkness, creates a strong base for us to step into as healers, and is constantly open to being taught the way. Then she shares what she has learned, which gives us an opportunity to do the same.

With Kathleen's support, my own Reiki practice has grown and thrived. Tera Mai has healed many of my clients; they report experiences that are truly inspiring. As you delve into the wisdom in this book, recognize that the energies of Tera Mai Reiki may open you up to embrace new techniques and knowledge. At this time more than any other, it's important to be connected to a path that is growing and responding to the needs of our earth and it's guardians. We all may participate in the revolution of light that is leading us out of the darkness.

Cathy Towle, Brooklyn, **New York**

Tera Mai Seichem Master, Mind Body Coach and Astrologer www.cathytowle.com

Wednesday Night Clearing / Healing Observations

You may read about this worldwide healing effort on pages 2, and 102

Six months ago I made the following wish... "I want to easily attract, recognize and begin working with the right spiritual teacher and mentor for me to learn from and actualize my own completion and fulfillment of my divine destiny." I sense at a deep level that I am on the right track.

Shirley Rosales, California

Another treatment that has become successful is your information about the treatment of the heart (page 64). A woman came to me with irregular heart activity. After that I have treated as you describe in the book, Reiki & Other Rays of Touch Healing, her heart now is good! When I am connected to the energy of the Golden Grids I feel peace and harmony, in meditation I see many beautiful colors.

Ratka Jovanovic´, Stockholm, Sweden

A lady from Canada on visit to India had a severe car accident with multiple head injuries. Admitted in ICU, she was operated for the same and put on life support with guarded prognosis. We did Hosanna Clearings (pages 129-31), as well as connected her with the Wednesday Night Clearing. The result – she is back in Canada well healed. Her relatives admit that she has been given a new life.

Dr. Naveen Mehra & Dr. Manupriya Mehra, India

During the Wed, July 22 clearing, I was joining in with all the other energy/light workers. I had been suffering with a severely torn shoulder rotator cuff for a very long time (5 years). In April, I was finally forced to have it surgically repaired, due to the chronic pain and weakness.

I was joining in with Kathleen to help heal the two women that she has been working on during the Wed. night clearing/healing sessions. During the evening, I had also asked the universe to help heal Mother Earth, as well as those who would do her harm. In addition, I had asked for enlightenment for those who would greatly benefit from it, and also the other things that Kathleen had suggested in her correspondence to Tera Mai Reiki healers throughout the world.

I was almost through when, almost as an afterthought, I placed my painful arm and shoulder straight out in front of me, as though I was placing it in a great glowing golden light. I asked for the pain to dissipate in order that I might be better able to exercise and thereby strengthen the shoulder. Miraculously, the pain immediately stopped!!! I have remained pain free since that time! My physical therapist had previously stated that she was sorry...but she feared that my surgery had not been as successful as she had hoped for. She did not think that I would be able to recover over 50% use of the arm and shoulder. But, now that I am pain free...I am able to exercise the shoulder and arm, and I have since regained approx. 90% of my muscle strength! I am certain that I will return to 100% soon!

I am a Tera Mai Reiki Master, Seichem Master, Cartouche Master. I have joyously facilitated the healing of countless numbers of individuals (as well as animals). I am not really accustomed to asking for energy work for myself. I did not consciously plan on doing so. It was just totally spontaneous!!! The whole experience was so powerful.....I felt an intense glowing "peace" as well as 'lightness.' I really cannot put the experience into words. I also felt a humble "awe", for lack of a better term.

Each and every time that I experience the overwhelming power of Tera Mai Reiki....it is just as amazing, and just as uplifting as the very first time I ever experienced it (many years ago). Thank you, Kathleen, for giving the gift of Tera Mai Reiki to me and to the rest of the world!

Diana Abernathy, Atlanta, Georgia

On the one-year anniversary of the Wednesday Night Clearings, we participated in the 3 nights of clearings on August 11, 12 and 13. I dedicated those clearings only for our dog, Kiki. After the clearing on August 12, Kiki received the third Sakara initiation. She was very quiet. On Thursday evening, I asked all of the Higher Beings to help her to pass over. For the whole day on Thursday, Kiki did not want to sleep. She knew she would pass over, and she did not want to leave us. At 20:00 hours on Thursday, we lit candles representing all of the Sakara's colors, and placed the orange candle next to the Buddha. All the candles burned very restless, I think it was because she was fighting to stay with us. Only the candle next to Buddha was very quiet. André gave Kiki Reiki, and I drummed to help her pass over. I had heard from the angels that Kiki's time to pass over would be Friday. Late Thursday evening, we were getting ready to go to bed, and it was the only time I did not asked if it was all right to extinguish the candles. But the candles did not allow me to extinguish them. We let them burn out. When the last candle next to the Buddha went out, Kiki passed over in a very quiet way. It was Friday, 00.40 hours.

Marion Valkenburgh and André Beukers, Holland

We regularly do the Wednesday night clearings every week. At the end of the clearing, we also send lost souls to the light (page 97). For two weeks in July, we were very sick, and my husband and I did not have the strength to do the clearings. On the third week, my whole family started to sleep really badly. We could not figure out why. One night, spirits, who were tugging on my pajama and rubbing my stomach, woke me up. My daughter also saw two spirits from the corner of her eye, and started to hear some noises, like something opening or falling down, but no one was around. We quickly figured out that they were spirits, who were anxious to be sent on, and were not happy with us for not doing the clearings for two weeks. They did not want to hurt us, just trying to get our attention. On Tuesday, we asked the spirits to be patient, and said that we would do the clearing the next day. Tuesday night, they left us alone, and we were able to finally get a good night's sleep. On Wednesday night, we did the clearings and everything since then is back to normal.

Mariola Bitner, California

I took Reiki Level 1 Tera-Mai ten years ago with Maria Rawlins in Dublin, Ireland. Previous to that experience, I had had a number of profound healings with her. I had developed a condition called Erythema Noduosum, which was followed by Post Viral Fatigue after the birth of our first son, Philip, that persisted for over a year. During the treatments with Maria, she gave me a gift of that Initiation. It is hard to find words to adequately describe the incredible experience. Ultimately, this initiation was a significant step in my realizing why I am on the Earth at this time. Over the last ten years, I received all the Tera-Mai Initiations mentioned in this book.

I have been a midwife and nurse, and worked in a management capacity in a Gynae Ward in a local hospital for many years. I now work full time healing and teaching Tera-Mai. It has totally awoken in me my full life purpose, which is to serve others. This healing system, Tera Mai, really works and is its major credit. Tera Mai also allows one awaken to who and all they are. Anyone may experience the remarkable energy of Tera Mai firsthand by participating in the Wednesday Night Clearings.

Kathleen Milner has worked tirelessly on behalf of Tera-Mai. She works without Ego. She meets each moment as first or last. She teaches clearly and well. Enjoy reading her book!

Eileen Heneghan, Tipperary, Ireland

The following email was sent out by Kathleen prior to the Wednesday, September 30 Wednesday Night Clearing: *As more Light comes to Earth, it is becoming increasingly easier to see clearly what is really behind people's actions and what they say. All secrets are rising to the surface. Thus, it is easy to fall into the trap of judging people. Whenever we judge anyone, we attract the same negativity to ourselves. We get caught in a downward spiral.*

It is OK to find the actions of someone deplorable. But to call someone deplorable is a judgment.

It is OK to feel compassion for someone; compassion comes from the heart. But to feel sorry for someone comes from the mind and it is judging the path that another has chosen.

If it feels right to you, at sometime during the 8:00 pm Wednesday Night Clearing / Healing, work on releasing your judgments about anyone. If even 1/3 of the 4-5 million people who are participating do this, the potential for spiritual growth and understanding will be great. Science has proven that whenever two people put their minds to prayer or to a task, the energy and potential go up exponentially. We have 4-5 million people!

Hej, Kathleen, I just would like to say thank you for this mail. It was so important what you wrote. As it is easier to really see people and what drives them, it is also so much easier to judge them. I find that in myself and it is not good, as you say, you get it right back. I really needed to hear this right now! It helps me to see everyone with compassion and not judgment. The healing energy during the 8:00 pm Wednesday Night Clearing was very strong and gentile at the same time.

Annika Winkler, Sweden

Advanced Healing for the Aquarian Age

When the song, <u>The Age of Aquarius</u>, became a hit, not many people took the lyrics seriously; in fact, many considered the lines airy-fairy, hippie rhetoric. Since then, prophecies regarding the end times have been fulfilled. What is ending is an age of pain, not Earth! The word, apocalypse, means to unveil; in this case it is mankind's amazing potential in relationship to The Creator. Only one prophecy is left to be fulfilled regarding the great spiritual aspect of the Aquarian Age, which is called the Golden Age of the Return of the Angels: When all of the men who fought in the Great War (World War I) are dead, the New Era will begin. Only three survive, two, Americans.

We have become dependant upon other people telling us what the Bible means, rather than reading for ourselves without preconception. They put their own spin to the words and miss the meaning of the great metaphors. They think that December 21, 2012 is either the destruction of Earth, or an abrupt shift in gears. Neither assumption is correct. We are working up to an enormous change where there will be a prevalence of scientific inventions and new forms of knowledge. New discoveries and new ways of thinking will clash with limited rigid thought. The lost art of intuition will and is beginning to resurface. All secrets and hidden agendas are in the process of becoming known. Shadows and illusions are being lifted. It is becoming easier to see people for who they are.

By definition, the three Magi mentioned in the New Testament had to have been astrologers and astronomers. Over twenty-five years ago, by using historical clues and references from the Bible, the University of Wisconsin-Milwaukee's Astronomy Department proved that our Gregorian calendar is wrong. By using computer technology, to determine where planets' positions were thousands of years ago, they concluded that the three Wise Men were following the king planet, Jupiter into Bethlehem. According to Christina Molina, an astrologer from Argentina, in the year 7BC, the Magi followed the Great Conjunction of Jupiter, Saturn, Sun, Moon and Venus in Pisces. The Great Conjunction appeared very early in the morning, preceding the sun, and illuminating the sky. The Magi were following the light of 'the star." 2,000 years ago, planets were called stars.

Thousands of years ago, the great Mayan astrologers/astronomers accurately forecasted the Galactic Alignment on the morning of December 21, 2012, when the sun will eclipse the center of our galaxy, or the Galactic Rift. This conjunction occurs once every 26,000 years. 26,000 years ago, the Ice Age ended, and humans began using fire. Cro-Magnum Man disappeared, replaced unexplainably by Neanderthal Man. No evidence exists that Cro-Magnum Man evolved into Neanderthal Man, who simply appeared and mankind took a giant leap forward. The Galactic Alignment always ushers in great change. We are about to make another quantum leap!

December 21, 2012 is the end of the Mayan great calendar. The Mayans knew it was the ending of an age, not the end of the world. Egyptian astrologers/astronomers also depicted the Galactic Alignment and the coming of a great age on the walls of their monuments. The Hindu religion has other words describing the exodus from the Dark Age (Kali Yuga) into the Golden Age (Satya Yuga). Hopi Indians foretold this event with a simply prophecy, "Embrace change or choke in your own fear." Prophesy Rock on the Hopi Reservation depicts a timeline, signifying mankind's existence on earth. At the time of the Galactic Alignment, there is a junction of two distinctly different possibilities. The first predicts a dead planet with a skeleton crew of sad survivors, culminating with the inevitable extinction of humanity. The second predicts happy people at one with nature. With the exception of a small minority of people, the Dark Age has treated Earth as a disposable planet. It would be considered insane for a man to destroy his survival system. That is what Earth is; Earth is our life support! Earth is every bit a part of God's Creation as we are. Disruption between the ages will cause people to re-evaluate and know what is really important.

Nostradamus, Edgar Cayce, and the original teachings of Jesus also state that we have options. That is, the transition into the Aquarian Age may be as difficult or as easy as we wish to make it. For many thousands of years, people have prayed to God that we who live now might make the best choices. Because of the vocal insistence of Ramona Kirk and several other Tera Mai initiates, in August 2008, a handful of Tera Mai healers from around the world began a weekly Wednesday night clearing. To connect with one another at 8:00 pm (20:00 hours), wherever we happened to be, we got into a meditative state and asked the Angels, "Please connect me to the Tera Mai healers who are doing the clearings." (This simple phrase has become the key to connecting to the group.) Then we were each free to work for as long as we wanted and do whatever we wanted – clearings or healings, prayers, meditate, Buddhist chants, holding the energy, etc. By the end of 2008, one million people participated. Science has proven that when two or more people put their minds to a task or pray, the energy and potential go up exponentially. By the summer of 2009, we were 4 - 5 million people. We are helping to steer Earth into the second Hopi alternative.

During the Wednesday Night Clearings, people received healings, insights, observed noticeable changes, and experienced the energy in tangible ways. By December 2008, the group effort was paying off; a new, higher energy began replacing the evil that was lifting off of Earth. This lighter, more joyful energy came in shifts that created cycles, it began to feel like there was more room, clearer and that it was easier to breathe. Many people felt uprooted, like their feet were not on the ground, or having the sense of being temporarily suspended because of Earth's change in directions. However, for those who were not clear and conscious, or who were not coming from their hearts, the new energy made them feel antsy or angry; their actions oftentimes appeared illogical. Lots of people began sensing an upcoming big change, which would land them somewhere new. No one seemed to know where or when that would be, just that it would occur soon. Cathy Towle, an astrologer from New York, stated in July, 2008, "The planets have been supporting full out change since December 2008, and almost every full and new moon since then have been pulling us slowly through our paces to make constant little changes, which are adding up to a big full out change."

Christina Molina provided additional interesting information that I have put into language for non-astrologers, which further helps to explain these times of disruption leading up to the Golden Age. In the early morning of February 14, 2009, Jupiter and Mars, both in Aquarius, aligned in the twelfth house, and the Moon was in the seventh house. Just like the song! Unbelievable but true, this identical alignment occurred on the same day and at the same time in 1962. Because the February 14, 1962 configuration of planets was aligned to the South Node, The Age of Aquarius was a hope, a possibility. The 2009 configuration of planets was aligned to the North Node, signifying the beginning of the physical manifestation of the New Age. In addition, on February 14, 2009, other powerful planets were in alignment to support the embodiment of The Golden Age.

On March 1, 2009, the planets again conspired to fulfill the prophecies. In particular, the conjunction of Jupiter and Uranus throughout this time stimulated a noticeable interest in policy and social change. We can observe this happening today. When Jupiter and Uranus return to conjunct one another in zero degrees of Aries on June 2010, a new cycle of 84 years will begin for humanity. People will be thirsty for the establishment of new rules for communal property. Dedication to defending the rights of humanity and freedom of thought will establish a new planetary conscience.

To fulfill this promise, the Golden Angels have been in the process of reclaiming Earth for God. They have built a golden grid around Earth, which may be experienced in prayer or meditation. Then on May 30, 2009, a dramatic worldwide shift occurred. Matteo Renzi described the event as, "God turned the page." God changed the channel. The energy and presence of The Goddess was re-established on Earth in combination with God The Father Almighty. It is interesting that in the Holy Kabballah, Malkhut, the Feminine Presence, is banished. Well, She's back now!

When something really big or important happens on Earth, there are corresponding signs in the sky. On May 30, 2009, a great configuration, an extremely rare "Cosmic Comet", was formed by the grand trine between Moon-Mars, and Venus-Pluto; and the little trine between Mars and Venus-Pluto-Chiron, and Neptune and Jupiter. The head of this "Cosmic Comet", Chiron-Neptune-Jupiter, is considered vastly beneficial, as it brings healing, spirituality, and God / Goddess protection. The aspects also emphasize the need for integration of unconscious feelings with conscious thoughts. If these two avenues for information and analysis are working together, they form a great combination and are very therapeutic. The integrated psyche is a powerful tool for intellectual and creative endeavors. Trines, and especially this trine, are a gift from Heaven for humanity. Many people do not realize or even want to see this; thus, not everyone takes advantage of the opportunities.

3

Edgar Cayce is referred to as The Sleeping Prophet. He died just before the end of WW II, and he is the greatest modern prophet. People sent him questions regarding loved ones, or about their own health. All he required was their name and address, and he would go into deep meditation for the answer. He would go so deep that his conscious mind would not remember what had been said; so, his secretary transcribed. Most of the healing suggestions that came through Edgar Cayce were simple and involved such things as changes in diet, various types of exercises, chiropractic adjustments and caster oil packs. Sometime after his death, a study was conducted to see how many people who Edgar Cayce did a reading on were cured. The study concluded that the only people who did not benefit were people who either did not follow the advice of Spirit, or people whose bodies were too close to death.

Edgar Cayce had other predictions as well; he predicted the collapse of the world stock and financial markets now. He also saw people walking into the New Age with whole, healthy, youthful bodies. Just as Cro-Magnum Man evolved mysteriously into Neanderthal Man, in the Golden Age the physical body is changing. That is, the condition of the physical body will be less dependent upon chronological age, and influenced more by the condition of the mental and emotional bodies. The condition of the astral body has always been dependent upon an individual's thoughts and emotions. The astral body, connected to the physical body by a silver cord, is a part of the soul, but it is not the entire soul.. During sleep, the astral body travels. This information is in all of the great mysticisms. When an individual dies, the silver cord is cut, and the astral body leaves the physical body for the last time, taking with it the unconscious and conscious minds, and life's experiences.

Just two weeks before my father died, I was involved in a conversation with him. His attention wandered a bit, and then I saw his astral body above his right shoulder. Because my Dad's was outside of his physical body while he was awake, I knew that he was already beginning to leave. I also knew that he had done a lot of work on himself because even though my Dad was in his eighties, his astral body looked as he did when he was in his late twenties or early thirties.

Before passing over, most individuals prepare for their time to leave on another level. If a healer were to try to do a healing on the aura, that healer would find that the aura either wasn't there or was acutely weakened. If a psychic were to look at the aura, there would be a disproportionate amount of color over the head, which would increase with each passing day. If one felt on other levels, it would feel as if the body lacked energy or presence. However, sometimes, an individual has a really good day, days before death. While my mother-in-law was dying of liver cancer, her bridge friends came to the hospital ward. She picked herself up and walked out the front door with them to have lunch a few days before her death. While she was having fun and saying goodbye to her friends, the nursing staff scoured the facility for her. People are also often given opportunities to make amends before their passing; afterwards, it is very difficult if not impossible to do so.

4

God puts us on a three-dimensional planet and it is our choice as to whether we become Angels or demons. There is something called "the glamour of evil," but it is more than an illusion, it is a lie. Lies have no weight, and as more Light comes to Earth, the truth about many things is coming to the surface; delusions are fading. People who have built up a lot of Karma throughout their lives have closed their hearts, which also closes them to remorse or compassion. Their heads become blocked to anything except what they want to hear or expect to know. Their astral bodies reflect all of this. Black magicians are marked with a black cross across the face on the etheric level. One arm of the cross goes across the eyes; the vertical arm may go down the middle of the face or off to one side. If through many lifetimes there is no change in consciousness, or desire to seek forgiveness and The Light, the astral body becomes blackened and featureless, or darkened and twisted. These perverted etheric forms or astral bodies are barely recognizable as formerly human. It is possible to recognize such individuals in or out of body by their eyes, which are dark and soulless. For dark, unconscious beings, who try to hang onto the Earth plane, it will seem more and more as if the Light is crushing them. In the Dark Age, conscious individuals experienced darkness and evil as crushing. This was expressed by a saying in every culture that went something like, 'the good die young'.

In the Bible it is written that 1/3 of the Angels and 1/3 of the stars fell. These stars may literally be star systems or planets, or possibly other dimensions. Because of The Light, by December 21, 2012, soulless individuals, enmities and the like will not be on Mother Earth, or in any of the dimensions around Earth. God's Universal Laws are being re-established on Earth. As December 21, 2012 fast approaches and the density of evil is leaving, it feels like there's more room. The new energy has a dazzling presence; sometimes, accompanied by heavenly aromas.

The veil between this world and the Otherworld of Spirit is becoming thinner. Claire Campbell sometimes watches ghost-hunting shows, which go to notoriously haunted places. Claire was very psychic before receiving any Tera Mai initiations, and she is particularly good at feeling things on other levels. She told me a story of how she was watching one such show when a man fell unconscious. While he was out cold, she felt a demonic entity enter his body. Later, he said that he wanted to kill someone when he became conscious. That entity is still with him. (If you go to the *Index,* you will find exorcisms for people and places.)

Earth's reality is becoming more akin to the next dimension, the Otherworlds of the Shaman. One way to become acquainted with the Otherworlds is through Shamanic journeywork, or meditation. You would be surprised at how many 'ordinary' people, who have never meditated and have no idea what Shamanic journeywork is, have had some kind of unexplainable or paranormal experience. Because of my books, people tell me things because they know that I will not laugh at them. They are also looking for an answer. One woman told me the story of how she had gone into her doctor's office after her surgery. During her appointment, the doctor simply disappeared.

5

Needless to say, she was perturbed. She said that when she went back to his office for her second appointment, she kept her eyes on him the entire time. He disappeared anyway. Even though this was years ago, the incidence still brought up memories of fear. She wanted to know what happened. My intuition told me that the doctor had passed on a number of years ago, and that he was not a threat to her. Spirit told me to tell her what happened, and with understanding her trepidation would go away. There is a way for an individual to disappear. In his mind's eye the doctor saw the cells in his body. Then he willed them all to make a 90-degree turn. In his mind's eye there was now space between the cells, and the edges of all of the cells were barely discernable. The doctor had the appropriate metaphysical abilities, so, his physical body became invisible.

The Golden Age is not the end of the journey; rather, it is the beginning. Aquarian lessons are learned through groups, and emphasis is on what is good for the group. Retaining an expression of individuality will be the tension point of the Aquarian Age. Tension points are necessary because they create energy with which to move forward; thus, things get accomplished. In the Dark Age, the dark was drawn to the Light and visa versa. As December 21, 2012 approaches, the Light and dark are separating; thus, polar opposites no longer attract one another. Relationships where one individual is 'good' and the other 'negative' produce highs and lows, like an addition cycle. They are breaking up. Aquarian relationships support one another and contribute to group consciousness.

All healing comes from God, and healing abilities are a Gift of the Spirit. They are one of the tools by which to achieve Enlightenment. Like the Golden Age, Gifts of the Spirit are not the end of the road, or the final achievement. The Bible speaks about Gifts of the Spirit; it is how they are used that is important. Jesus was not the first healer! The High Priest Melchizedek, who established a healing order of priests and priestesses, is mentioned several times in the Old Testament. In the New Testament, Jesus initiates a priest into the Order of Melchizedek. Furthermore, the Bible states that Jesus taught his disciples how to heal, sent them out to heal AND to teach others how to heal. The ancient art of hands-on healing was a vital part of Jesus' teachings. Nowhere in any Bible has any devil been credited for healing anyone! There have been other healers; some are called saints. When I was young, a nun told me that 'saint' meant "friend of God." Praying to a saint is not a form of worship; rather, it is opening the heart and asking for help from a great soul who has passed on.

Some saints, such as, Saint Rita, have interesting stories. Shortly after her birth in Italy, a swarm of white bees covered her. When Rita's father tried to shoo the bees away, they landed on him and he was healed. As she grew, she wanted to become a nun. Instead, her parents betrothed her to an evil man. Through her love, he was healed and changed his ways. Later, his former colleagues murdered him. Rita's two sons were on their way to avenge their father's death, but Rita prayed that they die rather than sin by perpetuating a bloody feud. Both sons died before stabbing anyone. Rita wanted to enter a convent, but the nuns at the convent in Cassia would not admit her. Not because she had prayed for her sons' deaths, but because she had been married. Frequently during her life, Rita had gone to the top of a narrow, tall mountain outside of Cassia, where she meditated upon a large stone. This time when she reached the top of the mountain, she was teleported to the gardens inside the locked gate and convent walls. The nuns saw her appear from nowhere and allowed her to stay. After her death, a swarm of black bees covered Rita's body.

In May 2008, Elisabetta Pizzi and I traveled through Umbria to Saint Rita's Mountain, which stands like the Eiffel Tower in a large valley surrounded by mountains. A paved path zigzags to the top, where the stone that Saint Rita stood on is enclosed within a wood and glass structure. Within the structure, chattering people, who were missing the spiritual experience, kept the energy low. We went outside and looked at the view. That's when I knew how Saint Rita had achieved her enlightenment. At the top there would have been no structure; all around her beckoned a great panorama, an expanse of space and nature. By stilling her mind, she focused on the space and through her heart she felt the joyful, invisible world of possibilities. Through the invisible world she made her own connection to God/Goddess. Mysticisms and some religions talk about entering what has been called The Great Silence. It is helpful to get into a beautiful place in nature where it is easy to get out of oneself, but this meditation may be done anywhere by stilling the mind. It is tremendously helpful to work with someone who has done it.

More chattering people came, so Elisabetta Pizzi and I sat off to the side on stone steps. While she held the energy, I lowered my voice and called in Spirit using the Native American 20 Count, which recognizes God's Holy Spirit in everything – plants, Angels, saints, all of God's creatures, etc. (It also clearly states in the Bible that God's Spirit is in everything.) During the process of calling in the energy, I did the clearings for Mother Earth and Tera Mai by energizing healing symbols. Whenever I did this, the sun came out; as soon as I was finished, the clouds again covered the entire sky. We had been working for nearly two hours and were nearly finished; it was lunchtime, and the people and noise left the mountain. Peace! Then a group, who had just finished praying the Stations of the Cross, arrived. They paused and then began praying again. It felt as if they were praying for the salvation of my soul, but I also knew that on some level they had agreed to be there that day to assist with the miracle that followed. Shortly after they gave up and left, I finished the invocation and thanked God and Goddess and all who had come in the love of Maria and Christ. Absolute silence! Five second later, the bell on the top of the hill began ringing. We didn't even know there was a bell. In that moment, Holy Spirit blessed Tera Mai; the healing energy and potentials for Tera Mai increased dramatically. When I stood up, my back, hips and legs, which had been re-injured in a car accident, were healing. There was no pain after having sat on a cold stone for two hours. This healing continued for many months afterwards.

In May 2009, Elisabetta and I went back to Saint Rita's Mountain. It was lunchtime and nobody was around. This time when I stood near the stone, the power of the mountain made itself known. For a brief time in the silence, I was able to feel what Saint Rita felt - the preeminence of the mountain combined with expansive space, and the power of The Creator. It was a glimpse of what we might all look forward to in the Aquarian Age. To get there, a lot of people need healing.

What I have begun to do in my workshops and before a healing session is to ask the workshop participants or healee if I may remove manmade attunements (page 158). To determine if manmade attunements are blocking the chakras and etheric channels, I douse the chakras (page 156 + 157). Then I call upon Thoth, an ancient healer who was elevated to god status by later Egyptians. He is like the saints and may be called upon to assist with healing and issues of Karma. I stretch my arms and hands above the healee. Before moving my hands down the aura I call upon Thoth and ask him to please release any Karma that has already been worked out.

Jesus mentions "the sins of the ancestors" in the New Testament, and states that they go back for seven generations. These are inappropriate contracts, which have allowed dark souls to temporarily avoid their Karma. So, I stretch my hands in front of me with the palms facing outwards. While I push my left hand to the left and my right hand to the right, I ask Thoth, "Please return the sins of the ancestors back to the original perpetrators with love so that all might work out their own Karma and learn their own lessons." I ask the Angels to fill in any voids with pink love. Most people strongly feel a great sense of relief with one or more of these clearings/healings.

Psychics who tune into the individual that they are reading on rather than going up to Spirit for the answer typically leave black webbing in the client's chakras. If the psychic is devious, s/he may even pull good energy and opportunities of a reading for him/herself, leaving nasty energy behind. Such unscrupulous readers subconsciously leave etheric vampire-like tentacles in their clients; thus, taking more energy. With the help of Saint Michael and other Angels, I cut and pull off the cords and send them to the central fire for transformation. Then clear the chakras by curling my fingers to make my hands look like claws and rake them though the aura above each chakra. If there is still 'stuff', I do the clearing, Thrice Around the Circle Bound (page 103-104).

Most individuals experience a sense of relief from one or more of these clearings. During healing sessions, I go on to do the emotional healing (page 60), and mental healing (page 58 & 59).

8

At the heart of these issues are inversions, denials, misconceptions, distortions and omissions, which are masked with humor, sophistication, compulsive behavior and overwork. Behind the mask, problems fester, causing disease, pain, fear, depression and anxiety. Many people are not able to release all mental and emotional issues in one session. When the individual has released as much as s/he is able to release, I proceed to areas where there are physical symptoms (check *Index)*.

In healing sessions, I ask that my personal energy be set aside and that only the healing energies of Tera Mai flow through me. I ask the Angels to remove any darkness by moving my hands through the aura. Shadows, which hide dark energies, are typically in the chakras, but may be anywhere. They hide dark stuff. I claw through the aura with my hands. Once sent to the central fire, it is easier what was behind the shadows. Once seen, it is easier to release and transform it.

In absentee healing, it is very helpful to heal the individual's timeline (page 104). Issues that go back to other lifetimes may simply come up for healing during a session, or the individual may benefit from a past life regression. During a past life regression, Stephen Bogdon saw that he was an exceptionally high-ranking army officer in the Pentagon reviewing navy personnel at Great Lakes. The thought crossed his mind, *perhaps Hitler was right.* His hatred of homosexuals in that lifetime drew him to incarnating as a homosexual in his present incarnation. There are cases of homosexual men being regressed, having a similar experience, and as a consequence either releasing AIDS or becoming heterosexual. Stephen's AIDS did not leave him; his Karma was much more involved.

In the Piscean Age we were drawn to things and people we loved, and to those we despised and judged. However, Alan Okan said he felt that he became a homosexual later in life so that by working exclusively with the feminine aspect he softened his harsh and abrasive masculinity. Louise Hay, who feels that she was a homosexual man in another lifetime, says that homosexual men who die from AIDS agreed before they were born to do this, and that at their deaths they take a lot of negativity off of this planet. Homosexuality is not a sin. In nature homosexual behavior is observed in overpopulated groups to reduce overpopulation. Prior to the 1900's people did not care who other people slept with. It is documented that Abraham Lincoln shared a bed with one of his guards when his wife, Mary, was gone. He may well have been doing that to keep warm. Nobody cared!

Oftentimes, homophobics are closet homosexuals. Through the news media some of the more publicly verbal ones have unintentionally come out of the closet. There are also homophobic individuals who have no idea that they are homosexual. For example, Julie often complained that Mary was a lesbian and made public passes at her. Julie was the only one who saw this in Mary! What Julie saw in Mary was not Mary's sexual preference, but her own. Mary, who was totally into guys, was only serving as mirror that Julie might see who she was. Julie was utterly and completely in denial of who she was. Julie was a Mormon and there are no homosexuals in the Mormon Church!

Getting past denials is the first step, but that is often not easy to do. For example, while on Alan Okan's Mexican tour, a man asked me if I would help him do a past life regression. I just had seen him with my physical eyes walking up the grotto pool stairs, as he was in another lifetime, a masculine Roman soldier in full regalia. During the regression, it wasn't surprising that he ended up in Rome. He so repudiated his masculine nature that he could not see or feel his true nature in that lifetime. He wanted to believe that he had always been a homosexual male. He kept talking about his male Roman male lover; I kept seeing and hearing his own frustrated maleness trying to get through, yelling, "Female lover, not male!" As all past lives are experienced through the present brain, his experience could not get past his denials. While guiding a past life regression, I see what the individual sees, but without the filter. It is not helpful to dismiss anyone's experience. Guidance may or may not help people to get to the Truth. When he came out of trance, he told me that he had also had a Mayan astrology reading that day. In Mayan astrology, we do not have one sign, but five. One in the center, one to our left (feminine side), one to our right (masculine side), one in front (where we are going) and one in back (where we have been). He told me that Ken Johnson had told him that he had a strong male presence in back of him. In order to go forward, he needed to address his masculine past, and the issues from his male Roman incarnation. A good guess might be that one of those issues was either homophobia or the rape of captured civilians.

Recognizing our dark side involves more than paying lip service, and does not sit well. The following is based upon the work of Dr. Norberto R. Keppe, president of the International Society of Analytical Trilogy, and the author of Liberation. The numbers are part of sacred geometry and might be referred to as God's Telephone Number. The system of tap touch points on the human body is called the Gems of Excellence, which was channeled and designed by Dorothy Espiau. Charlotte Liss and Sean Grealy designed the formula below for the purpose of recognizing and integrating our shadow side so that we can accept and love ourselves for being human. If we cannot accept our negative manifestations, then we cannot accept our Light. Not accepting makes us contract our love and our life; it's what makes our bodies sick. We cannot push our "kill" away and hope that it disappears. If we push away our shadow, we push away our Light. By repressing one side, we repress the other. This results in either working out Luciferian pacts of destruction in the world, or self-destruction, which manifests as pain, disease and/or unfulfilled and unhappy lives.

To reclaim our Oneness and integrate power and love to form beauty and harmony: Cone the fingers of your right hand and continuously circle clockwise *(which will seem counterclockwise to you)* over your chest *(big circles)* and say, "8-7-3-1-2-9-5-7 to integrate the Hitler in me. 8-7-3-1-2-9-5-7 to dissipate the murder, denial, omissions, inversions, distortions and misconceptions in me. 8-7-3-1-2-9-5-7 to integrate this Truth at the deepest neurological and cellular level so that it will be 100% effective and in Divine Order for this body's highest good. 8-7-3-1-2-9-5-7 for all anchors, locks and seals (poke your left shoulder with your coned fingers). 8-7-3-1-2-9-5-7 for print and save (slash your left shoulder down to your armpit with your coned fingers)."

For those who are working out their Luciferian pacts in the world, begin by saying: "8-7-3-1-2-9-5-7 to integrate the Mary in me. 8-7-3-1-2-9-5-7 to integrate compassion and love within me." Power without love is what we call evil run rampant; love without power is what we call Mr. Milktoast. The integration of love and power to form beauty and harmony is 'strength' in the Tarot. In the Bible this is stated as, "and the lion shall lie down with the lamb. . and peace shall reign over all the earth."

3,000 years ago, the Mayans grasped the workings and the mind of the cosmos. They were far advanced beyond comparable European cultures of the day. Mayans were adept astrologers and astronomers, who perfectly understood where humanity is coming from and where we are going. When the Spanish landed, the great Mayan cultural centers, schools and cities had been left abandoned two to three hundred years earlier. At the same time, the Anasazi of the southwestern United States and Angkor Wat of Cambodia also disappeared. Spanish soldiers never witnessed a ball game. When they saw the relief on the ball court walls of the team's captain being decapitated, they assumed that it had to be the captain of the losing team. In fact, it was just the opposite. Captains of winning teams were allowed to die at their highest moment of achievement and glory for their benefit and the benefit of all society. Spanish soldiers burned thousands of Mayan texts and books to obliterate the Truth and rewrite history in order to vindicate their horrific acts of murder, theft and oppression. All done in the name of God!

Hitler used the Bible to justify genocide. Jews use scripture to justify their actions; others strap on the nitrate, blowing up the innocent in the name of God. Nostradamus, an accomplished astrologer, predicted that the 20th century would be the most horrific. He will find no arguments here.

Mayan spiritualism is understandable outside of western mental constructs. To be Mayan is not a color of skin; it is a state of consciousness. To the Mayans, knowledge belongs only to the memory of God and their name for God was Hunab K'u. We are held in the memory of Kunaku. We are God because we have memory. To go within, to meditate in silence, is to go into God Consciousness. The more understanding we have the closer we are to God. We become like Buddha or Christ.

Nature was the Mayan's teacher; trees were teachers and protectors. Mayans understood that we are a reflection of the cosmos. Hall describes the body's relationship to the cosmos in The Occult Anatomy of Man. Quantum physics recognizes our holographic universe and that we are all in dynamic relationship.

Mayan day keepers, like Hunbatz Men, who wrote Secrets of Mayan Science/Religion, are revealing long-kept-hidden secrets to help humanity's evolvement into the Golden Age. In the Mayan religion, the sun and its life force was the physical manifestation of Divine Light. Eagle represents the sun during the day; jaguar the hidden sun at night. Carvings in the Mayan temples of the eagle and jaguar holding human hearts do not represent two warrior factions. Rather love is a mandatory precursor to high spiritual work. The heart is the fulcrum between what we refer to as the lower emotions and the upper emotions. The third eye is the center for Buddha or Christ Consciousness. Love from the heart stimulates the brain and opens the third eye. The heart is the gateway to higher psychic development. Because there is some brain matter in the heart, there is also a physical relationship between the brain and the heart. Without heart love energy, evolvement of higher faculties is unattainable.

To the Mayans, to be Quetzalcoatl or Kukulcan, the feathered serpent, is to be initiated with spiritual knowledge and empowerment, and to be able to manifest through these faculties. In other words, make the invisible visible. The true initiate balances between the heavens and the earth and has a perfect understanding of energy. To the Mayans, the beautiful Quetzal birds perfectly represented these spiritual concepts. The male's brilliant ruby-red breast and long emerald-green tail feathers are a sight to behold. In flight, with his undulating tail, he looks like a flying snake. Snake was closest to earth, bird nearest to the sun. Thus, Quetzals physically represented the knowledge, integration and mastery of the Laws of heaven and earth. Mayans also knew that energy, as well as the cosmos, moves in a wavelike motion, like the undulating, crawling snake and the Quetzal in flight. Temple reliefs depicting the image of the initiate's head inside the mouth of the snake represents transformation, like the snake shedding its skin, like the initiate's own transformation.

Gifts of the Spirit come from God. When the initiate uses them consciously, the initiate and the world moves forward. Some unconscious individuals were endowed with metaphysical or other gifts in the hope or understanding that they might use them to work off their own Karma and make the world a little better place. Some have done just that. As the Light separates from the dark, for those who have remained unconscious, these gifts are being pulled away as well. The separation of the Light from the Dark has unimaginable, far-reaching consequences. In the Golden Age, Edgar Cayce saw a reversal in the haves and have-nots. This will be interesting!

12

What is Reiki?

Stories about Dr. Usui begin predictably. One hundred years ago, Mikao Usui sought knowledge of enlightenment. Most of what we know about Usui comes from a few western books. Books on Usui usually tell of how he was a Christian who turned to Eastern teachings when he was unable to discover in Christian doctrines and texts how Jesus performed his healings and miracles. They say that at one point he went so far as to earn a doctorate of theology at the University of Chicago, which is why he is commonly called Dr. Usui. There is a problem! A rather big problem! The University of Chicago has neither record of his graduation nor of his ever attending the school.

I was born with psychic and healing abilities in a time and a place where these Gifts of the Spirit were not seen as gifts. After my divorce, I asked God to reconnect me to the abilities that I had put aside so long ago. God heard my prayer and slowly my awareness of those things outside of this world trickled into my consciousness and healings began to happen. After taking a meditation class, my perceptions and healing abilities took a big step forward. When I heard about the story of Reiki and the discrepancies within the story, I was impelled to ask God for the Truth. That question brought about another journey. I have studied with diverse spiritual teachers and Shaman in a variety of workshops, seminars and spiritually guided tours held in a wide range of locations, from posh hotels in New York City to the jungles of the Yucatan. From my search for self-healing and discovery, what follows herein is what I personally feel to be true about Reiki, healing and Mikao Usui:

What has also been taught about Mikao Usui is that his journey lasted a lifetime. Unable to find knowledge of healing in translations of the Sutras, Master Buddha's teachings, he sought out the original version, hoping to find the wisdom of healing and the means of empowerment. Earth was held bound with dark, heavy energy. Thus, Universal concepts were not spelled out in detail anywhere for anyone to see, learn and misuse. Ancient doctrines and truths masked in rich Sanskrit verse waited for the right time and the pure of heart to decipher spiritual codes.

Mikao Usui was a Buddhist monk. In order to read Buddha's Sutras, Usui's search led him to India, Mongolia and Tibet where he mastered Sanskrit and studied with the Tibetan monks. Afterwards, he spent considerable time reading these venerable manuscripts. Sacred law was revealed to him in much the same way as when we read the Bible and suddenly find ourselves in an expanded state of mind. Truth of this kind comes in not through the brain, but through the solar plexus. It is like a gut feeling but goes beyond; a knowing that encompasses many aspects at the same time. In the same way, Universal mysteries vibrated through Usui's solar plexus or gut. He remembered - in another lifetime, he had been one of the Tibetan masters.

13

Mikao Usui found his answers. However, wisdom without the power to implement it is like trying to catch water with a sieve. You know you have something, but you can never get hold of it. In order to be able to manifest healing, transformation and manifestation, and bring back a way in which he could transfer healing ability or initiate others, he had to go through a consciousness-raising experience. Merely meditating would not bring healing initiations into form!

A consciousness-raising experience entails considerably more than most people would imagine. In order to grasp this concept; let us look to Egypt. Whenever a pyramid is opened and archaeologists go into the Pharaoh's ornate burial chamber, they always find two things: First, the pharaoh is buried in another part of the pyramid. Second, there are air holes in the sarcophagus. Air holes are the last thing a society intent on preserving its dead would drill into coffins. The King's Chamber in the Great Pyramid is not a tomb; the empty coffin is actually an initiation chamber . . . an initiation chamber with multiple covers or lids, allowing precious little air in and absolutely no circulation. A chamber where the aspiring initiate would lie in a high state of sustained meditation for three days; a state of meditation so deep that very little oxygen was required to sustain life. The successful initiate was rewarded with the ultimate prize; s/he retrieved psychic knowledge as well as the power to perform advanced metaphysical tasks and healing abilities.

Mayan funerary pyramids are oftentimes initiation chambers. While the King's Chamber in Egypt's Great Pyramid at Cheops is 2/3 of the way up, the initiation room at Palenque is below the ground level of the pyramid (there are pyramids, which have a mirror image of a pyramid constructed directly underneath them). At Palenque, the chamber (after the priests helped the initiate achieve a deep trance state) was covered with a large, inscribed stone, which is still there for visitors to see. As in Egypt, once the process had begun, there was no turning back.

Maintaining a high state of meditation in a confined, sealed chamber for 72 hours was not embarked upon haphazardly. With no possibility of escape, lids were raised only after the allotted time period. Prospective initiates would prepare themselves for years for the 72-hour initiation. They studied, practiced meditation and went through many minor initiations. One minor initiation involved swimming the crocodile-infested Nile River to reach an underwater entrance to a temple on the opposite bank. Fear resonates like a dinner bell. One of my students had a past-life recall of going through a similar initiation, making it to the other side, only to find that a jealous fellow student refused to open the door. Too exhausted to swim back, the once-hopeful initiate drowned.

Even if the aspiring initiate had the emotional, mental and physical skills to make it through minor initiations, there was no guarantee of surviving the initiation in the King's Chamber. Another of

14

my students came to the realization in a past-life regression that she had unsuccessfully attempted the initiation in the King's Chamber. At the time, she knew instinctively that she was not yet ready. However, rather than listening to her own inner knowing, she went ahead anyway and died as a consequence. One of her lessons in this lifetime has been to learn to listen to her intuition.

In Egypt, the royalty and elite, and religious, state and secular leaders had access to metaphysical schools of initiation and instruction. It was not only considered an honor to be able to go through these schools, but it was expected of the Pharaoh and those in line of succession. Egyptians always used their left-brain library knowledge as well as their right-brain intuition in all highly involved tasks, be it engineering, embalming, leadership, etc. Egyptian culture understood that the physician performed surgery or the Pharaoh ruled by developing all higher mental skills.

In the story of Moses in the Old Testament, we read that the Pharaoh's oldest daughter, who was without child, found Moses as a baby and raised him as her own. The Pharaoh's oldest son always married the Pharaoh's oldest daughter. This singular fact places Moses in line to the throne of Egypt, which means that Moses would have had to have gone through all of the initiations and learned all of the metaphysical teachings available in Egypt. After Moses led the Hebrews out of Egypt, his name was erased from all of the stones, monuments and documents. Thus, we do not know whether or not he was actually Pharaoh. In the Bible, we also find testimony to the fact that Moses was an accomplished metaphysician. The story of Moses and the Amman high priests transforming sticks into snakes is not a story of mass hypnosis. Rather it is a tale of dueling alchemists. They literally altered the vibration and changed the mass from stick to snake. The jurisdiction of all alchemists (and master healers) is mastery and connectedness to all four elements - earth, air, fire and water. Moses manifested his intent and parted the Red Sea by being in touch with the changing forces of nature and his knowledge of the four elements.

Moses taught the Hebrews, who had been "chosen" to learn sacred mysticism and to keep the ancient lore of Mother-Father God, the secrets of Egypt. Afterwards, the Hebrews transformed from a simple nomadic culture to a viable force in the Middle East. The Book of Genesis contains variations of Egyptian stories, which are variations of Sumerian stories. Was the message within the burning bush to rewrite Egyptian stories using metaphors that would be familiar to the Hebrews? Did Moses return with white hair because he had been gone for a long time, visiting India, Mongolia and Tibet in order to extend his mystical learning and understanding? When he returned to the Hebrews he discovered that many of them were abusing the Universal energy in their own way, just as the Egyptians and Atlantians had done previously. It is our birthright to be co-creators of the Universe. When we don't respect our gifts and the rest of Creation, they are taken away. We are sent back to learn the basics. Once again in human history, the "Law had been defiled." It was then that the mystical secrets were handed down orally through a Jewish sect called the Essenes. It is no coincidence that Mary, Joseph, Jesus, John the Baptist and Lazarus were all Essenes. Jesus was called the Nazarene because that was the sect within the Essenes to which he belonged.

Lazarus was the last known man on earth to go through the three-day initiation of sustained high meditation described earlier. Lazarus' sisters had sent for Jesus so that he might bring their brother back from "the land of the dead." Yet, when Jesus arrived, he was told that he was too late, "Lazarus is dead." Lazarus had been unable to break the state of suspended animation by himself and his physical body perished. Jesus then performed his second greatest miracle.

Looking again at the Bible, we are told that at Jesus' birth the Magi, who by definition were wealthy magicians, astronomers and astrologers, had been following a star. Utilizing historical clues from the Bible itself, the University of Wisconsin's Astronomy Department speculates in a program they put on at Christmastime, that Jesus was born 13 years earlier than 1 AD (we entered the year 2,000 in the year 1987) and that the Magi were following the king planet, Jupiter. Upon the Magi entering Bethlehem, the constellation of the Virgin hung over the city. These three Magi then gave Mary and Joseph, a skilled carpenter, expensive gifts of gold, frankincense and myrrh. Jesus, the Greek translation for the Hebrew name, Joshua (God is salvation), was born in a humble stable in Bethlehem so that the prophecies might be fulfilled. The Bible prophecy, "and David will walk among you in the city of Bethlehem," predicts that "the Savior" will be a reincarnation of King David.

Jesus and his family were not poor. In his day, Saint Francis' poverty was a discomforting embarrassment to the pope and Catholic hierarchy, who lived high on the hog by selling indulgences and church offices. They engaged in other crimes as well. For example, Gregory VII reinvented history through his school of forgers. Sixtus IV, who sanctioned the Inquisition, licensed the brothels of Rome, bringing him a yearly income of 30,000 ducats. Leo X invented offices and then auctioned them off. In stark contrast to Saint Francis' goodness and poverty, they felt he called attention to their promiscuity and opulent lifestyles. In fact, the Pope came close to burning Francis as a heretic. It was after Saint Francis' death that the church promoted poverty, having discovered that asking the masses to emulate Jesus' poverty made it easier for them to secure donations from the faithful.

To protect their son from Herod, Jesus' parents used their wealth to flee into Egypt, where their son was educated. Did Jesus receive instruction and initiations in the Egyptian temples? As a young man, it may well be that he studied in India, Mongolia and Tibet. India's legend of Saint Isa is the story of Jesus, who was called back to Jerusalem at the age of 30 when his father died.

16

Beginning in the third century after Constantine conquered Rome and incorporated the church into the state, Ignorant Romans altered Jesus' true teachings. In 553 AD, the Roman church-state took out all references to reincarnation in the New Testament because they found out that they could not control a population who believed in it. However, there are passages they missed. For example, Jesus said that one of the Caesars had been Caesar twice. Yet, there was never an overthrow of a Caesar and a subsequent climb back to power. Jesus' disciples asked him if he was Elijah. Rather than reprimanding them for believing in reincarnation, Jesus responded by saying that John the Baptist had been Elijah. Rome desired that the masses look to and pay the Church for salvation. (Reincarnation: The Phoenix Fire Mystery, compiled and edited by Joseph Head and S. L. Cranston) Balloting, by one vote, Rome made Jesus divine. A stroke of genius! With the stroke of a pen Jesus was made more than he ever claimed to be; that is, the only Son of God. Jesus ascended to a pedestal for our admiration, never our emulation. "The Messiah" means "the chosen one" not "the only one." The one chosen one was to lead the people into spiritual awareness.

Ways and means of developing psychically are found within Jesus' original teachings. The original manuscripts (there are over 50) are currently locked away in a chapel in the Vatican. Jesus' teachings were still available in the 3rd century when Saint Patrick brought the knowledge and ability to heal to Ireland. Men and women referred to as saints (friends of God) by the Church demonstrated psychic and healing skills. While they lived, most of them were a discomfort to the Church, and were uplifted to unearthly status only after their deaths. Again, the masses would never think that they, too, could possibly strive for out-of the-ordinary accomplishments and extraordinary abilities. According to the Church, one would have to be an egomaniac to think such thoughts.

The Holy Inquisition, ordered and prolonged by the popes, silenced women who, like Joan of Arc, worked with Spirit, herbs and the feminine aspect of God. The other victims were the Essenes; those who carried on the mysticism handed down by Moses and later added onto by Jesus. During this period, 9,000,000 European women met their deaths (many historians actually believe that this number is too low). A woman's holocaust, around which developed a whole economic structure prospered. It took only one accusation by one individual to set off a whole chain of events. People were paid to find and get the witch; others were paid to hold her in captivity and torture her. Lawyers and judges had to be paid, and those who murdered her were also paid. The defendants had no defense. Their accuser was never revealed, and the accused was not informed of what it was that they were accused of. The guilty were either burned alive at the stake, tortured to death, or drowned. To pay for all this and to add to the coffers of those in power, the witch's property and that of her relatives was seized. To escape the Holy Inquisition and to protect their families, to this day in Europe, there are stories of the gathering of hundreds upon hundreds of women. "Holding hands, in a refusal of betrayal, chanting to the Mother Goddess, chose their deaths in the sea." (Christy Moore, Burning Times) "In this age of evil," while it was not unheard of to burn children and even whole towns, the majority of the remaining people burned were Essene mystics.

Under heavy Catholic control, the burning laws were not even taken off the books in Ireland until the 1940's. Witch trials began in Massachusetts, but with the need for women in the wilderness, and with other colonies, like Virginia, outlawing the practice, the witch trials halted. The United States Bill of Rights insured individual freedom and the right to a fair trial in the New World. The separation of church and state guaranteed that a church would not control American politics the way it had in Europe, where popes literally dethroned or controlled monarchs. The Three Musketeers and In the Name of the Rose only scratch the surface of Church political and social interference (Peter de Rosa, Vicars of Christ: The Dark Side of the Papacy). The founding fathers never intended to take God out of the state; rather they sought to protect citizens from extreme religious fanaticism.

The point is that one hundred years ago, the only ancient documents on healing and spiritualism left unaltered and available were Buddha's Sutras. After studying the same passages Jesus had read 1,900 years earlier, Usui realized that he, too, had to attain a high-altered state of consciousness in order to be empowered with healing energy. He was then guided to return to Japan where he climbed to the top of one of the mountains. The mountains in Japan are sacred. There he meditated and fasted for 21 days, at the end of which time, he was literally struck by a bolt of lightning. In his own unconsciousness, he became conscious to the healing rays from Mother-Father God that he had searched for.

Upon awakening, he found healing vibrations strongly emanating from his hands. He also knew how to, and was capable of transferring elemental healing energies of earth, air, fire and water through a series of initiations. These were the same types of initiations that Jesus gave to his disciples. It was in this manner that Jesus transformed illiterate fishermen (the only educated apostles were Mark, a tax collector, and Luke, a physician) into master healers and knowledgeable metaphysicians in a relatively brief period of time. Jesus instructed the Apostles to heal and to teach others how to heal as well. Trials and tribulations endured in ancient Egypt initiations were no longer necessary. Jesus, the Shower of Ways, provided a means for anyone to tap into God Consciousness, and a way ultimately to end the last enemy, death.

Mikao Usui then began his healing mission and he initiated other men into the elemental healing rays. They were called Reiki (energy) Masters. They had control over the elemental forces of earth, air, fire and water of which we ourselves are composed. It is the nature of the hologram that

18

all parts are in relationship to all other parts. The forces that combine and bind the energy of the four elements provide a theme in variation in our holographic universe. One simple example of the inter-relationship between the elements is that earth and air both have the ability to hold water, but in different forms. Elements are multidimensional in that they exist on this planet, other planets and other planes of existence. Space probes are finding water on other planets, and where there is water, there is possibility of life. Within each one of the elements is a ray of healing. Japanese Reiki Masters, and masters of the Chi (or Qi), were capable of performing miracles because they were able to work on all aspects of the physical human body and subtle bodies with these four elemental forces. Misqualified energy had nowhere to run, so to speak.

Hawayo Takata's story is that in the 1930's she heard of healing miracles of the Reiki Masters. She was a Japanese-American woman living in Hawaii and dying of cancer. She went to Japan, was healed of her disease and then relentlessly begged them to initiate her and teach her Reiki. Dr. Chujiro Hayashi at last obliged. After World War II, Takata practiced healing in the United States and taught others how to heal under the banner of Alliance Reiki. The price tag for Reiki Mastership was $10,000. The problem is that none of Takata's 22 Reiki Masters were able to do the same miracles that she did. There is a documented, witnessed account of Takata raising the dead (Hawayo Takata's Story by Helen J. Haberly). Every now and again, there have been sudden and dramatic healings, but not with any kind of regularity or consistency, or by a significant percentage of Reiki initiates. All of the Reiki Masters know this; all of them know that something was left out. Could Dr. Chujiro have left out initiation procedures because Takata was not a man? Was she was not told everything because in the old Oriental tradition, the master withheld key knowledge from his students until just prior to his death? On his deathbed the master would reveal what he had withheld in life to his best student. Hopefully, the master was lucid.

Later, after I began to reinitiate Reiki Masters from many of these 22 lineages, I discovered that in some cases there were subtle differences in what Takata had taught each of them. (The three original Alliance Reiki initiations had never been standardized.) In her defense, Takata was only following in the tradition of her Eastern teachers, giving more to one student than to another. She just didn't think that they had done it to her.

Like the Japanese men, Takata charged for her services. Others who have received Gifts of the Spirit are rewarded for their time, proficiency and efforts. For example, musical talents are also a gift, yet Yo-Yo Ma does not leave the concert hall unpaid. Some kind of energy exchange on the part of the healee is required; something for nothing does not exist. If something is offered free on a silver platter, look again, it's probably tin. On the other hand, and equally important, healing work or anything that is done foremost for monetary reasons is destined to failure. As Sai Baba says, "Work for the love of God and leave the fruits of your labor to Him." Julia Cameron, author of The Artist's Way, says, "artists supply the quantity, God supplies the quality." Thus, when labor comes from our hearts and our desire to attain higher consciousness, we are rewarded with money, success and all other earthly pleasures. Buddha says, "There is no way to happiness. Happiness is the way."

In order to retrieve the complete wisdom and empowerment of all of the elemental rays, we cannot return to Japan and learn from the Reiki Masters that Mikao Usui initiated. Why? Because Japanese in Japan learned Reiki from Westerners, who trace their lineage back to Takata. Why? Because traditional Japanese people find Dr. Usui's story difficult to believe for cultural reasons! First, there is the matter of the large, newly discovered, modern tombstone dedicated to Dr. Usui. Land is so expensive in Japan that it can cost a half-million dollars to simply widen a driveway a few feet. Only the exorbitantly rich are able to afford to be buried rather than cremated. What monk is this incredibly wealthy? Secondly, religion and spiritualism are eclectic and openly discussed in Japan. New ideas that work are incorporated into the body of religious knowledge. In Japan Buddhism and Shintoism are nearly identical in their practice. If the many stories of healing miracles attributed to Dr. Usui were true, Reiki would have been incorporated into religious life and Dr. Usui would have become legendary. There would be many stories told about the healings Dr. Usui and his masters facilitated and of Dr. Usui himself. There are none! Thirdly, the University of Chicago is not the only institution that has absolutely no records of Dr. Usui's attendance. The Kamura Temple has no record of Usui's membership or association. And fourthly, no Buddhist monk who practiced Shintoism would name a healing system (Usui Reiki) after himself. However, the whole term "Usui Reiki" is controversial because Takata called the Reiki she taught "Alliance Reiki."

What is the answer? Did Takata receive a minor initiation that originated with a simple monk called Usui? Did this cause her to discover her own innate healing abilities? Did she elaborate on the initiations that she had received rather than asking God for a consciousness-raising experience to find the answer? Did Takata make up the story of a Buddhist monk, who had been converted to Christianity, knowing that the world she lived in would never accept the knowledge and capabilities of the ancient art of hands-on healing from either a Buddhist or a woman?

All of the participants to this story are dead. Some say that there are nameless, unavailable old people in Japan, whom Dr. Usui supposedly initiated. Verification is thus impossible, What is known is that if a Japanese healer were facilitating the same kinds of healing miracles that even Takata was able to do, it would not be kept a secret for long in Japan! One option to finding the truth is to discover where real healings are occurring regularly and consistently.

The Reluctant Reiki Master

Totally unaware of the Reiki drama, I became initiated into Reiki I and II in 1983, after watching a Reiki demonstration for several reasons. First, emotions had been in my paintings and drawings from the time I was a little girl. I wondered if the initiations would add healing qualities to my artwork. Secondly, I was hoping that it would help me to understand the extraordinary psychic and healing experiences I had had as a young girl and woman. When I was young, the fact that I could pray for someone and changes would occur overnight, or that on occasion, dramatic changes occurred while I spoke to someone frightened me. Never prayed for myself because at a very young age a nun said that that praying for oneself was selfish. However, she also impressed upon us to ask that God's Will be done when we did pray. Thirdly, besides the power of prayer, as a young child I watched with my inner eye as the Angels worked, working as a Shaman without understanding what was happening. Helen Borth taught me how to heal with my hands. She also impressed upon her students that we were channels and not responsible for another person's healing or lack thereof.

Books on healing in the 18th and early 19th century, warn that healers ran the danger of contracting the disease and pain of the healee. The healer also tended to give away his/her own energy. For example, in the movie, <u>Resurrection</u>, which is based on the life of a healer, Ellen Burstyn gets into the hospital bed of a woman with spasmodic seizures. While medical professionals watch, the sick woman slowly stops her jerky, uncontrollable movements and Ellen slowly takes on the woman's disease. After a week, the healer recovers. However, if there is a Universal connection to the elemental healing rays from Source (God/Goddess) either through a Gift of the Spirit at birth or a Universal initiation into healing, these worries do not apply.

After the first two Reiki initiations, it would have been nice to complete the course. However, with a price tag of $10,000 for the third initiation or Reiki Mastership, and the fact that I wasn't channeling any more healing energy that before I had started Reiki, I put aside the idea of becoming a Reiki Master forever. Forever proved a short time in coming. In 1988 after two automobile accidents, I was left at a standstill with my artwork and my life. Wright Gallery in Chicago represented me and was selling my artwork; but after the accidents, I was left frustrated and closed down with a concussion, brain trauma and severe muscle spasms. While my doctor went so far as to prescribe massage therapy, stretch exercises and even Rolfing, I remained in acute pain. Sometimes it literally took me an hour to get out of bed in the morning.

In the summer of 1989, a brochure from a New Age retreat, The Haven, in Walkerville, Michigan offered Reiki Mastership as one of the workshops, not for $10,000 but for the reasonable cost for a weekend class. I had an irrefutable inner knowing, a sensation that comes from a Divine Connection, that I had to go. I told several friends, who were Reiki practitioners, about it. Because the class was offered over Thanksgiving weekend, none of them could get away. After making holiday arrangements for my two children to spend Thanksgiving with their father, my ex-husband, I went alone. Once there, I made some friends, had a good time and walked in the woods of this once Girl Scout camp. It was one of those beautiful places in nature willed and entrusted to an organization that supposedly would preserve the wilderness forever and later sold. After being initiated into the third level of Reiki, we were taught how to do the initiations, and we all began a cleansing cycle. That was it, and I kept my secret to myself.

One day, it occurred to me that I had missed Thanksgiving with my family, paid a sum of money and traveled a long ways to take Reiki Mastership. The cleansing cycle, which the initiation instigated, had released and healed much of my pain. The breathing technique, which is used to do the initiations, had been taught, but not stressed. Later, I discovered that Takata herself never emphasized the breathing in her teachings; while she taught the breathing techniques to most of the Reiki Masters, later Reiki Masters did not always teach it. Recalling how difficult it was and how much energy it took for me to do the breathing, I decided to practice the breathing for the purpose of healing. Wasn't exactly sure why; just impelled from within to do it each day.

The following March, a young man held a crystal workshop in my home. One of his students, Michelle Lichtman, was an acquaintance whom I had seen at other metaphysical functions and classes. My daughter, Jennifer, was also in the crystal class. Sometime during the course while we worked in front of the fireplace, Jennifer told Michelle, "My mother's a Reiki Master." With those words, my own daughter changed the whole course of my life. To this day, I can see Michelle's face; her mouth open so wide that one could count all of her teeth. When she discovered that I did not pay $10,000, and that I could initiate her and teach her how to do the initiations, she asked me what it would take for me to teach her. I thought for a moment and told her that if she could get 3 other people together, I would put together a class.

I have two college degrees, a BA in fine arts and a BS in elementary education. Having taught both the first grade and higher level reading skills at Alverno College, there were several goals I had in mind for the class. Since experimenting with the breathing, I was convinced that it was important and should be highlighted. While I learned what I needed to in Michigan, my personal teaching preference was to incorporate more structure into the class than. At the same time, I wanted to make the class fun and enjoyable. Later, I discovered a way in which to use the ancient symbols from Egypt and those of the Rune Masters to teach the breathing.

First Reiki Mastership class was set for April of 1990, and rather than 4 students, I ended up with six. I would have had seven, but one woman flew to Texas that weekend. To accommodate her, another class was set up on a weekend the following month. Eight students attended. Another four women made their own arrangements with me to teach them the following Monday and Tuesday. And so it went through the summer with people calling me and asking me to teach them, until my very own Judas came unsuspectingly into my life and into my classroom.

Then in the summer of 1990, my own personal Judas took all three Reiki classes. During sharing times after the initiations, Judas verbally expressed her amazement at the energy she had experienced. Afterwards when we practiced hands-on-healing, she was astonished at the heat that came out of her hands. The people whom she worked upon praised her healing abilities. During one of the meditations during Reiki Mastership, she had to sit out because she had experienced too much energy. She praised my teaching and brought me small, unexpected gifts. Then about a month after the last class, she sent me a letter with the news that she wasn't a Reiki Master, and that I was a fake. She informed me in writing that she was helping the community out by Xeroxing and distributing copies of a letter that she had received from a Florida Reiki Master, who claimed that I was a fraud. Thank you! My students stood by me; the only one who didn't was Judas' friend. The thought that crossed my mind, *Jesus only had to contend with one Judas, so why did God feel it necessary to send me two?*

Many of my students had taken my class so that they could teach. While they called to say that they had felt the energy pass to them, and that they as well as their own students were satisfied with their healing abilities, I felt that they deserved more. So, I asked Mother-Father God for the Truth. It is an interesting fact that much in our lives is dependent upon asking the right questions. So, for this I will always be grateful to these two women. What initially could have been a disaster became the impetus to alter my life forever. My prayer was heard and answered; artwork left behind!

Shortly after Judas' relentless campaign began, an interesting series of events occurred. My Reiki Master, Margarette Shelton, started her last semester of graduate school, her father was dying, and she detested written correspondence. On that note, she informed me on the telephone that while she had documentation proving that I was a Reiki Master, I would have to wait for it. Secondly, I had written to the Floridian Reiki Master, who had declared me to be a fraud, and asked him to further clarify comments he had made. Interestingly enough, his reply was filled with numerous contradictions from the initial letter that he had sent to Judas. In fact, he had gone so far as to change his story completely. Thirdly, when Margarette's documentation and the copy of Rick and Emma Ferguson's Reiki Mastership certificates arrived, the Floridian Reiki Master's signature proved authentic. The Floridian Reiki Master's reply to this was that Rick and Emma had stolen the certificates. Writing back again I asked, "How could they have stolen signed and dated blank certificates from you?" Eventually, I ended up with three different letters, each with its own unique set of facts and circumstances. Fourthly, I was invited to speak and give a workshop that November at the Whole Life Expo in New York City, in the company of people I had seen on television and whose books I had read. In 1992, I had the opportunity to ask the director why out of all possible Reiki Masters, he had asked me to be a presenter. He responded by telling me that he intuitively scanned all of the applications. I responded by telling him that I hadn't sent in an application; I hadn't even known at the time that the Whole Life Expo existed. He didn't have an answer.

Arriving in New York, I stayed with a friend of Marcy Miller's, Charlotte Liss. Marcy had taken Reiki Mastership with me in Michigan. Even though I had been given a time slot of late Friday afternoon, a time when everyone in New York is still busy working, I lectured to a full audience and followed it with a packed workshop. As I drew in so many people, the Whole Life Expo asked me to be a presenter at the Los Angeles Whole Life Expo in February 1991.

When I returned home to Milwaukee, Marcy called to find out how the New York Whole Life Expo had gone, and inquired about her friend, and now my new friend, Charlotte. Marcy also shared with me something very interesting. She had just been with a channeler in Arizona, who told Marcy that a woman named Kathleen had taken Reiki to higher levels. Since I was the only Kathleen that Marcy knew, Marcy made immediate arrangements to fly from California to Milwaukee in December (something most Californians would not do) to retake Reiki Mastership with me. I am typically skeptical of channeled information from people who leave their bodies. Wanting to know the truth, I prayed, and was struck with the realization that it was the exercises in the Runes and Egyptian Cartouche that awakened former lifetimes I had spent in Egyptian temples. In addition, my paintings of the Holy Kabbalah (see Tera, My Journey Home), which I placed around my living room, allowed Spirit to raise the energy of the Reiki initiations. Thus, initiates received more healing abilities.

Marcy paid me for the class, but she was a guest in my home, as were all who traveled long distances to take my classes. Before she left, she wanted to return my hospitality and invited me to stay in Los Angeles with her after the Whole Life Expo there in February. When she left my home, she left for India to see Sathya Sai Baba. Since his birth on November 23, 1926, Sai Baba has manifested supernormal powers and his mission in one phrase might be, to raise humanity's consciousness to God Consciousness. While he never went beyond the first grade, Sai Baba is able to communicate in languages he has never studied and quote passages from texts he himself has never read, at least not in this lifetime. His healings and manifestations are sometimes imminent and dramatic. He is able to perform many of the same miracles that the Master Jesus did: Manifest, heal, transform, and bi-locate. There are countless stories and many books written about him, two by western medical doctors. When Marcy left, I wished her well and told her that I was looking forward to seeing her in Los Angeles and hearing about her trip.

The next time I saw Marcy was at the exhibition hall of the Whole Life Expo. While she was in India, Sai Baba had told her in meditation that Takata had left out a symbol and over half of the initiation procedure for each of the three Reiki degrees. Smiling, Marcy told me not to worry. She said that Sai Baba had gone to the inner planes to retrieve the lost information and power Dr. Usui had originally discovered, and he would be giving us the information shortly.

In the City of Angels at the Siddha Ashram where Marcy was staying, a Higher Being appeared ethereally. His presence filled the ashram, and I watched as the walls and ceiling expanded to cathedral size. During this consciousness-raising experience, my physical body and conscious mind were in the Otherworlds. He initially appeared in orange robes, brown-skinned, and with thick, black Afro hair. From what Marcy had said, I assumed that it was Sai Baba. The missing symbol the Higher Being retrieved contained within it the symbol for infinity. Infinity was a symbol that I had seen repeatedly in many different ways and from many different people at the Expo.

Energy was still running through my body when I woke up the following morning. Recalling the events of the preceding night, I lay still for a long time with the sensation of being displaced or misplaced in time and space. When I was able to take a good look around me, it was shocking to see how small the living room and the house actually were. On the beach later that day, the Higher Being's presence was felt and I reviewed the initiation procedures he had given me the night before, and I was told to call the missing symbol Zonar (pages 120 & 121). I was to reinitiate Marcy first, and afterwards, she initiated me. I decided that when I returned home I would reinitiate all of my students and teach them the full initiation procedures. Reading my thoughts, the Higher Being asked me how much I intended to charge them for this service. My response was that I would give it freely. I felt that my students had paid me once to become Reiki Masters and they should not have to pay me a second time. Rather than rewarding me for my spirituality and humility, he admonished me for not honoring my time and myself. I then cautiously asked him if charging ten dollars would be all right. Holding my breath, he responded by saying that that would be fine.

For the sum of ten American dollars, the cost of lunch at a relatively nice American restaurant in 1991, I reinitiated and taught my interested students. They practiced on me and in this way the energy of the initiation was established. Everyone felt the increase in energy both during the initiation, and afterwards pouring out of their hands. Several people broke out in tears crying, "This is it!" I even reinitiated Reiki Masters from other associations, and they felt the increase in healing energy. As I moved closer towards the energy I had as a child, those whom I had reinitiated moved up right behind me. When the process had been completed, however, we still were unable to do the same things that Mikao Usui and Takata could do. *What else could be missing?* Again I was heard.

In April 1991, I was once again in New York. While sitting in Charlotte's New York apartment with a group of my students, I mentioned that I was going back to California to teach a class in May, and that I would also be seeing Marcy. Colleen Zurawski and several other psychics present told me that the masters had more in store for me. Gasping, I wondered, *how in the world am I going to explain this one?* Received a similar message upon arriving home in Milwaukee. Rosemary Schoenenburger asked me if I had a symbol with a cross in the middle of it? I did not have one to give her, at least not yet.

In May 1991, in California, I again met with Marcy and I re-entered the Otherworlds. Thus, I was not caught unaware when Zonar was replaced with Harth. This also raised the Reiki vibration. Watching the symbol was being drawn, it was clear that the first lines were those of a cross, around which a pyramid was drawn. Several years later, one of my students from New Jersey, Aaron Sapiro, told me that he had met a man whose family had left Japan just prior to World War II. When he was a young boy, his family had done some work with Mikao Usui's Reiki Masters. His family had been given HARTH (pages 121 & 122).

Everything happened just as before. I re-initiated Marcy and then she re-initiated me. Again for ten dollars, I reinitiated former students and shared the initiation procedure and symbol the masters called Harth. Each person I reinitiated felt the increase in energy, and how more effective the healing energy was. Again there were cries of joy. Several of my students had instant past-life recalls of working with Harth in Egypt or Atlantis. Each one said the same thing; that is, that Harth had been altered slightly. When I asked in Divine Truth why this had been done, Spirit replied that it had been done intentionally. Spirit said that it was like advancing one number on a combination lock. This stopped anyone who had lived in Ancient Egypt and had known the symbol, and misused the energy from corrupting the energy again. Again, we were able to do more for those who sought healing from us, but we were not able to do the same consistent miracles that Usui and Takata were capable of. Hesitantly, I asked, *why?* I remembered as a very young girl, being conflicted by the abilities I had, which my mother teased and berated me for. Yet, one Sunday morning, during the reading the Gospel, the priest quoted Jesus as saying, "Ye shall do great things than I have done." Looking around at the blank expressions around me, it seemed that I was the only one who heard.

Earth, Air, Fire, Water

From the beginning, my unconventional experiences with the Higher Being created a stir. These facts were included in biographies used in programs where I lectured and in other promotional material. I made it perfectly clear to individuals that the Reiki initiations I had received from Margarette Shelton had been altered and the reason why. I would have been taken for a fool or madwoman were it not for the fact that real healings were beginning to happen regularly.

During healing demonstrations I let the healing energy speak for itself. Once in Chicago after giving a lecture, a woman volunteered to receive a public healing. When I placed my hands on her neck, she suddenly flipped into a past life where she had been hung. Her neck literally elongated, her face became puffy and her eyes looked as if they were going to pop out. Moving my hands to her shoulders, I wanted the audience to see that I was not strangling the woman. However, that seemed to be my concern, not theirs. It was also a Shamanic-type of session, because during her release and healing, everyone in the audience received a major healing.

While in California with Marcy in February of 1991, we went to several powerful group Light-channeling sessions conducted by a former 'yuppie' (many of whom live in California). He went into a trance and held the doorway for healing energy from higher realms to come through. This is also a Shamanic-like ceremony because attendees may receive healings, or take advantage of the energy by entering deeper states of consciousness. An everyday example of the channeling of Light phenomenon is during the consecration of the host during the mass. The priest or minister (and some of them are conscious of what it is that they are doing) brings the body of Wholeness, the Light of Christ Consciousness, into the bread. This is the body to which Jesus referred; the fact that we are all one, we all belong to the same Wholeness. Interesting enough, scientists have discovered an invisible energy that connects everything in this universe. The more Light energy a psychic channel is able to hold, the more that can be accomplished by the individual participants.

After returning home, Rosemarie and Michelle told me about a psychic surgeon who was teaching a class the following week. Unable to attend the training, I scheduled a healing appointment with him. He worked with the Angels in a powder blue color that was strangely familiar. I asked, *what is this?* To my surprise, I experienced a knock on my head, and my guide, Straight Arrow, said, "Remember the Light sessions in California!" I looked to my dreams for the answer.

It is possible to **problem-solve in the dream state.** A common practice used by many very famous scientists, mathematicians, leaders and intellectuals through the ages, including Albert

Einstein and Thomas Alva Edison. It is easy and effective. Just prior to falling asleep, write down all aspects of the question. Narrow the question down; rhymes work particularly well. Repeat the phrase over and over again while falling asleep. Immediately upon waking up, write down all aspects of the dream. The answer is received either through dream analysis, or if psychic abilities are developed, by an unmistakable inner knowing. The subconscious provides appropriate symbology. Dream analysis books are helpful. If our intuition is open, we are the best interpreters of our dreamscape metaphors. Within the imagery of our dreams lies the answer; and interestingly enough, there is often more than one answer or level of interpretation. Sometimes, it takes several nights before the answer comes. Some people set their alarm clocks to four o'clock in the morning, at which time they begin recording their dreams by writing or speaking into a voice-activated recorder.

My question concerned the connection between the Light sessions and the psychic surgeon. The message I received the following morning was, "Each of the two men is working on the outskirts of something larger." Shortly thereafter, I was told to call the powder blue ray **Angeliclight**.

In June 1991, I returned to California to teach another Reiki class. August Starr, a Seichem Master, asked me if I would do an exchange with her for Reiki Mastership. August did not know who had discovered **Seichem**, but I was strongly impressed to barter with her. Seichem was a different kind of energy from Reiki. Reiki ran hot and cold out the palms of my hands; Seichem sparkled, like effervescent bubbles or small electrical impulses. Seichem worked in either the healee's aura or in the aura of a group. Later, one of my Native American students, Roxanne Struthers, told me that Seichem was the energy she had experienced many times with Shamans in sweat lodges.

Seichem initiations were both complex and lacking. Yet, Seichem healing facilitators were able to initiate healing. The Seichem symbols were identical to the Reiki symbols, only slanted. Even the master symbol, the Dai Koo Mio, which is used to fully open the initiate to the Seichem healing ray, was the same as the Reiki Dai Koo Mio. What really caught my attention was a symbol that Buddha had told me that Takata had made up, Hon Sha Za Sho Nen. Buddha said it was a combination of Hawaiian Shamanism and Buddhism. I had to ask, *if Takata made up thirteen variations of Hon Sha Za Sho Nen, what is it doing amongst the Seichem initiation symbols?*

The surprising answer came the following morning as clear as a bell: Seichem played on the outskirts of a larger ray, which in full manifestation comes in like a sparkling rainbow of color. I was told to call this energy Sakara. Later, I found out that Patrick Zeigler had a consciousness-raising experience after spending the night in the crypt in the King's Chamber of the Great Pyramid, and that through the loving Grace of God he was able to go through his fears. Afterwards, he held Shamanic-like circles where people might experience the same Oneness. One of his students, Phoenix Summerfield (a.k.a. Kathleen McMasters), used this energy to change the original Alliance Reiki initiations. Somehow, her initiations produced fire energy, which was experienced as pins and needles in the palms of the hands and the fingertips. However, the Seichem initiations she made up were volatile. Spirit strongly advised not to pass these unstable initiations on. Phoenix has since died. One of Phoenix's students suffers from severe health problems, and has publicly mentioned her encounters with Dark Beings posing as Light Beings. Other students of Phoenix refuse to talk about the entities they invoke. Today, these initiations do not pass on fire energy.

Neither the three-dimensional world of logic, nor meditation fails to produce into physical reality **Universal initiations** into healing energy emanating from God. It takes a consciousness-raising experience whereby the physical body and conscious mind fully participate in a higher reality. The participant knows where s/he is, and a Higher Being is met in this Otherworld who instructs and takes responsibility for the Gift of Spirit. So, I was at a loss to understand why I was guided to do the exchange with August Starr. Answers only come when questions are asked. Buddha wanted me to re-experience fire energy that I had as a child. Afterwards, he cleared me of the initiation.

Upon returning to Milwaukee, an array of 5th-dimensional beings moved me upwards from being a Seichem Master to a Sakara Master. At the same time they initiated me into Angeliclight. Getting closer to the healing and psychic abilities I had as a child! I was guided to meditate and travel, though it was not always to visit places of power. Performing simple earth magic on full and new moons helped connect me to Earth and nature (see Scot Cunningham's books).

During an astrology reading, Larry Peterson told me, "You traveled a lot during the eight years prior to your becoming a Reiki Master." When I said that I hadn't, Larry said, "Well, then you moved a lot during those eight years." When I said that I'd lived in the same home for eleven years, Larry became deeply agitated. He responded, "These aspects are too strong. You had to have traveled or moved around a lot!" Larry Peterson asked his spirit guides to explain the conflict, and was told that during those eight years, masters, Angels, and Higher Beings had taken me out of body at night to other planets, solar systems and even to other universes to teach me Sacred Mysteries and Laws of Healing. It was as if becoming a Reiki Master flipped a switch, and since then I have been in a process of remembering what I was taught in my dreamtime.

Larry's insight made a great deal of sense. Before learning about different Reiki associations in serious conflict with one another, and before speaking in New York and Los Angeles, whenever I taught Reiki, I felt that the energy needed to be raised – a lot! During the Reiki I initiation I had

29

received from Helen Borth, I kept waiting for something else to happen. After Reiki II, I asked Helen, "Are you sure this is all there is?" She just looked at me.

Before teaching a Reiki class, I stood the series of oil-on-canvas paintings on the Holy Kabbalah on the floor along the walls of my living room, creating a ring of energy. Within this vibration I initiated my students and taught them Reiki. I learned a lot as well! What we call Reiki comes from the elemental earth-healing ray, which emanates from Source. The energy runs hot and cold just like the surface of our planet. Since my encounter with the Higher Being in the Otherworlds, the color of the Reiki attunement changed immediately from purple to gold. When Mantak Chia found this out, he called me to make arrangements with me to reinitiate him as a Reiki Master in New York City. Jack Schroeder came along. Mantak Chia told us that he considered the Reiki Mastership initiation to be the initiation of the Taoist Masters, and he wanted his full initiation.

Tera Mai is close to meaning 'my earth' in some languages. Interestingly, that while traditionally a variety of hand positions are taught in the first Reiki class, the most effective hand placements are those where the palms of the hands are parallel to the earth. Other characteristics of **Reiki** or earth energy are grounding, foundation, introspection, physical healing and prayer. (Prayers that God or Spirit answers readily being with, *I am open to receive,* or include, *I wonder?)* Because of the qualities of earth, Reiki is fundamental to all other elemental healing rays. Those who facilitated remarkable healings (Jesus, the Priest Melchizedek, some Shaman and saints, etc.) have command over all four elements, the same four elements that comprise our own physical bodies.

Sakara is fire, the energy of transformation! Fire itself is a phenomenon that cannot be explained or defined by any scientist alive on a three-dimensional planet using left-brained logic. Fire comes from the fourth dimension and lightning comes from the fifth. It is virtually impossible to explain fourth and fifth-dimensional phenomena using limited three-dimensional terminology. What the masters told me was that Sakara or fire at the healing level is the vessel or vehicle, which holds Angeliclight, the healing aspect of air. Sakara brings a rainbow of protective light, which surrounds the aura. More precisely, it is this merkaba or body of light created by Sakara that holds Angeliclight. This merkaba also allows an individual to astral travel into the higher realms, as opposed to out-of-body explorations of the physical universe, which in itself is a variation of a physical trance state.

In healing, Sakara works in the **aura**, the electromagnetic field surrounding the body. It is helpful for the healer to work through the aura first before 'laying on of hands' or even Shamanic journeywork. Sakara also releases blockages and resistances in the physical, emotional, mental, and spiritual bodies. As Higher Beings took me into higher levels of Sakara, low voltage electricity and later, what seemed to be lightning (both aspects of fire), moved through me. Healees would use the words like "electricity," "lightning," "sparks," and "sparkling" to describe their healing process. Later, I was to discover that Sakara further aids in **pranic healing** and balances the electrical-magnetic field. Prana is the vital Universal energy that surrounds us and sustains life. In pranic healing, one uses what the Taoists call Chi to clean the electromagnetic field or aura, the chakras and meridians. After the healer cleans the chakras, s/he then projects prana or Chi and healing colors to the healee, specifically through the chakras.

Typically, we bring in energy through our left hand and foot and out through our right hand and foot. When people talk about their "receiving hand," they are referring to their left hand; when they refer to their "sending hand," they mean their right hand. Using Sakara in the aura above the body, a healer might bring healing energy in through the healee's right foot and hand, across each chakra, and out the left. The effect is as if we were to suddenly reverse a river; that is, debris that has been neatly tucked and filed away can be loosened and released. (See page 54 – **chelation**)

Auras contain layers of electromagnetic energy fields, commonly referred to as the subtle bodies, which directly correspond to each one of the **major chakras**. In East Indian mysticism, chakra means wheel. They understand that chakras whirl outwards both clockwise and counterclockwise from the vertical energy line located within the physical body. This vertical energy line comes from Source, moves into the crown and out the root chakra, which grounds into the earth. The crown chakra spirals up; the root chakra at the base of the spine spins down. From this vertical energy line, the other major chakras (third eye, throat, heart, solar plexus and at the belly) spin outwards both front and back into the aura. Clockwise spin draws prana or Chi into the physical body. Counterclockwise motion releases spent or misqualified energy. However, to **dowse for the health of a chakra** with a pendulum, the movement of the pendulum over a healthy chakra will be a clockwise, balanced circle rather than an oval or a straight line. If the major chakras are in harmony, the circles will be roughly the same size. The navel chakra and the chakra at the small of the back (the Meng Ming or the Door of Life) will be about 2/3 the size of the 7 major chakras. There are exceptions! For example, when dowsing the crown chakras of autistic children, the pendulum will swing erratically; it's as if the souls of these individuals are not able to fully come into the physical body. After a Tera Mai Reiki I initiation, the pendulum will swing back and forth in a straight line; after a Tera Mai Seichem I initiation, the pendulum will swing in a clockwise circle. (The younger the baby, the more dramatic the healing results from these initiations.) However, dousing may be done before and after any healing sessions. Problems with major organs will be reflected in the swing of the pendulum. It also might be interesting to dowse the crown chakra of anyone offering Reiki or other initiations into healing.

There are **smaller chakras** throughout the body. For example, the palm chakras of a healer are large and become larger during healing sessions. The **three major chakras used in healing and psychic work** are the solar plexus, heart and 3rd eye. The heart and inner visions are telling if the mind is clear. Inner knowing and gut feelings from the solar plexus bypass the brain, and are reliable. The solar plexus connects to the higher self and God. In addition, there are **three knots**, which are located between the heart and throat chakras, between the solar plexus and heart chakras, and at the pubic bone. The knots prevent us from being who we were meant to be and keep us from God. They may be cleared or untied by the combination MT and SMF Light Waters, which is the work of Italian biologist and author, Enza Maria Ciccolo. They may also be cleared by strong intent, or by a healer who works in the aura, literally untying the knots s/he sees. However, if the individual returns to evil or corrupt behavior, the knots return. Each time the knots return they are harder to remove. When they are removed energy is able to flow clearly through the body.

Aura **healing** removes thought patterns before they enter the physical. Aura healing bypasses the ego, which oftentimes masks the root cause or the issue behind physical pain. Physical pain or disease does serve an important purpose by calling attention to the fact that issues must be addressed. These issues tend to gather in particular place in the body, which may or may not be the origin of pain. Dr. Deepak Chopra, Dr. Bernard Siegel and other qualified medical doctors state that drugs or surgical techniques alone serve to mask symptoms. If the root cause is not addressed, the patient is not healed. Unfortunately, there is no monetary incentive for a doctor to prescribe herbs and homeopathic remedies. Ralph Nader's group has a book, available through his organization that was researched and written by medical doctors. Worst Pills Best Pills lists roughly 100 pills that should never be taken and about 700 deadly drug combinations.

Changes in the aura alter the energy pattern of the electromagnetic field, and will cause repercussions on all levels, which includes corresponding changes in the physical body. Changes may be for the 'good' or the 'bad,' but will manifest sooner or later. When positive change results because of healing work, regardless of what form of healing is used (hands-on, Shamanic or aura), if core issues are not resolved, dis-ease or pain will return. As Earth moves into The Golden Age of the Return of the Angels, it is like God Himself is changing channels on Earth and new possibilities will become a reality. At some point, it will be possible to reconstruct missing limbs and organs through aura healing. Salamanders have an active electromagnetic aura, and they have the ability to regenerate. Interestingly, the Greek word for a fire elemental is salamander.

Layers of the aura correspond to the major chakras. The root and throat chakras correspond to the first and fifth electromagnetic fields, which are associated with the physical body.

The second, or creative chakra, and the third eye (mind's inner eye) correspond to the second and sixth fields. They deal with the emotional body. The solar plexus and the crown chakras relate to the third and seventh fields. These are the mental bodies. The heart chakra and corresponding fourth subtle body acts as the fulcrum. The heart is the entrance to higher levels of physical, emotional and mental expression. Without heart love energy, the passageway to the higher chakras is blocked, and so too, is joy. Without joy it is not possible through the silent mind to reach The Unmanifested Potential with compassion. Heart love energy directed to the upper chakras helps the psychic centers to open. While the heart is a muscle, there is also brain matter within the heart. Thus, on a physical level there is also a connection between the heart and the brain.

Sue Szymanski moves the pendulum straight up through the aura over each chakra. In this manner, Sue measures the astral, emotional, and mental bodies that are mentioned above. For example, I once demonstrated this phenomenon on a woman who used her will center (solar plexus - first mental body) to extremes. As the webbing (necessary, protective interweaving of energy lines) in the solar plexus was worn thin, the pendulum moved in a straight line in each layer of the aura above the solar plexus. As a matter of fact, the pendulum arched back and forth higher than my fingertips, which quietly held the chain. Interestingly, the pendulum moved in a straight line through the layer of the aura corresponding to mental body (third electromagnetic field) of every other chakra. **If a major chakra is compromised, it will adversely influence major glands and organs, which are associated with that chakra.** For example, the woman's depleted solar plexus will at some point adversely affect her liver, kidneys, stomach, spleen, gall bladder and/or pancreas.

It is also possible to find thought patterns behind current physical pain in the aura. As I work my hands through the aura, the electrical impulses in my palms and fingertips sometimes 'zap' or transmute thought forms, which may feel like hard stones or energy currents. **Possession**: I found a dark, heavy area about 3 feet in diameter just above and to the left of the head of a man who felt that he was possessed. Awareness of this ethereal object lasted for only a moment. Suddenly, it exploded in my hands. The man, who had been lying calmly on the massage table, jerked up and doubled completely over. He lay sweating with his head on his knees for fifteen minutes. His possession was gone, but he still had other issues that he needed to work out in order to stay clear. All healers who work effectively in the human aura are working with Sakara or fire energy.

One of the greatest benefits to working with Sakara energy comes immediately after **accidents**, when the aura is literally shattered. Misqualified energy is on the surface and will not solidify until three days afterwards. Within this three-day time frame, energy patterns are easily transformed and pulled out of the aura by using the **pain drain** (left hand over the area, right arm and fingertips pointing down to the central fire). Then healer's hands work back and forth through the aura, re-establishing healthy electromagnetic energy pattern in the aura.

For example, Marcy Miller flew in from California and was helping me paint my living room. Foolishly managed to fall off the ladder and sprain my ankle! She worked on it and within the hour, I was able to put weight on it; the next day, I was fine. **The process for clearing injuries** involves draining off misqualified energy with the pain drain, and putting in beneficial energy. In addition, the palm of the left hand may be held up in a receiving position, while the palm of the right hand radiates healing to the healee. If the healer keeps wrists and elbows unbent and his/her arms away from the body, this may increase energy flow, as this opens the chakras in the armpit. It also helps if the healer does big spirals in the healee's aura with his/her arms – both spirals getting bigger and spirals getting smaller. Because an accident shatters the aura, the other good news is that disease or pain unrelated to the accident itself may also be released and healed. The problem may be found away from the point of injury. The bad news about an accident is that after three days, the misqualified energy takes more permanent physical form. Time etches in undesirable energy patterns. The more time that is involved, the deeper and more ingrained alternative, destructive patterns become. At this point, if physical healing is possible, it may involve more time and effort.

If Karma is worked out and there is no dependency on the injury, healing may be instantaneous when removed by a healer. At the Whole Life Expo in Los Angeles in September 1992, while I was doing a healing demonstration in front of a packed lecture hall, in less than 10 minutes Beverly K. Henson released an arthritic hump on her thoracic vertebrae.

"I am not sure what led me to attend Kathleen's lecture at the Whole Life Expo in Los Angeles, in September of 1992. But, it changed my whole life.

My husband and I were without a baby-sitter and had taken our eight-year-old son with us that Sunday morning. He promised to sit quietly while Kathleen spoke. He found her lecture very interesting and paid close attention.

On the other hand, the arthritic hump on the upper part of my spine was aching so badly, I could not concentrate on everything Kathleen was saying. It had been hurting constantly for the past several days. Walking around the Expo for two days, carrying my purse on my shoulder had not helped the situation either.

When Kathleen asked for a volunteer to come up on stage, my hand shot up before I could give it a thought. She asked where my problem was and then put her hand on the spot. She could easily feel the hump. As she began to work in my aura, she asked what emotional problem I needed to deal with. I couldn't identify with this, simply because I had shoved it to the back of my mind.

She worked on pulling a very heavy plug from my crown chakra and said that I would begin to deal with the problem soon. She worked on me for maybe five to seven minutes. When she finished, she asked how I felt.

34

I put my hand on the hump and it had definitely gone down. It was tingling like your hand does after it goes to sleep. I looked at the audience and told them it had gone down.

Over the next few days, the hump continued to disappear. Every single time I bent to pick up something heavy, I expected it to hurt. It never did. Two days later, I was watching a TV show about a person going back in time and telling his father how much he loved him. I broke into uncontrollable tears. These were the tears I had held back since my father passed away two months earlier. This was the emotional problem that Kathleen had pulled the plug on, enabling me to deal with it."

Angels and Ascended Masters processed within my being the energies of Sakara and Angeliclight throughout the summer of 1991. On two occasions when I was deep in meditation, my heart stopped beating totally. Lying in a strangely silent body, an etheric hand dropped easily into my chest to massage my heart until it resumed beating. The experience with Buddha in the Otherworlds left me with an inner drive to complete my assigned task from the Universe, and an inner knowing that God would provide. Moving ever closer to the Gifts of the Spirit I had been born with.

Consciousness-raising experiences engrave the reality of God's Presence into the fabric of consciousness. With that comes the knowledge that God is not an old man in a place far, far away, and that this is not the only reality. **To establish your own inner knowing that God is at hand** you may be impressed to say the following before praying, facilitating healings, etc.: *Divine God, Divine Goddess, I know that You hear me, and are here for me whenever I pray, ask or in my hour of need. Please work with me and through Tera Mai, Shekinah, God The Father Almighty, Holy Ghost, Holy Spirit, Christed beings, Buddhas, Angels, Elementals, Blessed Ones, Ancients Ones, Star People, Power Animals, Saints, Shaman, the Brotherhood of Light, and Spirits of the Land who have come in the love of Buddha, and the light of Maria and Christ.* You may add the names of higher beings you work with. Each being or group brings in a different vibration, which may be seen as colors.

Angeliclight is a twofold ray working with both the element air and the angelic realm. Air's qualities are wisdom, communication, gratitude and mental healing. It is through the silent mind that the heart opens to joy, which opens the possibility of The Unmanifested Potential. (Eckhart Tolle The Power of Now). The third eye (inner eye or mind's eye) is comprised of a chakra at the forehead and another between the eyebrows. Watching and serving as a silent witness with the mind's eye while healings take place strongly intensifies the healing energy. Angeliclight increases dramatically the healing effectiveness of the third eye. Angeliclight works through the throat chakra by raising the impact of the spoken word. Angeliclight acts like an Angel magnet. The first healee whom Madonna Peters worked on after she received these initiations told Madonna that she had never seen so many Angels gathered in one place in her whole life.

Angeliclight initiates required a disciplined mind, and awareness of speech. As Angeliclight increases the power of the spoken word, it helps to establish another energy pattern. If higher being's names are repeated 3 times, it helps to raise the healer's vibration; the vibration of the masters is already raised. For example, within The Magician's Companion by Bill Whitcomb can be found the names of 12 Archangels translated from the original Hebrew. They are: Advachiel, Ambriel, Amnitziel, Asmodel, Barachiel, Cambriel, Hamaliel, Hanael, Malchielael, Muriel, Verchiel and Zuriel. The suffix "iel" means, "of God." Chanting these and other high-vibrational names in a monotone is like the droning of the Shamanic journey drumbeat; imagery in the mind's eye becomes clearer.

With Angeliclight healing, when the healer speaks about what is occurring during the healing process, the energy is magnified and the experience is intensified. **Aromas** from invisible flowers or herbs may come in during the healing session. The healer or the healee may catch a sweet whiff here or there on the same inhale. Other times, the fragrance is constant, but only in one particular square foot of space. Sweet smells indicate the presence of a master or Archangel and are healing in themselves. On the other hand, vile odors are a signal that the issues are very old. Either phenomenon is incredible proof of the existence of another reality beyond the ordinary 5 senses.

Angels, what are they? In March 2009, I went to Saint Mary's Guildhall in Coventry with Anita O'Hagan and some of her students. William Shakespeare's writing desk is there, and people have seen his ghost. I called him and he came. The next day, Anita saw him during a group healing session that I was facilitating. He said that he had come as an Angel to help with the healings. I have also seen demons find love and step into the vortex to go to the Light. What I have come to believe through these and other experiences is that God put us here on Earth, and it is our choice as to whether we evolve into Angels or demons. Those people who are going into the Golden Age are becoming more angelic. On the other hand, Alice Bailey, whose material is heavily right-brained, says that **elementals** exist in a parallel universe, where they take forms that the Greeks call Sylphs of the air, Gnomes of the earth, Salamanders of the fire and Undines of the water. Rather than going through a reincarnation cycle, they evolve into Angels. What we do know is that stories of the elementals are found in Greek, Celtic, Oriental and Native American lore; to mention a few. Dwarfs in the folk tale, *Snow White,* and tales of Irish leprechauns represent Gnomes. Elementals may change forms and look like small people. While in Hawaii, I saw them as balls of rich, earthy tones of color. They are spiritual forces that care for nature. Without nature, Earth is a dead planet. Doing simple Earth magic helps us to connect to nature, and to the missing Universe.

All **psychic surgeons** work with the energy of Angeliclight.   After initiation into Angeliclight, celestial Angels are able to project themselves over the healer. In one definition of channeling, a disincarnate soul enters the body of the psychic and the psychic (channeler) leaves. In Angeliclight, healing, Angels gently overshadow the healer's body in such as way that they are able to reach through the healing facilitator and into the body of the healee <u>without cutting the skin</u>.   This initiates physical changes.   The healee may feel angelic hands moving within them or organs being moved.   There have been instances where people have experienced the sensation of cutting away of tumors or diseased tissue.   These healings are looked upon as miracles because the common elemental phenomenon and structure of the angelic universe is uncommon to our own.

There are 333 levels of Angeliclight, which the healer may receive through initiations and these are given along with the Sakara and Sophi-El initiations.   The levels are for our point of reference on this 3-dimensional reality.   After the last initiations into Angeliclight are given, the healing energy of air evolves upwards on its own as the healer uses it.   There comes a point, however, when Angeliclight becomes out of balance with the other elemental healing rays, and it is then that the other elemental healing rays - earth (Reiki), fire (Sakara) and water (Sophi-El) - are pulled upwards to re-establish balance.   There is no end to Angeliclight!

Sophi-El is both gentle and persistent; a powerful force, like the water element from which it comes. It's attributes are healing, love, compassion, development of psychic abilities and emotional healing. *(Originally I did not have the name for this ray, and one of my students suggested that it be called Celestial Star Fire. Sophi-El was the name the masters gave to me later.)*   The ray's color includes all of the various hues of silver, plus white, and the velvet black of the void.   The Great Void or Hidden Mystery is black, like the Universal womb from which the Light emerges.   Without black, there is no Light.   Black magicians are called so because they use the color black, which is a dead black, to hide their magic.   Whenever any color is murky or dead or smells badly, it is an indication that the energy is sour or is in need of clearing.

Sophi-El helps heal the heart and inner child by finding the core, cause and ramifications of disturbances. Sophi-El may help heal deep rage and defuse outrageous anger bottled up in the emotional bodies of child abusers, wife bashers and other molesters.   Battered women have been known to break their attraction to physical abuse through things like assertiveness training, where they begin to regain a sense of self-worth.   Sage Oh'hne, the founder of Ishpiming, and author of <u>Our Journey Home - A Guide for Conscious Ascension,</u> recovered from both alcoholism and being a battered wife. **Addictions** are a substitute for the full expression of joy.   Psychics may see this void as a small black ball within the brain.   **Healees help when they are able to visualize their bodies, tell the body to release and heal or affirm, "I deserve to be joyful and healed.".** As the liver takes a beating from alcohol and drug abuse, it is wise to take Vitamin B and detoxify slowly.

Sophi-El also opens the heart to receive love and feel compassion.   A woman once brought her boyfriend to me.   He had multiple sclerosis, which Louise Hay says is caused by hardheadedness as well as hardheartedness. He was exhausted and having a particularly bad day. The energy, Sophi-El opened the "iron doors" of his heart. Within two hours, his head was clear, he was walking normally and he had his energy back. Several weeks later, his girlfriend said that he was only doing, "So, so." When I asked the Angels why, they said that while his heart had opened, it had not opened enough. That his old habit of closing his heart began immediately after the healing, as he was financially capable of donating much more than $9 for the healing he received.

Sophi-El further aids healing by re-establishing the feminine-masculine **balance**. A woman has 2/3 feminine and 1/3 masculine energies. A man has 2/3 masculine and 1/3 feminine energies. Feminine energy is creative, nurturing, psychic and healing. Masculine energy is logical; it is the teacher, the consoler and the true and valiant warrior who protects. Where is the rest of our masculine and feminine energy? Each one of us has a counterpoint, which has been called a twin flame or split-away. This soul mate has our other 1/3 - 2/3 balance and may well be what we refer to as our Guardian Angel, who watches out for us from the world of Spirit. On rare occasions do both aspects of the twin flame come into body at the same time. If a soul is not evolved, this double incarnation is not always beneficial. The point is that regardless of what sex an individual is, being fully open to both masculine and feminine aspects enables an individual to become a fully integrated personality. When one aspect over-dominates it maybe that the other is blocked. Or it maybe that there are issues, which the over-dominating aspect must deal with. We are all here to learn in our own way, and it is important to stay out of judgment with those whose paths are different from our own. Focusing on other people's issues is a way to avoid our own issues!

In addition to emotional healing energy, Sophi-El enhances the healer's **psychic awareness**. Increased intuitive abilities aids the healer in visualizing, hearing Holy Spirit, and receiving psychic impressions while s/he is facilitating healing. Additional psychic insight comes only through doing the inner work; clearing the mind and emotions, and through meditation. It is through our healed feminine nature that we have access to the Akashic Records, which has within it all memories and all experiences. If a Shaman journeys to the Akashic Records with a specific question, a brand new question or rewording of the original question may be provided by Holy Spirit! For example, Anita O'Hagan journeyed to find the answer to, *when is the big thing going to happen?* She found herself at the Akashic Records and was shown a calendar, which flipped rapidly through months until it came to May 30. She heard, *now you are here* (see page 3).

Initiations into Sophi-El and the other rays of touch healing are not a replacement for working on personal issues. They will bring up deep, buried issues. For example, anger may protect us or move us to positive expression. Anyone who has had even one event where s/he failed to speak up when someone unjustly criticized them has unexpressed righteous anger bottled up inside their solar plexus. **Righteous anger** that was never expressed requires a constructive outlet.

Outrageous anger needs to be defused. Andrew Vachss (http://www.vachss.com) would say that it is better to feel righteous anger as long as we need to, rather than keep it bottled up inside. However, until anger, fear, and sorrow are released, they act as magnets for negativity. Louise Hay feels that anger is the cause behind cancer. One woman was able to release the resentment she felt towards her mother for the total lack of love and the humiliation she experienced as a child when spirit pointed out to her that her mother's conduct is now and always has been inappropriate (mental illness). How could she hold her sick mother responsible? How could she reason with insanity, which has its own twisted truth? When she gave up her need for her mother to love her in the way that she wanted to be loved, when she stopped caring what her mother thought about her, and loved her mother, she was able to heal and release her childhood issues. Understanding opens the heart. When we totally reject our parents, we reject the gifts they gave to us on all levels. When we blindly accept our parents, we take on their heavy baggage. When we heal our relationships with our parents, we heal ourselves. When parents heal they help to heal their own children.

Sophi-El also works indirectly on the physical body because our body is mostly water, and trauma may be held anywhere in the body. When all four elemental healing rays are used together, the 'negative' energy has nowhere to hide. **In emotional healing the idea is to feel the emotional pain or shame, and release it.** Monsters shrink, and the physical body has an opportunity to heal. We may then embrace ourselves and love ourselves for being human, just as Mother-Father God has always done. Some people need to look at lifetimes where they were the ones who did the killing and let the furies run rampant. There are people who say that they will do anything to heal themselves, anything that is, but look within. Looking outside and seeing a world of chaos, they blame God. While looking within and unscrambling misperceptions, is a way to recreate the personal world. In this way, the world mirrors back to us our fears, or beauty and harmony. For example, if one does not want to participate in a recession, stay out of fear and look to God/Goddess.

Elemental rays of healing also carry feminine and masculine energies. Reiki (earth) and Sophi-El (water) are the feminine expressions of the Godhead. Sakara (fire) and Angeliclight (air) are the masculine. These forces are a theme in variation throughout this holographic universe. Other universes may or may not have physical laws that are similar to those in this universe. In a hologram, all parts are in relationship to the whole. The choices we make and our deeds impact everything. When groups unite in a common effort, the results significantly impact the hologram.

Earthbound spirits existing on other planes of existence are also comprised of these same four elements. It is possible, therefore, to send elemental healing energy to disincarnate souls if they

39

are open to receiving healing. When we see these spirits on other dimensions, they oftentimes appear to be ethereal and airy. They do not think of themselves as see-through! You have heard stories of ghosts who do not know that they are dead. That is because the astral body has physical form on the astral plane. The astral body is only a part of the greater soul. Many mysticisms talk about the silver cord that connects the astral body to the physical. The astral body travels during sleep. **In death** the silver cord is cut and the astral body leaves with both the conscious and subconscious minds. Being in the physical depends upon where you are. In higher dimensions, form becomes less dense and more flexible, in part, because the soul is enlightened. We are a paradox; both form and formless, individuals and a part of the circle of All There Is.

All four elemental healing rays emanate from Source or Mother-Father God. They work individually or in combination. When they interface with one another in such a way that a new energy is created, it is called **Cahokia**. The initiation into Cahokia is the intertwining of the full expression of the 4 elemental rays. Oftentimes after the initiation, Cahokia initiates will describe the initiation process as the sensation of Angels weaving patterns within them. Cahokia is the combined force of elemental power, the three-fold ray of the alchemist. Its colors are blue, metallic silver, sapphire, purple and rich deep gold. Cahokia uses the nuclear, electrical and water components of creation to bring about transformation and manifestation. In some healings, diseased tissue is numbed or frozen while the Angels diligently heal or replace tissue or organs.

If an initiate has never facilitated healing before, universal initiations bring about the realization of other realities, and that real healing does exist. With the three Tera Mai Seichem initiations, the 4 elemental rays and the sensations each produce come in together. The second and third degrees of Sakara, Sophi-El and Angeliclight are given separately and each healing ray is experienced differently. Either way, it is important to own the initiation afterwards and experience its effects. In my classes after the initiations, everyone has an opportunity to share what happened during the meditation and initiation. Verbalizing helps the left-brain to remember what the right brain experienced. This also helps to integrate the two hemispheres of the brain. Then we jump right into doing hands-on healing. Students learn to trust that the healing energy from God does not deplete their own energy, and that "stuff" may be pulled off and sent to the fire or light for transformation. The word "work" is found within the word "workshop."

Universal elemental healing energies flow from Source, through the healer and into the physical, mental, and emotional bodies, as well as into the electromagnetic field that permeates and surrounds the physical. Universal healing energy alters the energy and changes the manifestation. This healing energy works with many techniques; and many different kinds of therapists, nurses and, yes, doctors take my classes. Doctors, who <u>only</u> work with allopathic medicine, focus their attention on the chemical aspect of the human body, and mask the symptoms with drugs and surgery. Physical bodies are electrical and mechanical as well. If we weren't electrical, then the electrical machines they hook us up to in the hospitals to take readings with would not work. It is impossible to take an electrical reading from something that doesn't have an electrical charge!

The elemental rays may transform and manifest in other ways besides individual healing work. They allow the healer or Shaman to **hold ceremony** through the second chakra. In teaching a class or holding a full moon ritual, the teacher's second chakra creates an energy pattern, which supports the Angels and spirit guides who are called in to be of assistance to those in the class or group. This ability to hold ceremony is the reason why, when I give a demonstration on one member in the audience, many other people who are watching receive benefits of healing as well.

Mother-Father God has promised that the psychic powers found within the healing rays, which have been abused in the past, will not be misused in the Golden Age or New Era. **Abuses** of Sakara and the forcible manipulation of Sophi-El sank Atlantis and brought Egypt to her knees. Stories are also told in cultures around the world about jealous Shaman, who when their egos were threatened, used their powers to destroy another Shaman. Rune Masters, through the use of symbols, created and sent harmful energy to those whom they perceived as their competition or enemy. The tale of Aladdin has its roots in Atlantis where magicians used crystals in healing and magic. They easily entered and left crystals until physical reality became denser. One of a pair of dueling magicians tricked the second into going into a crystal by daring him to do so. Once the second was inside, the first magician sealed the crystal so the second could not come out. **Jealousy is supposed to draw our attention inward so that we might discover what similar aspect that we are jealous of is missing in our lives.**

At the beginning of this journey, I was told that Angels and masters were working with two other individuals on earth at that time to bring back the elemental healing energies and Angeliclight. I am not, nor could I be an anomaly. The masters said that these two individuals had different names for the energy, and simply that we were all at different levels of development. I do not know who these individuals are, where they are now, or if they are still involved in the process. The only way to recognize them will be by the healing work they do.

Angels asked me to re-establish the **academy for the healing arts**, where Universal initiations into healing will be given and taught in their purity. In this way, each initiate receives the identical initiation, and channels the same Universal energy. Each individual who has been taught how to do the Sakara, Sophi-El and Angeliclight receives the identical information on how to give these initiations. Sakara, Sophie-El and Angeliclight initiations are now available through a school without walls. The complete and only list of qualified individuals who are able to give these initiations and teach individuals how to use the energy is on www.kathleenmilner.com - click on FIND INSTRUCTOR and scroll down to Advanced Instructors. At the present time, these instructors are neither authorized to pass on the information on how to give these initiations, nor have they been instructed on how to connect prospective initiators to the Angels in such a way that the Angeliclight initiations are passed on to the prospective initiate. Without Angeliclight, there is no vessel for fire; thus, the Sakara initiations leave. These precautions are in place because of the Reiki wars and the reckless abandonment with which some people have taken upon themselves to change initiations.

There is major **price variance** amongst various Reiki and other initiations. Some people paid almost $30,000 and never did get Reiki Mastership. Some people paid $300 for Reiki I, II and III and received absolutely nothing in the bargain. Some Reiki instructors give the initiations away because they say Reiki is nothing, so nothing is passed on. Equally amazing, price also does not determine the quality, quantity or validity of the material presented or the energy that is transferred.

Group initiations are at the best group healings. As the Internet is a portal through which anything might come through, it is not advisable to use them for initiations. Universal initiations are given one-on-one. That said it is possible to pass on Tera Mai Reiki initiations over the telephone because the telephone offers an immediate and personal connection through a physical apparatus. Personally, I believe that this is Divine Intervention because some people are not able to travel, and want to learn how to heal. In such cases, I give one initiation at a time. The initiate practices healing techniques, using symbols in healing, and they read this book.

Before going to any teacher, it is good advice to look to see if they are doing the healings that they say that they can do. Look to their students. Are their students able to do what the teacher says s/he can teach them to do? Does the energy transfer hold? If it is possible, dowse the crown chakra of the teacher. In every profession there are always some people who will say anything to make money. However, "Ye shall know them by their works." *Jesus Christ*

Ascended Beings do not think in terms of better or worse; there are no judgments. The Reiki initiations Buddha revealed simply are what they are! As is true with any healing system, **what works is obvious; what fails to work will not stand the test of time**. This is true for allopathic medicine and all other aspects of our lives. For example, there were many Impressionist artists. Those whose work we still admire are those artists who touch our souls. Their artwork expresses a quality of Universal Truth, which goes beyond the mastery of form, composition and color. These artworks literally have the ability to move us emotionally, as does Yo-Yo Ma's playing. The Bible quotes, which people use to frighten people away from healers and psychics, are taken out of context. Those who read the Bible find out for themselves that Jesus is actually admonishing false prophets, false teachers and those who claim to heal but cannot. Healing and teaching others to heal was an important aspect of Jesus' original teachings, and the work of his Apostles. **Taking the Bible or parts of the Bible literally** has produced atheists, as well as assertive, unbending individuals. Literal interpretation removes the possibility of a Spiritual experience, which allows firsthand insights. It is like the words lift off the page, and an inner knowing sweeps through the body and consciousness.

Allopathic medicine, or modern medicine sees the physician as intervening in the disease and death process by counteracting symptoms through surgery and medicine. It is big business! **Homeopathic medicine** utilizes toxic substances in a process that dilutes them down systematically with water. The herb that is chosen matches the symptoms of the disease. In a homeopathic form it stimulates the body's natural immune system. This causes the body to actually heal itself. As herbs in their natural state have spiritual qualities, and these spiritual qualities pass into the homeopathic, the core issues are addressed. Plants, like everything else, come from God.

There are medical doctors who **combine several healing modalities**. For example, Janet Goodrich, Ph.D. (psychology) and author of Natural Vision Improvement, and Deborah Banker, M.D. both recommend eye exercises, meditation, palming (placing the palms of the hands over the eyes, not pressing) and slowly decreasing eyeglass prescriptions with the help of an eye doctor to assist their patients move out of glasses. Janet Goodrich stresses healing emotional and mental issues behind eye difficulties. Deborah Banker utilizes aromatherapy, which aids in both the healing of the physical and emotional. For example, inhaling combined scents of eucalyptus, lavender and peppermint or Chinese herbs helps to clear the cavities behind the eyes and sinus cavities. Healing ability of herbs in their natural and organic form has long been known. Bilberry helped U.S. pilots to see when flying night missions during World War II. People owe night vision improvement to Bilberry.

Releasing emotional and mental attitudes behind ailments or disease is crucial. According to Louise Hay, blindness or poor eyesight is an unwillingness to see the whole true. Seeing clearly involves being willing to look at all aspects of truth, and to feel safe while doing so. Advancing beyond our own fears, suppressed anger, mental torture chambers, judgments, repressions, etc. is vital to any healing process.

Tera-Mai™ Seichem: Awakening from a deep sleep, I found myself half in and half out of my body. My astral body had not totally re-entered my physical body. My visual perception was as if I was looking through cut glass. This had happened to me once before, so, I wasn't frightened; just wanted to go back to sleep. The Higher Being came and told me that he had something important to show me. Fighting to stay conscious, I listened and watched. The Higher Being added two more symbols and two more colors to the Tera-Mai™ Reiki attunements. He said that through these three initiations the first degrees of Sakara, Sophi-El and Angeliclight would be passed along with the three Tera Mai Reiki attunements. He told me to call the three new initiations Tera-Mai™ Seichem. Again, I would be a mad woman were it not for the fact that the initiations that the Higher Being showed me worked. Energies of earth, fire, water and air were clearly felt by many who were attuned. Initiates were able to do consistently remarkable healings with the four elemental rays of healing. (More information about Tera-Mai™ Seichem may be found in Tera, My Journey Home: Alternative Healing.)

Higher Being: I assumed by his façade. and because Marcy had said that Sai Baba would appear to us, that the higher being who came in a consciousness-raising experience in Los Angeles was Sai Baba (see pages 163 & 164). Later, I asked Buddha why he had originally presented himself as Sai Baba. He told me that at that point in my life, I knew of Sai Baba's miracles and accepted him. Buddha said that if he had come as himself, I would have questioned my worthiness to have Buddha come to me. Doubt would have cast me out of the Otherworlds and the work to get me there would have been lost. Tera Mai energies have been used on a wide variety of symptoms, including those that are off limits with other Reiki systems. The Reiki taboo list, which is found on Reiki websites and Reiki books, includes: Broken bones before they are set, pregnant women, burns. cancer, tumors, schizophrenia, babies, individuals with a heart pacer, or people undergoing surgery. **None of these restrictions apply to either the healing energy I was born with or to Tera Mai**. Maybe that is why Tera Mai initiations do not combine well with other Reiki initiations? In addition, manmade initiations are becoming increasingly toxic; they also drain the initiate's energy. It is possible for a healer to **clear away manmade initiations** with the individual's permission. Standing in front of the individual, the healer circles his left hand counterclockwise and right hand clockwise in the aura over the chest. The healer asks the individual to take a deep breath. As the individual exhales, the healer pulls the initiation off and throws them into the central fire. The healer repeats the process at the individual's back heart chakra.

What Triggers Healing?

We only see who we are. What we do not like, even hate in others, is where our own healing begins. Many homophobics are repressed homosexuals. Just look at J. Edgar Hoover, and the radical-right homophobics who have recently been outed! Rather than judge another, look within and ask, "What is this individual mirroring in me?" Then great change, release and transformation are possible. Denial is easy. For example, one of my students repeatedly criticized and judged a fellow classmate's actions, I asked, "What is it within you that Diane is reflecting back? We all serve as teachers to one another. How might Diane's behavior help you to look within yourself?"

She turned chalk white and walked outside. Standing in the middle of the street, she called me over and asked me to look down the road. "Who do you see?" she asked me. When I answered that I saw nobody, she retorted, "That's exactly the number of teachers I have!"

We go to healers with proven track records because they are able to accelerate our healing process by facilitating or channeling Universal energy. **As a healer, during the healing process**, I talk with, pray to, and work with Angels, saints and spiritual guides. I am not there to tell the healee whether or not to divorce their spouse or move to Tibet. I ask questions and encourage the healee to participate in the healing process by sharing what they are experiencing in their minds and bodies. However, some people have lost the ability to perceive on other dimensions – so, I must focus harder. Sometimes, the healee will ask for an unrelated reading. My answer is, "Have you come for a reading or a healing?" However, when I am doing psychic readings for an individual, the healing energy I channel helps to remove blockages and bring about healing. **When I am a healee**, I am an integral key to interpreting psychic impressions. I do not have to 'buy into' anything that I am told. In fact, it is up to me to go within, so as to discern the Truth for myself, and ask if I am in denial or blocking the Truth. As all psychic messages are interpreted through the physical brain, limited vocabulary and restricted concepts influence psychic messages received in any reading, be it in a healing session, channeling session, out-of-body experience, near-death experience.

The healee's higher self is in charge of the **healing process**. Core issues that are ready to be healed are brought up. Healees may be guided to make lifestyle changes or see other healing specialists such as colon therapists, reflexologists, massage therapists, herbologists, acupuncturists, Ayurvedic doctors, etc. Healing is a process and each soul takes its own course in its own time.

Sometimes, **instantaneous healings** occur, as with Beverly Henson at the Los Angeles Whole Life Expo. However, what appeared to the audience as a sudden and dramatic physical

45

healing was in fact the beginning of a process that lasted for over a month. During that time, she faced the pain and tears of her father's death. A past-life regression dealt with core issues surrounding the arthritic hump on her thoracic vertebrae. For most people, the emotional and mental issues heal first and then the physical body follows. Beverley's was the opposite.

Layers of misqualified energy from many lifetimes come up for healing. We heal one issue, feel good, and then something else comes up for healing. For many people, total spontaneous remissions would be too much of a shock; the process has to be gradual. **How quickly or how gradually the process unfolds** depends upon a great many factors. How ingrained is the negative thought form? How many lifetimes has this thought pattern been repeated? How much work has the individual done on him/herself before coming in for a healing? How much energy is the healer able to channel? And is the healer focused and concentrating on the healee? In group sessions it is beneficial for healees to focus attention on the healing energy emanating from the healer.

All healing energy comes directly from God; healers are channels through which healing energy flows. **Healing techniques** described in this and other books may be utilized. Many healers pray for or invoke the help of Angels, guides, Jesus, Mary and other masters, whom Mother-Father God works through them. **Charismatic healers** work with the energy of the Holy Spirit, which effectively but unpredictably flows into their crown chakras, and out the palms of their hands. To increase rays of Universal healing energy, the tip of the tongue may be placed on the roof of the mouth. **Breath is powerful**; the soul enters the body of a newborn with the first breath and leaves the body with the last breath. Healees may exhale misqualified energy through his/her mouth and breathe in beneficial energy through his/her nose. Rays of healing may also emanate through the healer's breath, and healers may use their breath to blow away gray cloudy areas in healees.

Sometimes, Angels **release misqualified energy** through a burning sensation, which may be very intense. During a healing demonstration in Ireland, a man with severe kidney problems sweat through his jacket – but at the end, he was better. Sometimes, fire burns and transforms immediately; other times, the 'stuff' comes out and fills my hands. I may place my hand directly on the body where the pain or disease is and ask the healee to visualize the Angels working within, or to will the pain or disease into my hand. Blockages have different energy patterns, and produce different sensations. For example, cancer cells often feel spongy. Pain may be electric, sharp or dull. Oftentimes, I am able to describe the healees' pain to him/her without actually being in pain myself. When pain fills my hands, I grab it and slowly pull it off. It is then either thrown downwards to the central core of fire, or I lift it upwards and then push it to Light for transformation. Making counterclockwise circles with my hands helps release unwanted energy patterns; however, sometimes a few clockwise circles in

46

between help to loosen the blocks. Hot, cold or electrical, the healee may or may not feel the same sensation that I do. Regardless of how "stuff" comes off, when my healee realizes that I personally am not taking on board his/her 'stuff', it is easier for him/her to release and heal. Sometimes, the only thing that people perceive during and after a healing sensation is that they feel better.

Another method for releasing blockages works with electromagnetic energy and is actually the first step in becoming a psychic surgeon. Stretch your arms out straight and place the palms of your hands on the healee. Visualize and feel yourself becoming an electromagnet. See blocks, like iron pellets, being drawn up into the arms of the magnet. Ask the healee to visualize or feel this process; or to will unwanted physical, mental or emotional 'stuff' into the magnet. Slowly lift your arms above your head, keeping the palms of the hands facing the ground. When you've reached up as far as possible, flip your hands over, reversing the polarity of the magnet. Push misqualified energy to the Light for transformation. Wash your hands and arms in the Light. Repeat this process at least 2 more times. What do healees think about my strange behavior? They are grateful! Altering the foundation of disease or pain in the etheric initiates changes in the physical.

Sometimes, I need to excuse myself and run my hands and arms under real water; coldwater breaks up any remaining vestiges of unwanted energy patterns. When blockages leave, the healee often experience emptiness. This void needs to be filled so that the same energy or something like it isn't drawn back. So, I simply place my hands on the body or in the aura, and allow Angels and other spirit helpers to fill the area with healing. Angels know what is required. A healer might also focus above the crown. Then by following the vertical energy line upwards, s/he may contact the Universal palette or rainbow of colors, which is available to everyone (see page 56). **Once the blockage is released, the healee should not talk about the way s/he used to feel, or s/he will call the misqualified energy back to him/her by reweaving the old energy patterns.** This is difficult for women, because talking is a way in which women release. Talk about negativity during the session!

While releasing blockages, many people are not aware of what it is leaving. If they do not need to know, these individuals have worked out their **Karma** and learned their lessons. If the lesson is learned, physical healing can and will occur. A healer may also pull off Karma that has been worked out off the healee to usher in healing. (Typically, Karma that has been worked out during an individual's lifetime is released at the time of death.) On the other hand, if disease or pain is caused by a present mode of thinking, emotional pattern, or behavior, then it is helpful for the individual to be aware of what it is they are or are not doing. For example, there are people in this world whose utterances are more poisonous than a viper. Like mosquitoes, their words have a nasty and incessant sound, which stings and leaves behind a mean welt. If no one has ever asked these individuals, in the moment these words are spoken, to listen to what they are saying, then it is up to the Angels to guide the healing in such a way that they can see for themselves how harmful and destructive their words are both themselves and others.

If the individual is unwilling to change, healing will not hold. I realized in the middle of one healing session that the individual was an alcoholic. He was loaded with demons because alcohol and drugs create real holes in the aura through which low-vibrational energies may enter. He had distain for others. A lot of his pain, dizziness, and uncontrolled movements were removed during the session. Angels tried to tell him through me that other realities do exist, and not to worry about the recession – its just money. I worked on him for almost two hours, at the end of which time, he pulled out a large wad of large bills and threw $50 on the counter, scoffing, "It's just money!" Yet, I was still impressed to try one more time to get through to him by encouraging him to try to give up drinking. His face softened and he said, "My doctor tells me the same thing!" After he left, the massage table and room required an exorcism as well as a clearing. Later that night, I saw a psychic impression of the man back on a barstool and his symptoms returning.

Bad movies, haunting scenes from the past, and **self-destructive CDs playing in the brain**, may be released and transformed in the healing process. Mental chatter, judgments, mental torture chambers, and worries prevent us from thinking. The idea is not to "stuff" these thoughts, but breathe them away. As mental clutter leaves, breathe in peace of mind. When the brain is clear, ideas come in. Some actors and actresses become addicted to drugs and alcohol because their positive affirmation is the final product, rather than all of the necessary qualities, abilities and personality traits it took to get them the part and carry it off. It is always the process that is the product! The end NEVER justifies the means. When we die, all we take with us is our experiences.

Looking past masks of pain and disease to discover and accept what is in us that is creating the problem is not easy! It's also difficult to accpet that Mother-Father God has always loved and forgiven us. We do not relish the idea that we are not only the actor/actress in our lives, but that we are every bit as much the screenwriter, director and producer. We take solace in thinking of ourselves as victims, rather than seeing that we are co-creators of the events in our lives. **When ego creates a world of denial, justification or our state of being is numbed out**; warped personal truth separates us from Universal Truth and Oneness. There are people who participate in extreme sports because it is the only way in which they are able to feel anything. However, when we clearly see how we create our 'negative' role, then we call a halt to the game. Egos are necessary. It is always the extremes that are detrimental. In the case of ego, the extremes are narcissism or self-deprecation.

What is masking us is denial, distortion, omission, substitutions, misunderstanding or inversion. In extreme reversals we may see evil as good and good as evil, which causes us to do just the opposite of what is good for us. For example, while there are many possible reasons for being overweight, excess pounds may serve as protection. In the Piscean Age, many psychics subconsciously put on excessive weight for protection, which caused health issues. Other people ask for or put up **too much psychic protection** to shield themselves from other people's thoughts. In excess nothing is able to get in or out – that includes healing and Universal initiations into healing. Because energy is not able to move, it becomes stagnant, heavy and black. The only way in which a healer may take down the barriers is with the healee's awareness and change of mind.

Fasting is counterproductive for losing weight because it throws the metabolisms off. However, a juice fast may help to clear the body and bring up the emotion hiding behind the disease or the weight. Heal the emotional issues, and the pounds come off. There are many good **juice fasts**, each for a specific organ or gland, listed in Hanna Kroeger's book, <u>Old-Time Remedies for Modern Ailments</u>. On the third day of a fast or cleansing, hunger comes up the strongest. Eating feeds the emotion; resisting hunger brings emotions up for healing. Some people find it beneficial to work with a professional or healing facilitator while fasting. The physical release provided by colonics encourages mental and emotional release as well. However, some individuals hold on so tightly that colonics do not work on any level!

True, many individuals have childhood and adolescent pain from this lifetime to heal. For most, wounds go back further. Brian Weiss, M.D. has written books on **reincarnation**, the most familiar being <u>Many Lives, Many Masters</u>. The greater majority of medical doctors who are presented with past-life facts in their patients ignore them; thus, the issue is ignored. In experiencing a past-life regression, if we are with a trained therapist or qualified healer, when the unresolved issue or misunderstanding surfaces, then the disease or pain is transformed, released and healed. Past life regression is not to find out who we were; it is important to live in the moment rather than the past.

Reincarnation means that God is much more loving, because he give a soul more than one chance to 'get it right.' How appropriate to experience our thoughts and actions coming back to us in future lifetimes. However, this remained conceptual until I experienced a past life for myself. Getting into a past life is not just watching a nice visual movie played in the brain, although visuals of having lived before are experienced through the brain. Getting into a past life is just that, feeling and knowing it in one's core. **Realization of having lived before may be momentary, but the impact of the experience is life changing.**

My first experience with a past life came after I watched a series entitled <u>The Six Wives of Henry VIII</u>. Henry's first wife, who had been his older brother's wife, was very popular and nobody in England liked his second wife, Anne Boleyn. Nobody cried when Anne was beheaded. I didn't like her either. Shortly after the series, I was in a place of no mind and no thoughts, simply making my bed. All of a sudden, it felt like someone punched me in my solar plexus, leaving behind an autobiography of Anne Boleyn's life, her feelings and thoughts. I knew things, like the fact that Anne had a lying and abusive brother who raped her when she was a girl, she was an excellent horse rider, played a stringed musical instrument, had a lovely singing voice, and her family was secretly connected to Celtic magic and healing. Anne remained earthbound after her death, protecting her daughter, Elizabeth. Within a week's time, a psychic approached me. Apparently, my aura was so traumatized that she took one look at me and said, "You were Anne Boleyn, weren't you?" Openmouthed, I could say nothing. She went on to say, "You have been carrying a burden of shame for hundreds of years. You didn't have to be beheaded in that lifetime; it was your own guilt that brought you to the executioner. Just think of it this way - you didn't ask Henry to marry you. Henry asked you to marry him." With that, overwhelming self-hatred that I had carried since a small child was lifted from me. When I met Henry VIII in this lifetime, he was a Roman Catholic priest.

One thing that remains active in this lifetime from my Anne Boleyn reincarnation is what I call 'the voice.' It has always been with me, and I never know when it will come out. I used to teach first grade at a Catholic school under my former married name, Kathleen Owrey. One Good Friday, several church members were playing modern renditions of old Bible songs. As I walked down the aisle on my way to kiss the cross, all of a sudden I found myself belting out the melody with the boys in the band. For what seemed like forever, everyone else stopped singing. It felt like my whole body was blushing. Other symptoms included an occasional recurring stiff neck, and the ability to rideHealing paid off! In April 2009, I was able to connect to the roots of Celtic Shamanism, magic and healing at Kelkenny Castle, the childhood home of Anne Boleyn's paternal grandmother.

Child prodigies bring in with them talent developed in other lifetimes. Often these children are finishing this experience and move onto other things as an adult. However, there were several 20-year-old+ reincarnations of former singers in the 2009 *American Idol* contest; including Elvis! People who have remembrances of past lives when they travel on vacation or business are being given a gift from Spirit, whereby that individual might know that other realities do exist. In addition, if a misunderstanding, fear, etc. from that past life has manifested in their current life, there is an opportunity to heal then or to see a professional psychologist or healer.

When I intentionally guide an individual through a **past-life regression**, or if one comes up suddenly during a healing session, I suggest that the individual will be able to rise above his/her body at any time and observe the process. In this way, fear of physical pain is not an issue. While the healee is regressing, I meditate and journey along. In this way, healing comes through my third eye, and I am better able to see if the individual is observing someone else or is living the experience. It is similar to Shamanic soul retrieval. However, in soul retrieval work, the healee is in a non-active meditation, while I am actively participating in a deep meditative state. In regression I guide the experience and listen. A healee's guilt or fear may cause denials. For example, Mary reached the end of the tunnel *(which actually represents the birth canal)* and she saw herself as a woman in ancient Egypt. As we walked into the pyramid, she saw a craftsman and said, "I don't understand this; at the bottom of the tunnel I saw myself as a woman and now I see myself as a man. Who am I?" When I asked her who she was, Mary said, "I want to be the artisan." I suggested that she ask her Guardian Angel who she was. Her Guardian Angel told her that she was the woman. There was confusion because she didn't want to see who she really was. It turned out that Mary was a high priestess *(in her present life she didn't even know that there was such a thing)* who was excessively cruel and abused her power. In two other lifetimes we visited, and also in her present lifetime, Mary was and still is a 'victim.'

In another past life regression Mary saw the reason why she had been unable to leave her current husband. In the past life regression Mary had been a badly battered woman. She left her husband and took their two children to another town where she became a beggar. One of her children died shortly afterwards. Later, a man took in both her and her surviving child. He ignored her child, who later ran away, and the man abused her. She died in shame, guilt and fear. Mary now understood the reason why every time she wanted to leave her present husband, a terrible, unknown fear totally and literally consume her. Somewhere in her subconscious was the memory that if she left her husband, things would only get worse. Now Mary was free to make a clear, fearless decision as to whether to stay in her current marriage or get a divorce.

In order to get the healee to the particular moment where the misqualified thought form originated, I suggest that they **go to an important day in their life**. Their higher self or subconscious knows what I mean and will get us to the right place and time. I then ask the healee questions so that they are able to describe what is going on. There also may be more than one misunderstanding in more than one lifetime, but the first incident is usually the most important. I may ask, "What do the Angels want to show you?" The final step is to ask them to go to the last day of their life and observe the death process. Hovering over their body, the healee watches the soul leave with the last breath. The process is empowering in itself - seeing and knowing that personality survives death.

51

That individual need never fear death again. I then ask the healee to call in his/her Angels and spirit guides.   Depending on the situation, my questions go something like this: "What did you come into this lifetime to learn or experience?" "Where was there a misunderstanding?" "What and who needs to be healed?" Using the healee's own visualization and feeling process, Angels heal, resolve, transform and release pain. If we have gone to other lifetimes, I will ask, "How does this lifetime relate to the last lifetime? How are both of these lifetimes related to your current life?"

Sometimes a healee has a specific request. Samuel Minond had told Charlotte that she needed to go back to one of her Egyptian lifetimes in order to meet the scribe of Isis. This wasn't going to be easy! We were going down the tunnel. One moment Charlotte was with me, the next moment she was nowhere to be found. I asked her where she was, and she replied, "I don't know." So I asked her to ask Chris, her son who had passed away, where she was. Chris said, "Ma, you're in Never-Never Land." Good avoidance strategy; go look for the mermaids, pirates and seals! After getting back on course and down and out the tunnel, we were in ancient Egypt. Temples and monuments were very large in comparison to the human figure, so that mankind might keep a healthy perspective with Mother-Father God. We found the scribe of Isis, who was angrily accusing Charlotte of a crime. Charlotte sniffed burning rubber. Suddenly, she realized that she smelled herself on fire. She had been found guilty of stealing secret esoteric writings. As punishment she had been tarred and was now burning.   Horrified, Charlotte experienced old shame and guilt, coming up to be released and transformed. She observed the death process from a distance and watched the soul rise out of the body. I asked her to consult with her spirit guides and Angels and ask them, "What was my lesson in this lifetime?" She was told, "Listen to yourself." Apparently, someone else had asked her to steal the documents and she had never questioned within as to whether or not it was appropriate for her to do so. By looking at the event from another angle, she could see her lesson, release shame and horror, and heal.   When I told Charlotte that it has only been recently that people have been encouraged to look within and ask God questions, she was relieved.

Then the scribe took Charlotte to the Akashic Records, which contains the Truth of all memories and events. I was then guided to help Charlotte find the screen to the Akashic Records in her inner laboratory. Charlotte's male guide, David, had always actively assisted her, while her female guide, Shoshanna, came in only for group hugs. Now it was Shoshanna, who led Charlotte to this sacred well of wisdom. Shoshanna said that the knowledge found within the Akashic Records is available only through the healed feminine. In order to access the portal into the Mind of Mother-Father God, we must be willing to do the inner work by looking at events, lifetimes and attitudes where power is abused and love is cast asunder. Letting Light and Love into all of the dark corners through visualization in meditation helps heal issues and ushers in forgiveness. The only question Charlotte was allowed of the Akashic screen was, "What is it I am to know?"

In dealing with emotional patterns of their clients, modern psychologists may work with the **inner child**. From the time of the first trauma, or the day the youth began taking drugs, that child's emotional body stopped growing. Charlotte says that what psychology fails to do is to put the horror that the child experiences in perspective. If we are dealing with an inner child who is overwhelmed, the burden of shame is magnified in the child's eyes and looms toweringly overhead. By seeing the guilt in another viewpoint, it becomes at first manageable, and then healed and released.

Sometimes a healee will flip into a past life during a healing session without being regressed. Before he even came to me, a former priest objected dramatically to the possibility of past lives. He even asked me if it was necessary for him to believe in reincarnation in order for him to schedule an appointment to see me. I responded that it didn't matter to me whether or not he believed in reincarnation. Then he asked me if I was going to try to talk him into believing in reincarnation. I answered, "No!" During the healing session, suddenly he found himself dramatically experiencing another lifetime as a Mayan priest. While journeying through the temple, we found souls held earthbound within a dark room. We were asked by the Angels and spirit guides present to lead the lost souls into the Light. It felt as if there was an aspect of the priest's soul that had been held in the temple as well. As the priest led the trapped souls to the Light in his past life meditation, he was also guiding his own past life to healing. My perception was that because of his misuse of power in that lifetime, others had fallen off the path, or in this case, into a pyramid after they died. He was now the best one to offer them a way to the Light. His subconscious and super-conscious were aware of this; it was not necessary for his conscious mind to know. Therefore, I did not share my perceptions with the healee. If he needed to know, his guides would have told him.

Numerous people who have come to me for healings have flipped into past lives where they were burned alive as witches. If an individual is reluctant to do psychic or healing work in this lifetime, his/her fear may stem directly back to an experience where s/he died because of his/her beliefs. When the past life is healed, the individual no longer needs to make fear-based decisions. The inner clutch is gone. Other times, people see themselves being burned as witches because they are paying Karma for times when they burned others at the stake. **Everything we do comes back!**

Sometimes a past life surfaces for a healee after I receive an impression. I was working on a woman at Ishpiming when I heard the name, *Constantine*. As there are relatively few 'famous people' in history, my left-brain jumped in, stating emphatically, *No!* Heard the name again. Feeling the power of the woman's spirit under my hands, my left-brain conjured the possibility that perhaps this was one of Constantine's generals. The name, Constantine, persistently repeated! Reluctantly, I spoke the name, "Constantine," to her.

Her eyes opened wide, amazed that I had picked up what she had known for most of her life. She told me her story. Ever since the age of three, she had cried irrepressible tears at every new and every full moon. Thus far, Transcendental Meditation was the only working method of controlling her uncontrollable remorse. She went on to say that she carried within her heart a heavy object. She longed to return to the Light and trusted that I had released my own judgments and was channeling the healing energy she needed to heal. As past lives were being healed during the session, I pulled off many past-life cloaks and garb, which represented the shedding of and healing of old issues. Included in her etheric closet were many red hats as well as pontiff hats. However, there was one particular bishop's hat that was too familiar to me. Suddenly, the realization came that this man had had me burned alive as a witch. Singeing smoke filled in my lungs. Her friend and one of my students were observing the process. Later, they told me that my face went white when I saw the bishop's hat and they expected me to either start choking the healee or throw her off of the table. Instead, I helped her to release her guilt and even explained to her that many ascended masters had lived lifetimes as warriors, and were still fighting for the Light. As Constantine and the many past lives between then and now were healed, it felt as if smoke was clearing out of my lungs. Because I put aside judgments and aided my 'enemy,' great healing came to me. Angels told me that I would never fully be conscious of the rewards bestowed upon me because of this single act of compassion. Your enemies may or may not come to you for healing or forgiveness; if they do, heaven will reward you for your generosity of compassion.

Sometimes during past-life regressions, I utilize the opportunity to satisfy my own left-brained curiosity. The Illuminati or the Illumined Ones date directly back to Constantine. These are the seven families, who own the greater majority of the world's wealth. The Illuminati is the 7-headed beast in the <u>Apocalypse</u>. Larry Abraham says they call themselves the Illuminati because they think they know something that the rest of us do not know; that is, that there is no God. They also refer to themselves as the sons of Apollo. Peter de Rosa, a former priest who worked in the Vatican archives for years, wrote a book, <u>Vicars of Christ, The Dark Side of the Papacy</u>. In this book he describes how Constantine was praying before a metal statue of Apollo, the sun god, the day before he and his men marched upon Rome. They did not have a chance of victory. Suddenly, Constantine saw black rays pouring out of the statue and he knew that his prayers had been answered. I asked the healee, who was experiencing her past life as Constantine, about the incident. She told me that Constantine knew in the moment that the rays were evil and assumed that God was evil. It was not God that answered his prayers; Constantine only assumed that it was God. More likely it was Lucifer himself. If Constantine had asked in Divine Truth who was answering his prayers, he would have known. But then, how many people today are taught to question? Rather many blindly accept or assume. (Peter DeRosa's book is well researched and documented. It made the *New York Times* best-seller list, but it is no longer available. Somebody bought up all of the copies!)

Another time while I was working with Charlotte in New York, she went back to a lifetime where she was a high priestess in the Temple of Isis. When I learned how to do Native American journeywork with one of Michael Harner's teachers, Myron Eshowsky, I knew that I had done journeywork in the Egyptian temples. The definition of Shaman means, "one who works in the dark". To help reach deep states of meditation and to be able to see clearly with the third eye, the Shaman often wears a blindfold while journeying. While working with Charlotte, I discovered that **the veil of Isis' is the Shaman's blindfold**. Looking deeper, I saw that journeywork was as much an integral aspect of Egyptian metaphysical practice as it was with the Celtics or Wiccans. It still is with indigenous people. We have not begun to fully comprehend either the use of, or how extensively Shamanic journeywork was practiced. Mary Magdalene was not a prostitute! One pope decided that she was the one that Jesus saved from stoning. Mary Magdalene was a priestess and one of Jesus' followers. When she comes to me she refers to herself as "Mary Magdalene of the Veil."

Healing past lives is a means of healing the present, but people do not have to go through a past life to face the emotional issues behind the pain and disease. **Rebirthing** is another means of bringing emotions to the surface. The rebirthing breath is the breath of infants, particularly during the birthing process. That is, there is no pause at either the bottom of the exhale or top of the inhale. Breathing is continuous. Rebirthing therapists guide their clients through the embryo stage in uterus, birthing and childhood. In this way, the breath surfaces negative emotions that are experienced, released and healed. Sometimes people are simply guided on their own to do this breath during a hands-on healing session. Often this happens when a healee has done rebirthing.

Re-birthers say that hope is for the hopeless; it is the last stage of hopelessness. Rather than Faith, Hope and Charity, re-birthers might see the three virtues as Faith, Trust and Charity. Hope is looking for a specific outcome; Trust is allowing Mother-Father God to handle the details of our desires. It is important in healing for both the healer and healee to trust that God through Holy Spirit and the Angels will bring up issues that are ready to be released. Along with the release there occurs a corresponding healing of the body, mind and emotions. The nature of healing is such that the healer gets out of the way and allows the individual to heal or not to heal in his/her own way, and in his/her own time. When healings occur, we are able to see God in our lives.

There are many techniques that a healer may utilize and the success of any technique is dependent on the healing energy that is being channeled. Two of my students had the following experience with a healer who dealt with emotional issues in the following manner: When **Eleanor Moore** facilitated group healings, she had one individual lie upon a massage table. Everyone else present touched, comforted and encouraged the healee. Then everyone began chanting, "Ohm". During each healing process, Eleanor would pay attention as to which side of the healee's body experienced pain or paralysis. If the discomfort was on the left side, the issue went back to a woman *(mother, sister or grandmother, etc.)* and Eleanor would have the healee yell, "Caw" *(like the sound that the crow makes)*. If it manifested on the right side, the issue went back to a man *(father, brother or grandfather, etc.)* and Eleanor would have her client yell "K" *(pronounced just like the letter K in the English alphabet)*. The words themselves carry no meaning, yet they allow unexpressed righteous anger, fear and other emotions to be experienced and released so that healing transpires. What I tell the healees is this, "Your parent *(or perpetrator be s/he alive or dead)* is literally counting on you to yell out and express your buried rage. In this way you might break the cycle of pain and negative experiences for you both."

Healers may use this process when working on individuals. I encourage healees to participate in the healing process by sharing what is going on. If a healee has a sudden pain or paralysis and I am inspired to use this method, I call upon Eleanor's spirit to assist in the healing. I place my left hand on the solar plexus and my right hand on the heart chakra. Depending upon which side of their body holds the pain or paralysis, I have them yell "K" or "caw" at their perpetrator. I have had clients who have had one whole side of their body become suddenly paralyzed; dramatically revealing how constricting and debilitating negative emotions may bind us. At this point, I reassure the healee that something has come up to be healed and that they will regain normal movement after they start yelling "K" or "caw," and they always do. Release may be encouraged if I stroke my hand up the healee's neck, and then grab and pull fear and rage out of their mouth.

Sometimes, people who think that they have an issue with one parent actually are angry with the other. For example, women who were sexually abused by their fathers as girls may have pain or paralysis on the left side. These particular women are mad at their mothers for saying nothing and allowing their fathers to rape and molest them. One of my clients in about an hour's time went from her left side (physically beaten by her mother), to her right side (sexually abused by her grandfather), and back to her left side (mentally and emotionally abused by her grandmother). In any of these cases, the healer may place his/her hand on the throat and massage gently upwards to aid in the releasing process. Depending upon the circumstances, to further encourage release, I might say, "This is a yell?" or, "See your perpetrator doing something to you, or saying something you hated them for. Feel your anger. Now yell at them." Or "Feel it and release it, feel it and let it go."

A client's throat may become sore after only yelling a few times or even once, which is an indication that it is time to stop and breathe in Light and Love from Mother-Father God. In this healing modality, it is not the yelling that makes the throat sore but rather the emotion that is finally being expressed. As the emotion is released and healed, the physical is released and healed.

Unexpressed, buried anger manifests as dysfunctional behavior. The following method works for many people, whose rage is so deep that they are afraid to bring it up. It is a safe way to voice fury. I begin by asking the healee if s/he would be willing to have the Angels bring into the mind's eye the people whom s/he is incensed at. And that one at a time, the healee will vent rage by killing the individual with a submachine gun, shark, fire, axe, or other means of destruction. I explain that the healee is NOT killing people or harming their souls in any way. **The individuals, or more appropriately the images that the Angels bring in represent only unexpressed anger. The healee is killing off childhood misperceptions, fears and attitudes that have distorted and 'messed up' his/her whole life.** Quite literally, the people who are represented by the forms in the inner eye are counting on the healee to break up the rage and stop the downward cycle.

For example, Connie began with her coldhearted mother whose form immediately turned to stone. Connie and the Angels dynamited her mother! Connie, to her amazement, felt a release of anger. She brought in her father. His form was a thick mucus-like substance that had a foul stench. She torched him! Again she felt a release. Connie was surprised when the Angels brought in her sister; Connie didn't even know that she was angry with her. When I asked Connie to ask her Angels why she was angry, she was told it was because she felt that her sister was a burden. So she stuck her sister's feet in a bucket of cement, waited for it to harden, and then Connie and the Angels threw her sister off of a bridge! Connie at this point was feeling strangely empty without the anger she had held onto for so long. So, I asked the Angels to bring in the colors of cobalt blue and pink, unconditional love, forgiveness of herself and others. She then began allowing herself and others to find their own way home. If the healee is not ready for this method, it is OK. In either case, the hearler does not interfere so as to make the healee's process fit the healer's preconception.

Oftentimes, the healee will see him/herself in his/her mind's eye as the last person to be 'undone' or 'done in'. The healee is dying to old perceptions, attitudes and fears that no longer serve him/her. Sometimes, God enters. Many people blame God because for personal or world chaos rather than looking within. This is not an unholy act! These people are blasting apart their

57

own limited misperceptions of God so that the Truth is able to shine in. The Aquarian Age will heal mankind's anger with God. This process of seeing oneself in the mind's eye is akin to what is called the death of the Shaman, whereby the Shaman in deep meditation sees him/herself being eaten by the thing s/he fears the most. **What is being eaten is his/her fear.** In healing **sessions the healer may also watch him/herself in his/her mind's eye to see what happens**. This keeps the healer's left brain occupied and out of the way, and the healing energy is intensified. When the healer sees his/her back, that means that another aspect of the healer is involved in the healing.

The Priest Melchizedek, who is mentioned in the Old Testament, established a healing order of priests and priestesses. In the New Testament, Jesus initiates a priest into the Order of Melchizedek. I believe that Melchizedek programmed **touch points on the body**, which aid in the healing process. (In self-healing, crystals may be held.) Using these touch points is not mandatory. They are certainly helpful when the area of involvement on the body of the healee would not be appropriate or too painful for the healer to touch. Healers might begin by feeling through the aura for static or blockages, or douse the charkas. By asking the healee to **breathe Light into a pain** or breathe away negativity, s/he becomes involved in his/her healing process. It is also a technique that the healee may do on his or her own. When the healing energy is Universal, the healer or healee may wear watches. Praying, visualizing or watching the Angels work, and wearing crystals or Trachyon products increases the healing energy. Trachyon is a technology! (www.tachyon-energy-products.com) As an example of how initiations have become marketed, some unauthorized Trachyon sites offer absentee initiations into a technology used on inanimate objects. Yes, the objects work, but how is it possible for a living being to be initiated into a technology?

After going through the aura, **clear the mental body and mind**. Place the palms of the hands on the head of the humerus (top of the upper arm bone) with fingertips pointing down towards their hands. Ask the healee to keep his/her hands off the body. Allow energy to work. Give suggestions; such as, "Bring up and release any judgments that you are still holding on yourself or others." "Bring up and release any thoughts of lack and limitation. We live in an abundant universe. We are the beloved children of a Father-Mother God who loves us dearly." "Bring up and release any old negative programs, mental torture chambers or judgments." **Healer works his/her hands down one arm and hand, pulls negativity out the fingertips, sends 'stuff' down to the central fire, and clicks his/her fingers.** Asks healee if s/he feels a difference in the two arms. Typically, the arm that has just been cleared feels lighter or tingly. This gives the healee his/her own affirmation that all of the work s/he is doing is helping. As the mind becomes quieter, it is more receptive.

To further aid in **mental healing** and to balance and integrate the two hemispheres of the brain, healer may place the left hand on the forehead and the right hand directly opposite at the back of the head. If there is a throbbing, something is breaking up. When it stops, take hold of the misqualified thought forms and lift hands and arms <u>slowly</u> up through the seven layers associated with each of the major chakras and release it to the Light for transformation, or throw it down to the central fire, or to the Violet Flame. Making counterclockwise circles with the hands before grabbing the energy is helpful. Whenever **the healer's hands start to feel heavy**, it is an indication that something is ready to be released. And again, by intention grab it, lift if off and send it to the Light, to the Violet Flame or throw it downwards to the central fire for transformation. Mercury, monkey's blood, formaldehyde and other toxic substances that are found in vaccinations may be pulled off by the healer as well through hands-on healing, working in the aura, using the pain drain (page 60), or a combination of the three.

Another method for pulling off negative thought forms is for the healer to **send negativity to the Light for transformation.** I place my hands on the healee so that the palms of the hands are parallel to the earth. Visualizing or feeling myself becoming an electromagnet, I keep my arms straight. I see the blockages moving up like iron pellets being drawn up to the arms of a magnet. I lift my arms slowly. When I reach the seventh layer, I flip my hands, which reverses the polarity of your magnet, and push the psychic debris into the Light for transformation. Keeping my arms elevated, I take my right hand and work it up my left arm to the fingertips and send misqualified energy to the Light. Then repeat the process with my right arm and left hand; thus, clearing my own hands before touching the healee again. If I have sent misqualified energy to the central fire, I wash my etheric arms and hands in a downward movement, or shake my hands and click my fingers over a visualized Violet Flame. If my hands at any point feel uncomfortably heavy after clearing, I will excuse myself and wash them up to the elbows in coldwater. I have never had a client yet who objected to this. The healee wants to release his/her 'stuff' and s/he is in a better position to will misqualified energy into my hands when they know that I am not contracting his/her disease. Washing hands and arms in coldwater up to the elbows is also a very good thing for healers to do after each healing session. Saying *disconnect* three times after a healing or psychic session to separate the healer from the healee. Ramona Kirk uses the earth to clear herself after doing healing or psychic work (page 103).

To **drain misqualified energy** from an area, the left hand is above the area in the aura. For example, for mental healing that might be over the head or the heads of the humerus. However, mental trauma may be held anywhere in the body. The right hand points downward towards the central fire within Mother Earth. There is actually a pulling up or vacuum-like sensation in the left hand. As misqualified energy is transferred from the left to right hand, it may be best to keep the right arm and hand in front of the body and out of the way of flying debris. The same routine is followed: After pulling off misqualified energy and cleansing the hands, fill the area with Light by placing the hands back on the body. When I was a little girl, I never did hands-on healing; I simply watched the Angels or prayed, and things would happen or healing would transpire. I learned the basics of hands-on healing in the Reiki I class that I took. Prayers are much more effective when they are poured out through the heart.   Likewise, a healee's open heart aids the healing process.

While reading The Four Insights by Alberto Villoldo, John Ostrovskis had his own insight. Anywhere in the body misperception may be trapped and concentrated; this is the **Assemblage Point**. John lifts his consciousness above his head, which puts the Universal healing energy he is channeling and himself in the hand of Archangels. John watches in his mind's eye and feels freezing cold in his arms, as an Archangel works through his arms and hands, grasps the Assemblage Point and release it to the Light. As emotional attachment to the issue is released, it helps the healee to deal with problems objectively.   (John also channeled in the Aqua Blue healing energy.)

To heal the **emotional body and emotions**, the left hand is on the solar plexus (repressed anger is held in the liver and adversely affects the solar plexus) and right hand holds the healee's left. Left hand remains on the solar plexus no matter what happens.   Once, a voice came out of a healee, saying that it lived just below where my left hand was. Smiling, I answered, "That's nice!" but kept my hand on the healee's solar plexus. My agreement with Mother-Father God from my first Reiki class has been that S/He knows how much healing energy can be channeled through me, and what my spirit guides and Angels are able to do. In cases of possession, the healee's solar plexus will expand, even pushing or punching my hand out six inches or more. Regardless of what happens, I keep my left hand where it is. If I need to pull off, I use my right hand only. I may pull off at the touch point where my right hand rests (in this case it is the healee's left hand) or where the healee is directing me. The healee is encouraged to bring emotions up, feel them, and then release them into the ring of fire in the palms of my hands. Oftentimes, it is uncomfortable for the healee to feel heavy emotions as they come up, but by holding onto them the constraint on the physical body is far worse.

One time, a man who had been raped, grabbed my left hand and threw it off of his solar plexus. Running off into another room, he cried for two hours. What he chose to keep with him was far worse than if he had gone on with the healing process for 5 or 10, or even 20 more minutes. It was his choice. There are no judgments. He was apparently not ready to release the issue or his trauma. Like each of us, he could only do what he was capable of in the moment. For those people who are ready to release or walk through fear, Angels encourage them to let go.

60

There are also people who enjoy wallowing in misery; it is easier to feel depressed than to make the effort to be joyful. For those who find it unpleasant to feel misqualified emotional energy patterns, the good news is that when the core emotions are felt, transformed and released during a healing session, that's it! They are gone! In order to do this, we have to be willing to look within. For example, people who want to control others live outside of themselves; thus, avoiding working on their own issues. The paradox is that in seeking to control others, these people are always giving away their own power. **True power comes from respect, not fear.**

Next, my right hand moves to healee's right shoulder. Fear resides around the neck, which may be seen on the astral plane as iron collars, ropes, swords, guillotines, etc. However, once I saw a golden rope tied around a man's neck. When I asked spirit what this was, I was told that his wealthy parents used money to control their son. I may or may not tell the healee what it is that I see. Sometimes, they have already seen it first in their own inner vision. Cut, untie, or pull out the implement of shame or death, using both inner vision and physical hands in the aura. What can I say? It works! Necks maybe a sensitive area, and the release process can be dramatic.

Next, holding the healee's right hand in my right hand, I use the same process as described above. Then I move my right hand to the healee's left shoulder. Here, I check to see if either anything is still going on in the neck or if something else is about to begin. In about 20 minutes, I have made an "X" over their body with my right hand. Then I use both of my hands to pull the heavy emotional debris out of the solar plexus, scoop out and then drain the pus-like substance, cauterize the area with cobalt blue color, and have the Angels fill the area with Light, colors, tones, herbs, flower remedies and healing symbols. Oftentimes, the healee will either smell or see the herbs or flower essences. Angels usually use cobalt blue for cauterizing. It is a color of healing and sanitizing, and it cools down irritated tissues of the etheric body. Cobalt blue also seals off areas of infection so that it will not spread. Angels use blue on cancer; red, orange and even yellow are too hot; green is a color of growth and violet is a color of expansion. For additional information on cancer, Hanna Kroeger's book, Cancer Begins in the Colon, is excellent. She believes that toxic, encrusted, and impacted fecal matter provides a home for parasites, which take nutrients for themselves. These parasites also travel through the body, spewing their toxic waste and cause cancer. Black Walnut, Wormwood and Pumpkin Seeds may rid the body of parasites; colonics and colon cleansers are beneficial. First thing in the morning, lemon juice and warm water help the intestines move. Lemon juice or 1/4 teaspoon of baking soda with water alkalizes the body.

After the mental and emotional clearings, I focus on the physical body, using specific touch points for different areas. I used to tell people that they are like the ones Jesus used. Every

61

clairaudient would respond by saying, "I am hearing that these are not like the touch points Jesus used; these are the touch points Jesus used."

For the **bones**, the touch point is between the seventh cervical and the first thoracic vertebrae. These two vertebrae form a bony protuberance at the back of the neck. The palm of the right hand is placed over this spot. The palm of the left hand is held inside the upper left arm. *(The back of the neck will be sore if there is a fracture or break in a bone.)* For the **spine,** right hand remains on the back of the neck; left hand is over the tailbone. Let energy and colors run through the spinal fluid. John Sarno, M.D., author of Healing Back Pain, is professor of Clinical Rehabilitation Medicine at New York School of Medicine and attending physician at the Howard A. Rusk Institute of Rehabilitation Medicine at New York University Medical Center. He says that **pain is a symptom, which results from repressed emotions, specifically anger and rage.** However, if the healee is in such extreme pain that s/he cannot get past it to identify their issues, I work on the affected area first and then go back and do the emotional and mental clearing.

For the **tendons & ligaments**, the touch points are on the upper right arm. Left hand is over the point where the biceps becomes tendonous. Right hand is over the point where the triceps becomes tendonous. *(Myrrh oil absorbs into the skin and tendons. MSM prevents the uptake of selenium; so, take MSM for 10 days and then go off it for 2 weeks.)* For **cartilage**, I use these same touch points, and by my intention, I ask that the healing energy be directed there.

The next six touch points are exactly the same as those that were used by Hanna Kroeger, a forerunner in the field of homeopathic and herbal medicine. The touch point for the **muscles** is the point just below the flexed calf muscles on the backs of both legs, where the gastrocnemius becomes tendonous. Ethereally, with **Lou Gehrig's Disease** there is too much energy in the muscles. Energy may be pulled out at the touch point for the muscles. Or pull misqualified energy down the body and out the feet. Or clear each charka by dousing; holding the left hand in the aura, and a douser in the right hand. The right arm is straight down. *(Like the pain drain on pages 33 & 34.)* The douser automatically spins counterclockwise, oftentimes, wildly. As energy is released, the douser slows and then comes to a stop. Go back to hands-on. Techniques may be used for other ailments as well.

For the **ovaries**, I place my palms inside the lower leg just below the knees. If this is done when a woman is pregnant, miscarriage may result. My students and I have found that these touch points will also work on the male reproductive system as well.

The points for the **central nervous system** are located just below the knees at the kneecaps on the front of the leg. For the **kidneys**, on the back, place the right hand over the left kidney and the left hand over the right kidney. For the **ears**, hold the left occipital lobe in the left hand and the palm of the healee's left hand in the right hand. Then work on the other side. For the **lymph system**, place the right hand under the left armpit and the left hand at the back of the neck. If there is cancer, the aura will feel spongy. Rather than tell the healee, I simply go back to the emotional healing, asking the healee to feel past rage and breathe it away.

Sandra's sister had **cancer of the breast**; it ran in their family. She lay dying in the hospital, not from cancer, but from the damage her heart had received from radiation. Now, Sandra's breasts had begun to become hard and swollen. The doctor wanted to start running tests on her. Sandra wanted no part of it! She felt better and more hopeful after healing session. She was also guided to begin a fast she had read about. For 3 to 4 days, every 3 to 4 hours, Sandra ate 3 to 4 fresh oranges, which were the only things she ate. She even set her alarm so that she could wake up at night to do this. People she worked with laughed at her, but she didn't care. Sandra also went to a natural clinic and bought a homeopathic remedy for the lymph glands. Sandra told me that when she went to the toilet it looked like brown beer foam was coming out of her. But her breasts went back to normal and the healing held. Linus Pauling advocated large doses of Vitamin C. Other people have cured cancer by only eating fresh, raw foods, or doing a juice fast. Some people eat a pint of cottage cheese with a generous spoonful of cold pressed flax oil or apricot oil. MMS, Resveratrol and some herbal cleanses may produce flue-like symptoms. If this occurs, I take a charcoal table or bentonite clay with water to absorb the kill-off effect (toxicity that is released from dying parasites) and other toxins that are released. I also personally feel that colonics are important!

Three points for the **eyes**: Behind the ear where there is a slight indentation in the parietal bone, the angle of the jaw, and at the temporal bone to the side of the eyes. The eyes are an extension of the brain, so the mental and nerve points may also be appropriate. In Mahikari healing, for 10 minutes, the healer's left hand is raised above the healee's head to draw in Light; the right hand in the aura radiates Light to the third eye, which is closely associated with the physical eyes. Placing the left palm over the third eye helps the physical eyes and the skin. Touch points for connective tissue may also work on the lens of the eye.

For the **teeth**: The bone or the nerve touch points. For the **gums**, place hands over the ears so that the palm is over the auditory canal. This will affect the third eye, physical eyes and thymus. It is a point that helps connect the third eye and the heart. Healing gums helps to heal heart.

For the **lungs**, right hand on the forehead and left hand opposite the right at the back of the head. A second touch point for the lungs is about an inch and a half to either side of the sternum at about the 2nd or 3rd rib. It is comforting and may be used for **weight loss**.

For the **heart**: Healer's right hand holds the heel of the healee's left hand (the rounded bump before the thumb). Left hand is on healee's right shoulder, which opens the heart chakra and works on the right ventricles. When healing energy stops flowing, place left hand on healee's left shoulder. This restores the electrical balance (lemon in water also does this) and works on the left ventricles of the heart. Healer goes to the other side of the healee, holding the heal of healee's right hand in his/her left hand. The process is continued as described above.

Healers work with healee's symptoms. For example, in **multiple sclerosis**, there is typically heaviness in the heart and cloudiness in the brain. Before working on the points for nerves, work with the heart and brain points, utilizing healing techniques for removing the blockages. Repeating **positive affirmations** helps to create wellbeing: "From the Lord God of my being to the Lord God of the Universe . . . *(I release or I accept, etc.)* . . . . . . So be it and so it is."

For all **glands**, place palms over the floating ribs. Most of the misqualified energy moves down the arms, but out the fingertips only. Beneficial energy comes in through the thumbs.

For tumors or cysts in the breasts & mothering issues: The healee is sitting or standing and healer faces her right side. First, place fingertips of right hand just to the right of healee's sternum at about the 6th or 7th rib so that healer is touching the edge of the sternum. Place the fingertips of left hand opposite right hand on the back, just to the right of the spine at about the 6th or 7th thoracic vertebra. Push gently and hold. Second position: Leave left hand on the back, right hand is under the healee's right armpit. Push with left hand and hold. Third position is identical to the first. Fourth position: Move left hand under healee's right armpit. Push with right hand, which is at the sternum, and hold. Fifth position is the same as the first and third. Then repeat the entire process on the other side. Facing the healee's left side. First, place the fingertips of left hand just to the left of healee's sternum at about the 6th or 7th rib. Fingertips of right hand are opposite left hand on the back just to the left of the spine at about the 6th or 7th thoracic vertebra. Push gently and hold. Second position: Right hand stays on the back and left hand is under the healee's left armpit. Push with right hand and hold the position. Third position is identical to the first. Fourth position: move right hand under the healee's left armpit, push with left hand, which is at the sternum and hold. Fifth position is same as the first and third. If necessary, I repeat either the entire process, or I will repeat it on only one side of the body, depending upon what is happening with the healee.

*(This technique, along with others mentioned, are demonstrated on the DVD, **Healing Hands: Reiki I***. Healers have seen cysts and tumors diminish or disappear completely within the short period of time it takes to do this. Specifically for **cysts** anywhere, the touch point is the inside ankle of the right foot.

At an Atlanta, Georgia bookstore, a woman named Christine, who was undergoing chemotherapy for cancerous tumors in the lymph, came in to experience a healing demonstration. I used the process mentioned above. During the process, she felt that the cancer and tumors had gone. I advised her to go to her doctor and be re-examined rather than simply stopping treatment. She did! The doctor diagnosed her as having had a spontaneous remission. However, he wanted her to continue on chemotherapy just in case. The cancer and tumors have not returned.

Three touch points for **Alzheimer's**: At the shoulders where the 'V' is formed, at the 2nd or 3rd rib (like the lung point), and above the floating ribs (like the gland point). People with Alzheimer's do not like their lives. To escape reality, they check out, they forget. For healings to be successful, individuals may need to make changes in his/her life, release those people or aspects that no longer serve the healee's highest and best good, and find the possibilities for creating a new life. Not easy!

Healer's preparation for magnetic healing may involve rubbing the hands together, and then rubbing each hand down the opposite arm. Then centering at the Hara, which is about 2 inches below the belly button. Feel the vertical line running through the center core of energy running from the crown to the root charkas. Follow that line down to the heart of Mother Earth. Ground and feel cobalt blue healing energies from Mother Earth coming back into the root chakra. *(Contacting healing from Mother Earth can be a powerful experience in itself; there have been instances where people have lain down on the earth, slipped into an altered state of consciousness, felt the heartbeat of Mother Earth, and were healed.)* Next, feel the will center in the solar plexus and follow the vertical line up to the Universal Source. Bring back the yellow energy of the sun into the crown and down through the vertical channel. Feel the energies of Mother-Father God meeting in the heart. Visualize clear colors running through all of chakras. <u>Placing hands parallel to the earth also draws in cobalt blue.</u> Healer may look above horizon line in mind's eye and see this occurring. Looking slightly above the **horizon line** when using the 3rd eye in any meditation aids visuals.

This form of magnetic healing **lifts dropped organs**. Once the healer's hands touch the body, one hand is kept on the healee at all times. A cup or depression is formed at the throat by the heads of the collarbones (clavicles) and the sternum. The healee lies on his/her back. If starting at the healee's right side, gently put the tip of the middle finger of the left hand in the cup and pull slightly. With the right hand, sweep <u>slowly</u> up the right side about six inches above the body and over the top of the head. As sweeping action is best repeated (3 or 4 times, or in multiples of 3), avoid sweeping the organs back down. Healer keeps the back of his/her right hand facing the right side of the healee, as s/he positions his/her hand in the aura below the root chakra. Check with the healee during the process to find out what s/he is experiencing. Then move the middle finger to the top of the sternum and push down slightly. Repeat this entire process, sweeping up the center. Walk around to the left side, keeping contact with the healee the whole time. Gently put the tip of the middle finger of the right hand in the cup, pull slightly. Repeat the sweeping process with the left hand described above. Healer moves down to the feet, placing his/her hands on the inside of the legs just above the ankles. Hold for a few minutes to ground the energy. It is best if healer is channeling Universal healing energy. When I went to Colorado to take Hannah Kroeger's class, people who were not channeling healing energy had little or no success, or they were giving of their own energy. One individual was working in reverse by pulling out the healee's own personal energy.

This magnetic healing is a variation of Rosalyn Bruyere's **Chelation therapy**. This works particular well for **clearing joints** and the **major chakras**. Healer starts by holding onto the bottom of both feet. Move to the right side of the healee's body, keeping hold of the bottom of the left foot with the right hand. Move the left hand to the healees left ankle. Healer wills healing energy to bounce between his/her two hands. Etheric left hand drops into the ankle where healer uses his/her inner vision and sense of feeling. If healer has inner knowing, it gives meaning to what is being seen, heard or felt. If misqualified energy is found, it may explode in the healer's left hand. If misqualified energy does not explode or dissolve, healer grabs hold of it with his/her etheric hand. Healer wills his/her etheric hand into the physical left hand. Physical hand pulls up slowly through the seven layers; turning the blockage over to the Light and asking the Light transmute it. If the dark spot is like a plug, oftentimes, there is mucus behind this blockage. In this case scoop the mucus out with the left hand, drain it, cauterize the void with cobalt blue color, fill the area with other colors and healing vibration, and seal it with gold. If the plug has a cord attached to it, the healer has discovered a time line, which means that the issue goes deeply into the past or past lives. Keep pulling out the cord and plugs attached to the cord until the last plug is found. This is the core issue. The plugs themselves may represent different occurrences or past lives or both. All the while the right hand remains on the sole of the left foot. Negative energy needs to be pulled off slowly. However, sometimes this last plug needs to be jerked out. Follow the directions above for scooping out the mucus-like substance, etc. Angels may bring in herbs, flower remedies, healing tones and symbols. The entire process of pulling out plugs and cords, clearing and filling may be done at any place on the body during a healing session.

To continue on with Chelation Therapy, repeat the above process at each joint in the lower limbs: Move right hand to the sole of the right foot and left hand to the right ankle and repeat the above process. Moving up to the lower leg: Right hand to the left ankle, left hand to the left knee. Then right hand to the right ankle; left hand to the right knee. Moving to the upper leg: Move right hand to the left knee, and left hand to the left hip at the hip joint or the trochanter of the femur. Then move right hand to the right knee, and left hand to the right hip. Keeping the left hand on the right hip joint, move the right hand to the left hip. Healer wills healing energy back and forth between his/her hands. So, I have worked back and forth from the left side of the body to the right side of the body, back to the left side, etc.

Chelation Therapy continues up the chakras: Healers moves his/her left hand to the second or creative chakra, the right hand worked in the aura above the root chakra in the same manner. That is dropping the etheric hand into the body, etc. After the foot chakra is cleared, healer moves his/her right hand to the second chakra and the left hand to the navel. Clearing/healing process continues with the second chakra – hands-on or in the aura. Next, the right hand moves to the navel, the left hand to the solar plexus, where the healer works on the solar plexus. Then the right hand moves to the solar plexus; the left hand to the heart. And so it goes moving up the chakras. Right hand moves to the heart, left hand to the throat. Left hand moves to the third eye, right hand to the throat. Left hand moves to the crown or the top of the head, right hand to the third eye. To complete the process, healer works up each arm; palm to wrist, wrist to elbow and elbow to shoulder joint. Healee may also turn over so that the healer has an opportunity to work on the back chakras or vertebrae. This is a very long process, which may take 1 1/2 to 2 hours. This same process may be done from the healee's left side, using the left hand to do the work while the right hand send healing energy into the body. If the healee has specific issues in organs or glands associated with a particular chakra, this might be the only area where Chelation Therapy is used along with other healing techniques. Every healee has different needs.

To fill in the voids, there is a **Universal palette or rainbow of colors** that is available to everyone. To reach the Universal colors, focus at the crown and then move up the vertical energy line, past the soul star chakra (located about 6 inches above the crown), and past the soul. Spirit guides and Angels will help the healer to find the rainbow. The right colors come back through the vertical energy line and out the hands. The more healing energy the healer is channeling, the stronger the colors will be. Strength does not necessarily mean the depth of the color; sometimes, pastel colors are required. **You might experience the rainbow of colors** with a clear and quiet mind in meditation. Focus above the head and call upon the Angels, or ask for healing. Then visualize yourself and see what transpires.

Another way to **clear the chakras** is to start at the crown and work down the front and then up the back. Healer spreads his/her fingers, **creating etheric claws**. Reiki energy acts like a magnet in the palm, drawing out misqualified energy. Healer claws slowly through the aura above each chakra from left to right three times, and then right to left three times. Misqualified energy is thrown into the violet fire, down to the central fire for transformation or to the Light for transmutation. People with low or no energy oftentimes benefit greatly from having the root chakra cleared; one woman told me she felt like she had suddenly awoken. We also have chakras at the navel and the small of the back, which is referred to as the Door of Life or the Meng Ming. To **clear the aura**, start above the top of the head, again make claws out of the hands and rake down the center and on both sides through the aura both front and back. Repeat each movement three or four times.

Reversing the energy flow and running colors through the chakras is another way to facilitate healing through the chakras. Healer stands at the healee's right foot and asks the healee to visualize red. Healer may mention objects that are bright red, such as, Santa's suit, apples, red tulips, etc. When the healee sees red, the healer slowly says, "See the color red going into and filling the right foot, to the right ankle, right knee, right hip, across the root chakra and to the left hip; to the left knee, left ankle and out the left foot. See what is being released out through the sole of your left foot." As the healer talks, s/he moves the energy up the right side, across the chakra and down the left side through the aura. S/he may touch various points on the body, as they are mentioned. The color red is repeated 2 or 3 more times, for a total of 3 or 4 times. Then the color orange is visualized in the same manner, but instead of the root chakra, the color orange goes through the second chakra. Yellow for the solar plexus; green for the heart; blue for the throat; indigo for the third eye and purple for the crown. Gold is then run up, through and down each of the chakras one at a time.

Pademo is the name of a healing system that seems to come from another star system. Namadja appears to be the name of the galactic medical team, who work on another dimension through the healing energy that is being channeled by the healer. It was given to Gieny Meester of The Netherlands. The healer says, "Pademo, Pademo, Pademo, be here now!" The healer watches with the mind's eye throughout the process. Then the healer says, "Namadja, Namadja, Namadja, be here now!" The healer may use hands-on healing, or have his/her hands in the aura. The healer watches as Namadja cuts into the astral body, and goes about doing the clearing and healing. Core issues are addressed! When the healing is completed the medical team brings in small etheric packets or sachets, which may contain herbs. The medical team slips the sachets under the skin, or they may pack an entire area before sealing the incision. While the effect of the healing is on the physical body, emotional and mental issues behind the physical problem are also addressed.

Time and space do not exist in the same way on the etheric planes as it does on the earth! It is possible to ask the Angels to go back into time and retrieve the healee's umbilical cord at the time of his/her birth. Ask the Angels to clear the umbilical cord of any trauma or drugs. Then ask the Angels to bring the cleared and healed **stem cells** back to the healee. The energy comes in through the soles of the feet. What is interesting is that even through the healer does not ask for him/herself, the healer receives the stem cell healing through his/her feet at the same time.

To **close the session**, work through aura and hold feet. You may also place the left hand on the solar plexus, and right hand on left groin (line made between the torso and leg when sitting down - there's a long tendon there). Then switch - right hand on solar plexus and left hand on right groin! This, as well as the solar plexus and second chakra are touch points for **childhood issues**.

Healing sessions typically last from 1 to 1 1/2 hours. It would be wonderful if everyone received a spontaneous remission. Claudia Collins came to a healing demonstration, and I worked on her for all of 20 minutes. Her long-time, severe back pain went and never came back. However, most healees come for 3 or more sessions. One man in Arizona came 8 times before his heart was healed. Sometimes, people call just prior to a session to cancel because they are not feeling well. However, that is when the illness is coming up to be healed.

Healers may work with **crystals**, each type has its own properties. Black stones, like obsidian, or red rubies may be used for grounding by placing them next to the feet. Red garnet is a stone for the blood and may be placed on the touch point for **blood**, which is over the heart chakra (sternum and thymus). The heart chakra is also the trigger point for **arteries** and **veins**. Laser crystals or the pointed ends of any crystal may be used effectively in the aura. Blockages in the aura, chakras and body may be cut out using the laser crystal or point of a crystal in the aura over the affected area. The healee's skin is never scratched, never cut; this type of psychic surgery is noninvasive. Using the pointed end or a lazer crystal, the healer may pull off misqualified energy straight out, or use counterclockwise circles. Diane, of the New Spirit Crystal Gallery in Milwaukee, was told by her guides that in using the point of a crystal for healing, it is important to convey to the crystal by thought or words what exactly it is that you want the crystal to do. Sometimes it is important for the healee to ask these blockages, "What is it I am to learn from you?" The answer may come as a visual, a feeling, auditory message or as an inner knowing. In **meditation or Shamanic journeywork** try the following: See yourself clearly in your mind's eye and look for a crystal in the Otherworld. When you find the crystal, ask permission to enter the crystal. Within the crystal, present your petition and listen to the wisdom of the crystal. You may feel yourself shifting and becoming the crystal. Go deeper within and experience the properties of the crystal.

After working through the aura with a crystal, **the base of a crystal** may be placed on the body over the diseased area or chakra with the point facing up. In this way, misqualified energy is pulled up and out.   While doing the **pain drain** (page 33 & 34), the healer might hold a crystal pointing downwards in his/her right hand. Sean Grealy holds a crystal pendulum in his right hand. The pendulum moves in counterclockwise circles as the misqualified energy is being released. The circles become smaller and smaller, and when the pendulum stops, the draining is completed. Some manmade attunements initiate the star chakra (6 - 12 inches above the head). Initiations made up by people may close the star chakra, as well as other chakras. Because the chakras are not able to 'breathe' in new prana and 'exhale' spent energy, the physical body is adversely affected.

The draining method just described may be used to **clear manmade initiation**s and open the chakras. Begin with the soul star chakra. After draining pain and disease, voids may be filled with Light by placing crystals on the body (Katrina Raphaell has some excellent books, or the healer may work intuitively in the placement of crystals). It is possible to draw healing energy by holding crystal in the hands. Raise the left arm (elbows and wrist unbent) towards the Light, and place the right hand either over or directly on the area. Use a crystal book to determine what energies you would like to bring in and which crystal carries these energies. When through **clear the stones** in coldwater, in sunshine, salt, or on a clear quartz cluster. Smudging with sage clears, and because the Universe does not like voids, cedar brings in beneficial energies.   This works with crystals. Crystals do not respond well to either scents or rubbing alcohol.

There are a wide variety of ways in which people **release** "negative energies." Some people shake ('shivering timbers' at their very foundation) and/or cry like Deborah Fiorill did while I worked on her on an Angel segment that was shown on Connie Chung's CBS program, *"Eye to Eye."* Other people get very cold and need to be covered by blankets. Some people sweat; sometimes, the Angels bring the heat up to temperatures that would under ordinary circumstances be fatal. Whenever the Angels do this, the disease is gone afterwards. Some people have to talk out their problems. This is particularly true for women. Everything that comes up in a session is absolutely confidential! People whose stories I have included in this book gave me permission to do so. Where examples were relevant, I used a first name only and it was always a different name.

Unsolicited advice or healing is unwelcomed! Once, Charlotte and I asked a friend if he would like healing from us. We worked for 4 hours. Nothing! People have to ask for a healing. It is not my job to track them down. Yet, with lessons learned and being fully connected to the healing energy I had as a child, and healings happening regularly, and even miracles occurring, neither Tera Mai initiates nor myself were truly healing in the manner of Jesus.

In September 2009, that began to change. Edyta Ponikiewski of Chicago and myself found our **direct healing connection to God through the solar plexus** (see page 161). Claudio Emilio Meléndez of Mexico helped to ground the energy. Ramona Kirk helped to verify the symbols for initiation. The TM Reiki IV, V, VI & VII and TM Seichem IV, V, VI & VII initiations at the solar plexus brought more healing energy to the entire Tera Mai healing system; thus, the healing potential of all Tera Mai initiations noticeably increased. The initiation produced a clearing out of all kinds of toxic stuff. Healing energy typically came in through the crown and feet; in self-healing, negativity usually left through the solar plexus. Oftentimes, the solar plexus would heat up during clearings and healings for others or in self-healing. Healings came quicker and more dramatically. Most blessedly, God's Protection became ongoing. Especially since the Wednesday Night Clearings began (see pages 102-103), forces of darkness have tried to stop this group effort. They targeted me in particular, falsely believing that if they took me out, that they would stop the Golden Age. Ramona and I worked vigilantly everyday for over a year. She'd clear me, I'd clear Ramona and then we would both clear everyone who participated in the Wednesday Night Clearing and Tera Mai. Since IV, V, VI & VII, it takes far less effort to do the clearings; black magic now flies back to the perpetrator(s) automatically. The only way black magic won't go back is if it is called in or by judging it. God Himself protects the energies. It would be very unwise to try to misuse the energy.

Dear Kathleen, I meant to write you sooner, but I have been so overwhelmed by the gift you've given me, I'm having a hard time putting it into words. I have fibromyalgia. After you did the clearings on your first day in Holland, the pain in my left foot, which had been there for a year, disappeared. I have thanked you for that, twice. I would like to thank you again. It never came back!

After the Ama Deus workshop, I received the new TM Reiki IV, V, VI & VII and TM Seichem IV, V, VI & VII initiations from you (they're a bit of a mouthful). I just cannot thank you enough for this. I am used to always having pain somewhere in one of my muscles or joints. But it's gone. And whenever the pain comes back, I just have to think of sending healing energy. It gets warm (or sometimes a little hot) and the pain goes away. Just like that.

The day after the initiations I went to a fair with some friends. Usually after a day of strolling around a fair, you have to carry me off. Everything hurts, head to toes. This time however, I was the only one who came home and did NOT collapse on the couch or in bed. I walked my dog, went to get groceries, cooked dinner and did the dishes, which was a lot even if I hadn't been to a fair all day. Before I would have to take breaks every hour or so, and that would be on a good day.

Last Wednesday, I drove out to see my friend from Norway who was visiting her family in the far North-East of Holland. This should be a 3 hour drive, but because of traffic jams it took me over 4 hours to get there. Before this would cause me tremendous pain in my legs, my arms and my back, and probably give me a headache as well. Not this time. And after spending the rest of the day there, talking, taking a walk, having dinner, fixing her mum's laptop and do some healing work on my friend's broken wrist, I still had no problem driving home again for 3 hours (no traffic jams this time). The next morning my arms and legs were a bit stiff, but after moving about for a few minutes and a nice hot shower, the stiffness was gone and … no pain whatsoever. It's difficult because I've had it for so long, but I am slowly allowing myself to believe fibromyalgia can be healed.

Thank you again and again and again! Love and Light!   **Kitty Hekelaar, HOLLAND**

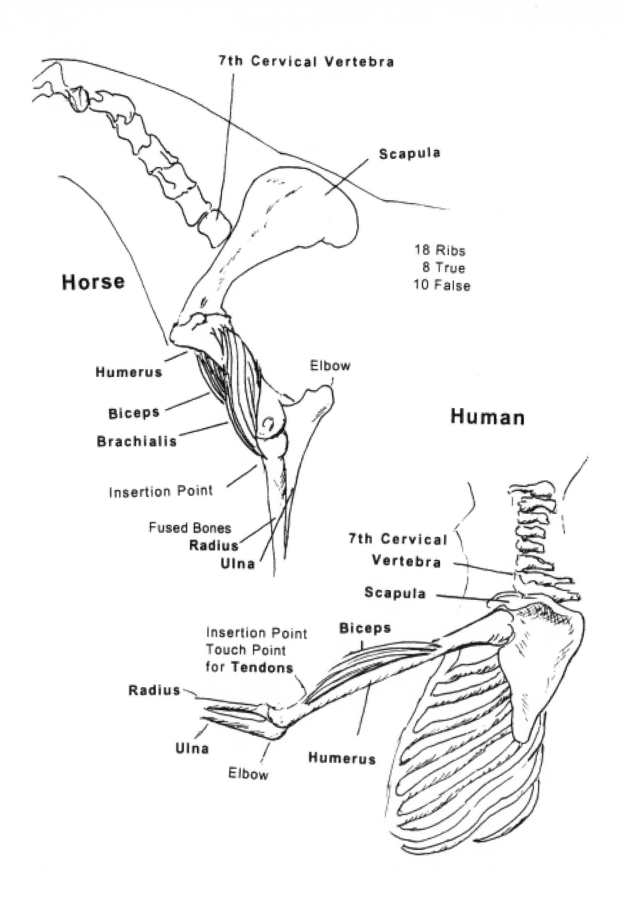

7th Cervical Vertebra

Scapula

18 Ribs
8 True
10 False

Horse

Humerus

Biceps

Brachialis

Insertion Point

Fused Bones
Radius
Ulna

Elbow

Human

7th Cervical
Vertebra

Scapula

Biceps

Insertion Point
Touch Point
for **Tendons**

Radius

Ulna

Elbow

Humerus

72

How to Heal Animals

If animals once had only an oversoul or group consciousness, because of their service, sacrifice and love for humanity, they each have their own individual souls. Maybe they always have? Ask any pet owner. They will tell you not only about the unique personality of their companion, but also of the quality we call unconditional love, which owners receive on a daily basis from their pets. It is why an animal's absence is experienced profoundly when they pass. Unconditional love, a quality of the soul, is an attribute that only a spirit that is connected to God is able to give. Psychics who communicate with the departed are often able to accurately describe diseased pets.

Each animal group brings to earth qualities that Native Americans refer to as animal medicine. These abilities are well described in story form in the book, Medicine Cards by Sams & Carson. There is joy of hummingbird, femininity of otter and power of horse. Even the 6-legged mosquito serves a purpose. Tonya Butts watched a mosquito land on her leg, and rather than smashing it, she communicated with it and asked, "I'm sure you have something to say, what is it?" The mosquito answered, "I suck out fear in small amounts at a time so that you won't be overwhelmed. I bring fear to the surface so that you can scratch beyond it." That particular bite left no welt. When humanity moves beyond its fear, there will be no more need for mosquitoes.

Many spiritual traditions throughout the world used an animal's hide, bird's feathers, etc. to connect to the animal's power. In our age, it is not spiritually correct to intentionally kill a member of a species on the brink of extinction; thus, there is no benefit gained from these hides, feathers, etc. In fact, the opposite is true! Bears in China try to commit suicide – this same energy is in the bear's gallbladder! The higher, stronger, conscious communication and expression of animal medicine is accomplished through Shamanic journeywork. The Sphinx is the guardian of the animal kingdom and the keeper of the secrets of animal medicine. In journeywork the holographic brain is activated through the constant droning of the drum, and by visualizing oneself in the Otherworlds working with what Native Americans call power animals. When hearts of stone are broken open and respect is shown to God's creatures, it is possible to access the gifts animals bring to Earth. Working to save wilderness and wildlife opens people to animal energy, as well as to nature. Artwork that is highly detailed does not necessarily contain energy; artwork that has energy may not necessarily have the quality of vibration we want around our homes and places of work. Charlotte Liss and I once went to see artwork that had been painted by a criminal on death row. While she raved about the energy, I could hardly wait to leave the gallery. This same sensation happened to John Ostrovskis and myself at a London art showing. We could both feel the negativity; however, this might have been due to subliminal messages in the recordings that were playing.

Like crystals; pets pick their owners. Watch a litter of puppies or kittens and observe how one particular puppy will make her or himself known, or perform when the right person comes along. When we fail to buy the things we love, be they paintings, crystals or pets, we are always sorry later.

Animals go through reincarnation cycles just like we do; it is one reason why some are wiser than others. For the most part, a soul stays within a particular species. When there is an exception to the rule, the animal's actions may be out of context with his/her species. Ziggy, a wondrous, fun-loving cat, was never a cat before. He was totally dependent upon Janis, his half-sister, to teach him how to be one. Among other things, as a kitten he had to learn to be graceful. Walking across the back of the sofa, he suddenly, and for no reason, fell off. Not slipped, but flipped off. He often acted like a horse that had been brought into the house from the barn. Psychically, the presence that precedes him was one of a much larger animal.

As part of a soul's lesson, people, who are extremely cruel to animals, may reincarnate as an animal to walk in another's hoofs, paws or claws so as to experience the animal's point of view. What we give, we get back by the power of three – oftentimes, more. The nature of this living Truth is reality and we call it Karma. Through Karma we understand another's life experience; we learn tolerance and perfect love. Humans generally go back and forth; in one lifetime, the slave trader, the next, the slave; in one lifetime, the Israelite, the next, the Palestinian; in one lifetime, the Hindu, the next, the Moslem. And so it goes round and round in a circle until we learn to see perfection in the Truth that God is in everything. We are both individuals and one.

People may ask to be reincarnated as a particular animal. I heard a story told that Christ once incarnated as a white horse, and anyone who saw this horse never forgot him. I do not know if it is true or not, but it is possible. The difference between having to and wanting to reincarnate as an animal is dramatic.

For example, my Great Aunt Hatti, who died in her 90's, said every day of her life that she was going to come back as an eagle. My Aunt June once reminded her that she would be eating rats and snakes." Aunt Hatti retorted, "I won't care." She's right! Undoubtedly, at this moment, she is a happy eagle catching her prey. What we focus on we create. We are drawn to what we love as well as to what we hate. Sometimes, people don't know what they are asking for.

I was watching "The Arsenio Hall Show" with my son, Lee, one evening. The comedian was holding up a picture of a man and laughing so hard that he could hardly speak. "What would you like to be when you grow up? Doctor? Lawyer? Teacher? How about horse?" That's what the man in the picture wanted to be; only he wanted to be horse a now! He lived in a stall in the barn by night, and pulled a pony cart during the day. What we ask for we get, especially if those petitions are made on our last day of our earth walk. Some problems are prayers that were answered.

Animals communicate with us; we are the ones who are not always listening. Oftentimes, our experiences with animals go beyond what could be called simple animal response behavior. One spring day, a robin was scolding wildly outside. I went outside and saw my first cat, Muffin, in a pine tree next to the front door. All that was visible were her twitching tail and rear end. She was going after the baby robins. Grabbed Muffin and took her inside, much to her dismay. Turning, I saw the adult robin looking on from a nearby elm, and knew that she would be returning to her nest. Several days later, I heard the robin calling wildly again. Looking around, I saw Muffin sleeping on a chair. Looking out the front window, I saw the robin sitting in the small cherry tree, which grew next to the pine. Blackbirds surrounded her. Blackbirds love to feast on baby robins. I went outside and chased the blackbirds away. The robin remained in the cherry tree the whole time. To this day, I know that robin was calling me to help her. Other examples of animal compassion and heroism show that they are capable of higher response patterns. As the Aquarian Age is being anchored, animals are relating to one another and people in new ways. These stories are all over the Internet.

Animal communicators work psychically with animals to help their owners find the cause of difficulties or disease and the nature of injuries. A stable was having problems with a horse that did not want to work, so they called in an animal communicator, who found out that in the horse's last lifetime he lived a particularly hard life as a man. The only horses he ever saw were out in a field grazing all day. Envying their life, and not fully understanding his request, he asked to be reincarnated as a horse in his next lifetime. (Might have been better to simply ask for a lifetime whereby he could rest.) Someone once said that God knows two words, Om and yes! Now reincarnated as a horse, this particular soul was resentful because he had to work rather than out in the sunshine eating grass and playing. The animal communicator had to delicately tell him that if he didn't work, his owners didn't want him and neither would anyone else except the glue factory. The animal communicator worked with the horse to help him find joy in carrying a rider.

Bear Shaman is an Alaskan Malamute (half Wolf/half Husky), who lived at Ishpiming, which was a New Age retreat center in northern Wisconsin. In his previous life, Bear Shaman was a Native American Shaman on the same lands. Through a channeling team known as Twin Trees, Bear asked permission to be born and brought to live at Ishpiming. I was working at Ishpiming the summer of Bear's puppyhood, and I was impressed to initiate Bear as a Reiki Master. Almost a year later, Twin Trees again tuned into the soul of the Shaman. Bear talked about the healing work he was

75

doing, "When I dig in the ground with my large paws, I unearth the prayers that have been said for Mother Earth. And when I roll on my back, I spiral them up to Heaven."

Animals think and communicate in pictures. Successful riders and trainers visualize what they want the horse to do before they physically ask the horse to do it. It is like playing a movie in your head. For example, at the specific spot in the arena you want your horse to change gaits and move in a 20-meter circle, visualize that place, your cue and the gait change as you approach your mark. It is like playing a musical instrument and reading a measure ahead of what you are actually playing.

To psychically receive messages from an animal, the first step is to open the heart and send love to the animal. This creates a connection. As the heart is the gate to the upper chakras, it also serves to open the channels and third eye. Love also reassures the animal. To make sense out of visual pictures the animal is sending, tune into inner feelings and knowing. Simply tell the pet's owner what is being seen, even though it may not make sense. Once in Santa Fe, I tuned into Chantel Quincy's cat and saw an unlikely desert home where Chantel's cat would disappear to for days at a time. I described it to Chantel even though I thought there would not be anything like it around. Chantel responded, "Oh, yes there is!"

I bought my horse, Abez, for $500, the price of horsemeat, because nobody else wanted him. He had been excessively abused and beaten by a spiritually unconscious man. Abez's behavior was that of a shell-shocked veteran of war. He had been with many different trainers afterwards, but nobody could do anything with him. Abez picked me and because of the love we shared, I was able to work slowly with him. Initially, I rewarded him for approximate behaviors; actually, I was giving him treats for things you would be reprimanding most other horses for. As he muscled back up and became ridable, he demonstrated 4 fantastic gaits, speed, power, agility and flexibility. We once jumped 6 feet from a standstill. It was not a planned event. I was riding him towards a small 2-foot jump. For some reason, he panicked and stopped just before the rail. I don't know how he was able to do this; maybe it was the quarter horse in him, but he picked up all 4 of his feet and moved to the right. Then he picked up all 4 of his feet and bounced to the left. At this point, we were directly in front of a 6-foot gray standard. Only my right foot was in a stirrup as he rocked back onto his haunches. At that point, I grabbed mane and rein because in the moment it flashed to me that if I tried to stop him, we would both go over. Never realized before that when jumping that high on a horse, as the rider moves up with the horse, there is a point when the rider is actually standing upright. Would have preferred not to experience this firsthand. Did manage to stay on Abez because when he landed, he didn't take off. One dressage trainer I worked with felt that Abez could have been champion of not just the Midwest, but of the United States.

Besides this, Abez was a beautiful chestnut horse; his body was the color of copper and his mane and tail were flaxen. One vet told me that Abez had the best qualities of all the breeds. He had wide quarter horse hips, tall shoulders like a Saddlebred, the racing line of the thoroughbred, and the graceful arching neck and dishpan eyes of the Arab. With all this, I can look back with absolutely perfect hindsight and see that rather than boarding Abez, he should have been kept on my own private farm. At the time, I was not in prosperity consciousness to be able to afford this. When Dolores Arechavala did a reading for me shortly after Abez's death, she told me that I was not to have any regrets because both Abez and I learned and grew greatly through our experiences.

Two owners of two different riding stables where I boarded Abez rode my horse without permission when I wasn't around. Inez, used to ride my horse early in the morning. When she couldn't, she would lease him out. When I came out to ride Abez, I would find him either worn out or injured mysteriously. They managed to injure Abez on four different occasions. Inez offered to buy my "miserable horse" from me and sell me a "decent ride." One day, one of her hands became frozen into what looked like a disfigured bird's leg and claw, and it stayed that way. I prayed for her, not realizing at the time what she was doing to Abez. Her claw went away. If I had known, I would have moved him first and then prayed for her. What can I say? I'm human. Inez's Karma didn't end with the claw. She put down a prize stallion only to find out later that the vet had misdiagnosed the horse; he could have easily have been saved. And there was more. Much more!

One of the lessons we are here to learn is to pay attention! Since I missed all of the small clues, the Universe threw larger and larger ones into my face. When Abez and I jumped 6 feet, Inez was present. She laughed loudly and rudely until she realized that I hadn't fallen off. Then she stopped. Everyone else was concerned. Another day, I was riding Abez while she was giving a lesson to another rider. Every time I rode Abez past her, he snorted at her and laid his ears back flat. Finally, one morning I went out to the barn after riding him the night before to have a look around. None of the horses had been turned out; they were still eating breakfast. When I went into Abez's stall, even though I had cleaned him up well the night before, he had mud packed solidly into all four hoofs and twigs and burrs in his tail. That is when I decided to move Abez.

At the next barn, Trixie, the owner, tried to sell him. Don't know how Trixie was going to tell me that an eleven-hundred-pound horse disappeared? Found out her plans quite by accident when I went out to meet the farrier (blacksmith). He wasn't expecting me. He was expecting the owner of the horse, who had explicitly instructed him to shoe Abez rather than just trim him. Trixie hadn't expected me at the barn that day either. When she showed up, I kept my mouth shut, so did the farrier. But I moved Abez a couple of days later, not wishing to pursue this particular drama further.

The next stable was uneventful; it was like God giving us a coffee break, as Pari Dulac would say. I kept Abez there for a couple of years. During this period, the owners became increasingly busy with outside endeavors to the point that they were hardly ever around. The day I saw an empty 4-horse trailer pull up with nobody on the premises, I made arrangements to move Abez.

The next owner/trainer where I moved Abez to had a good reputation. I learned how to relax on Abez and let him move my seat at all four gaits. With what I had learned from European and American instructors, Abez and I were getting the hang of riding. However, I could tell that he didn't particularly like her. One day, she walked over to us. Abez reached over and bit her on the arm. He had never done this before or since. I knew then that something was very wrong. I could also see it in her eyes. She had not been hurt, as she was fully padded in a ski sweater and snowmobile suit. The next day when I went out to the stable, my horse was injured and somebody had used my saddle. I knew this because I always uncinched both sides of my girth, not just one, and would then lay it across the top of the saddle. And the only person who could ride my horse or any boarder's horse and not be caught would be the owner of the riding stable.

We moved to a stable that was close to Inez's. Cathy, who had boarded her horse at Inez's stable, came out to greet us. She went on and on about the fact that there wasn't a resident trainer at this stable. Finally, I asked her what she was talking about. She answered, "There won't be anyone to ride your horse all of the time the way Inez used to do for you." She also told me how Inez would lease Abez out to a medical tech early in the morning when she couldn't ride him. Horrified at how unconscious I had been, I realized how much I had brushed aside, assumed or excused. During the entire time period Abez was boarded at Inez's stable, I was always doing healings on my horse. I even initiated him into Reiki and other rays of touch healing in an effort to save his life and help him heal. Cathy also told me that Inez had told people that I had put a spell on her hand. Maybe the Angels turned Inez's hand into a claw so that she'd stop riding him?

I could not believe how blind I had been. I stopped blaming other people for my horse's misfortune and asked, "What is Abez doing to draw unconscious people, traumatic events, and injuries to himself?" Stubbornness had helped Abez to survive horrific abuse and beatings; now it no longer served him. He needed to transform this energy, and use tenacity positively. One way to do this is to make a shift in consciousness by seeing in a different way. Willfulness without consideration is counterproductive; audacity and persistence to carry out a task to its greatest conclusion are attributes. When Abez made this shift, he and I became an even stronger team. Before this occurred, Abez reached his particular low point while I was in Los Angeles at the Whole Life Expo, the same expo where I did the healing demonstration on Beverly Henson.

78

Abez had injured his right eye, and because the owner of the barn had had an accident himself, Abez was left unmedicated and untreated in his stall for eight days, while I was in California. When I returned, his right eye was blind; it had turned a pale powder blue. There is a time and a place for allopathic medicine. I called the vet. When he arrived, I asked him to give Abez penicillin, but he gave me eye cream, which I already had. He said that it wasn't necessary to give Abez penicillin, because there was a triple antibiotic in the eye cream. There I was with two one-ounce tubes of eye cream and an eleven-hundred-pound horse. That night when I returned to the barn to reapply the eye cream, I found that my horse hadn't eaten; the infection in his eye had spread throughout the rest of his body. For a horse not to eat is extremely serious. I knew that if he didn't get penicillin that evening, he would be down by morning. If a horse lies down because s/he does not feel good, it's difficult to get him/her back up. If a horse is down too long, his colon stops moving. Made a quick trip to the nearest animal supply store and purchased penicillin. Administered the shot and laid my hands on him so that the Angels could heal him through me. Within a short time, Abez's energy level rose, he started eating, and he began healing. Between the eye cream, penicillin, hands-on and distance healing, Abez was seeing out of a brown eye within two weeks.

Now, Abez's only injuries occurred just prior to my making or considering making arrangements to show him. Abez was telling me that he did not want to be a show horse. Abez and many other animals, especially those higher on the reincarnation journey, understand what is being spoken. Carefully explained to him that I was OK and respectful of his wish. I just wanted to be able to enjoy riding him skillfully, and for him to be comfortable, happy, and healthy when I wasn't around. What Dolores Arechavala also told me in her reading was that Abez's subconscious was afraid that someone would steal him from me if I started showing him. When I asked her if his concerns were legitimate, Dolores answered affirmatively and added, "He was a wonder horse!" Three people told me within a week after I bought him that Abez was a reincarnation of Man O' War. But to the world, his greatness was never revealed. With my promise to him, Dolores told me that his fears were dispelled. He was at peace and healthy during the last several years that I owned him.

I bought Abez when he was 9 years old. I was his person, for nine years. When he was 18 years old, he made his transition. Dolores told me that Abez had accomplished his goals, learned his lessons, and as a sacrifice for me, he went on. He felt that if he moved to the Arizona deserts with me, he would hold me back by demanding too much of my time, keeping me from work I had to do.

I had called the vet out on a Monday for what I thought was a minor problem. It wasn't! The vet described surgery, which Abez would have to wait a week for, and afterwards endure a painful 4-week recovery period. And prospects were not good. Decided not to put him through arduous torture. He had been healed miraculously before; this time he wasn't taking any healing energy from me. What energy he was taking, he was using to control the pain. I could only feel his aura several feet away from his body. He was already preparing to leave.

Early Tuesday evening, I had Abez put down. I spent the afternoon in a field of clover with him saying goodbye. Watching him graze and patting him, I fed him an occasional apple. I knew his condition was going downhill quickly. On Sunday, he had rolled in the grass; Tuesday he couldn't even lie down. I told Abez what a joy he had been in my life and how much both of us had grown in those nine years. I told him about the beautiful place he was going to, and that soon all of his pain would be gone. All of nature came out to say goodbye and to help Abez. At one point, I saw a Galactic Confederation ship come down from the clouds saying, we're here to help, too. There were times that afternoon when the heavens seemed to open, and Abez and the sky and I were one. The vet came at 6:30. My image was the last he saw before he collapsed to the ground. As he slept, waiting for the anesthesia to reach his heart, I kept encouraging him to go to the Light. I can still hear his last breath. Just as the soul comes into the baby's body with the first breath, the soul leaves with the last breath. Three white swans had been swimming in the large pond in front of the farm when I arrived that day. They left unseen shortly after Abez died. The swans had never been there before, nor have they come back since. To this day, I believe that they were three Angels who manifested in physical form as swans to assist him.

When I got home that evening, I called my friend, Katherine Ettmayer, who is an extremely accurate psychic and healer. I asked her to help me tune into Abez to see if he had made his way to the Light. She felt that he was still at the farm. We both sent distance healing. He still wasn't going. In meditation, I journeyed to the farm to assist him. Angels were waiting to assist Abez into the Light; they motioned for me to step into the vortex as well. Together we went into the Light and came out into a beautiful place in nature, where he ran free. Sometimes, when a healee goes into a spontaneous exorcism, the demons will ask me, "How do you know what it is like at the end of the Light?" I believe that the Angels show them my memories, because without further encouragement, entities will suddenly drop their outer garb, revealing their Light. Then they go willingly.

Within the year before his death, Abez had completed the sacred marriage with his own **twin flame**, that aspect of his own soul, which held his other 2/3 feminine and 1/3 masculine energies. Abez and the white mare played and danced to the rhythms of the spheres, having great fun. At one point, they pretended to be carousel horses. A silver cord of love runs between their two hearts forever. When Abez died, he became what we call a master or an avatar; he became one with the Universe and co-creator with Mother-Father God.

Jake, who is channeled through a medium named Cocorah, told me that Abez's transformation and the July 1994 comet hitting Jupiter (Jupiter also represents horses) made it possible for the energy of horses to equal that of dolphins and whales on this planet. It is like this; the first millionaire in the United States created the way for a hundred more to become millionaires, and they, in turn, did likewise. It is also true that in order for any of us to go forward, we must bring at least one other soul up to our level. We get lots of help from the Universe along the way if we are open to doing this. Scarcity, be it money or illumination of the spirit, is an illusion. Emotions are ruled through understanding, not through suppression or outrageous behavior. For example, jealousy looks at the successful individual and has not the vision to see that a way has been opened. Opened not to recreate the identical life experience of another or take what belongs to another, but rather to take the core idea and create something that is unique. In this manner, humans and the planet we live on are able to evolve upwards. Begrudging is like being stuck in the mud and is a formula for moving backwards.

The evening that Abez transcended, Katherine Ettmayer said that he would be sending me healing energy that evening in a dream. Finally fell asleep that night with tears rolling out of my eyes. It felt like my heart had been cut out of my body. Left in its place was a large gaping hole. In the middle of the night, I was awakened. I had been dreaming about Abez and as I lay in bed, powerful waves of love and healing moved through me and continued into the next day.

Death is harder on those who are left behind. Having had any experience that personality survives death helps everyone enormously. Those who are dying know that life continues. For the survivors, when the grieving period is over, they are not left with a permanent sense of loss. Some people ask their loved ones to give them a sign after they pass. One woman, who had done this, told me that she walked into the bedroom as her husband breathed his last breath. Then for maybe a minute, his face looked young. When death came, the silver cord was cut. Her husband's astral body left the physical, taking with it the conscious and subconscious minds, and life's experiences. Because he was a good man, his astral body reflected this in youthfulness. This was the communication he gave his wife, telling her that he was OK.

With all this said, sometimes, when I was doing nothing and thinking of nothing, I would suddenly be aware of tears streaming down my checks. I was better off keeping busy and working. On Friday, I was facilitating a healing for a woman with a blockage that she could not release. Suddenly, in my mind's eye, I saw Abez's left rear leg come in and kick it out of her. I opened my eyes and stared at my client. Her eyes shot open and she said, "I don't know what you just did, but it was like a cannonball just left my body." How could I tell her that my horse just kicked her?

Numerous psychics told me that for a long time, the Angels took me up to him at night so that I could ride him. I know this is true. In those dreams he healed me.

It would certainly be my personal preference for everyone to be well, alive and happy. My job as a healer is to be a vehicle for healing energy to come through. Loving people where they are allows them to develop at their own pace. Free will choice is God's Gift to creation, and it is not up to me to judge another's choices. I once told the owner of a golden retriever that I worked on that I felt that her dog wanted to go on. Instead of looking within and checking my psychic insight out, she had her dog's badly- infected, left rear leg removed to the top joint. Six months later, the dog died of cancer of the lungs. The owner said that if she had to do it over again, she would not put her dog through all the pain it had to endure in her efforts to keep his body alive. In the same breath, there are other two-legged, four-legged or winged creatures whose task is to conquer and survive horrible physical calamities. These scenarios are realities on a three-dimensional reality. In the Golden Age or Aquarian Age learning will come in different ways.

Horses often sense impending disasters and even death. In Arizona I had a different horse, Buckley. One day, I was riding him towards the riding arena, as we had done many times before. However, this time, he refused to go anywhere near a palomino mare, whom we had ridden past many times before. Not this time! We had to turn back, go around the office and take another way to the arena. I found out later that day that the mare was colicing, and that the owner was getting ready to take her to the vet's for surgery. She died! He had seen other horses colic, and he was OK to be around them. What was different this time, was that Buckley sensed her impending death.

It is difficult to feel joy for someone who has gone home to the Light. In celebrating their life, we assist them in their transition. The grieving process is necessary, but to grieve without also recognizing that personality survives death, is to hold loved ones earthbound. Modern religions do not teach in any sort of practical way that personality survives death. Modern religions took God's Majesty away, and replaced Him with a vengeful, old man. Modern religions also do not prepare people for the dying process or death, with the result that some people hold tenaciously onto life, long after the spirit is ready to make its passage. They either suspect that they face annihilation, or they do not wish to sit on a white cloud for eternity playing a harp, and if they are lucky, an occasional French horn. The astral body is an aspect of the soul. During sleep, the astral body travels and returns by way of the silver cord, which attaches the astral body to the physical. In death the silver cord is broken, and the astral body leaves the physical body for the last time. After death, it has three days in which to go to the Light. All great mysticisms speak of this. In that three-day period, the soul must get through the thought forms, emotions and deeds that were created in life.

Dark, heavy mental attitudes, like control and greed, may make it impossible to even see the Light. If the soul cannot pass in three days, it becomes earthbound and confused. Sometimes, souls do not know that they are even dead because the astral or energy body looks very much like our physical body. However the condition of this part of our soul is a reflection of our thoughts, words and deeds. This is also true for animal spirits.

After traveling through a tunnel of Light, souls are taken to a place of healing and rest, where they review their lives and judge for themselves what was missed, what still needs working on, what was learned, etc. When ready, souls of people and animals may come back to guide and assist those whom they loved in life. Frequently, psychics in readings will describe a deceased pet, who is traveling spiritually with his/her former owner. When psychics pick up my father, he is typically with Arthur, a small black and white beagle mix. In a three-dimensional reality, whenever a spirit is seen or heard with a psychic sense, ask three times if they have come in the name of Jesus or if they are in Divine Truth. Even with animal spirits, remember to check. Spirits are capable of changing forms; dark, heavy spirits are fully capable of disguising themselves as Jesus. Also, look into the eyes!

Because animals have chakras and souls, if they are ready and willing, they may be initiated into healing energies. After initiating Abez into Reiki, I felt that my cats were asking me to initiate them. After their initiations, whenever anyone would come to my home for a healing, Janis and Ziggy would jump up on the table with my client. Ziggy would usually go to the feet to ground the energy. Ziggy does not under ordinary circumstances lie down at our feet. Janis would always go to the spot where the individual was having a pain or problem. Healees could feel healing energy coming from her paws. When she was doing healings, Janis' eyes changed, as if she was in a trance state. After initiating animals into healing rays, they become more intelligent and more aware on all levels. (*I demonstrate the effects of a Universal healing initiation on the crown chakra of a dog in the* **Healing Animals** *DVD and demonstrate how to initiate a dog on the* **Tera-Mai™ Reiki Mastership** *DVD.*)

All animals have the same bones, muscles and tendons that we as humans have. They are elongated or shortened, combined or slanted. For scientists to call animals' bones, muscles and tendons by different names than what we call the human equivalent thereof is actually confusing the issue. For example, a horse has more thoracic vertebrae than I do, but my femur bone (upper leg bone) is actually longer than a horse's. (The shorter the femur, the faster the mammal. T-Rex was slow!) The top of a horse's back leg is actually his knee. The femur then angles upwards and backwards, connecting to the hip at the joint. A horse's knee is actually his ankle, and all the bones from that point down are bones of the foot (metatarsal bones). Horses and other hoofed animals literally walk on their toes. Their nail or hoof is much thicker and more developed than our toenails.

The same is true for a horse's front legs. The top of his front leg is actually his elbow. His humerus (upper arm bone) angles upwards and forwards, connecting to the scapula at the joint. The scapula, which is quite large, angles upwards and backwards. The withers are formed by the cartilage extension of the scapula. In a horse, the radius and ulna (bones of our lower arm) are fused together. His knee is actually his wrist and contains the bones of the hands. His lower front leg is actually fused metacarpal bones; the hock is the sesamoid bone, and below that are the phalanges. He is walking on his fingertips. When a horse rears up, or when we bend over, we are better able to see our similarities. Look at the dinosaur skeletons in the museum; it is not just monkeys who resemble us. Science is a way of looking at how God creates. Physical bodies are a theme in variation, which serve as God's Reminder that there is more than one way to get to heaven.

What does this have to do with healing animals? The same touch points used on two-legged healees may also be used on my four-legged healees. Other healing techniques described herein may be adapted to animals. I acquaint myself with the animal before beginning. I want to be aware of the individual animal's character, as well as traits particular to his/her species. Typically, I place my hands on a spot that is not involved in pain. As with my humans, I work with an animal's current symptoms. With animals it is more difficult because their symptoms may have been going on longer than the outward physical manifestation. So, I end up using my psychic abilities more with animals.

Animal communication or inner communication is helpful for both owners and healers. After refusing a relatively easy jump several times, the trainer insisted that Maria's horse was being temperamental and that Maria should make Scotty jump. Even though a little voice inside Maria told her that there was something wrong with her horse, she listened to the trainer instead. Scotty's spine and back were severely injured in the subsequent and predictable jumping accident. Scotty's eyes went wild when I placed my hands on his shoulders; he'd never felt healing energy before. After he got used to the energy and found out it was helping him, I moved my hands to his spine. Also worked on his emotional and mental issues. Pulling 'stuff' off and sending it to the Light for transformation was a bit much for Scotty. So, I sent it to the central fire. Within a short time Scotty was being ridden again. Once when I was in England, a horse and rider were killed during a three-day event. At that same event another rider had withdrawn her horse because she had a 'bad feeling.' One wonders if the rider who was killed had a similar sense of danger or doom?

For the **bones,** I stand at the horse's left side at his left foreleg. As the division between the cervical and thoracic vertebrae is deep within the neck, my right hand is about one to two inches above the withers, which is formed by the 3rd, 4th, 5th and 6th thoracic vertebrae and the cartilage extension of the scapula. My left hand lies across the outside of the left humerus. As the inside of

84

the humerus lies inside the body, I will my etheric hand to wrap around the inside of that bone. Especially with animals, I incorporate Shamanic journeywork with hands-on healing.

Shortly after Abez's death, I worked on Sam, a 6-year-old thoroughbred who was off the track. Before Sam (and that is not his racing name) was 5, he had won $60,000. Like other horses who were ridden and raced at the age of 2 before the joints in their legs are locked, Sam's hocks in both back legs were bad. He also had an injury to the cartilage and muscles between the ribs on his right side, and the lower joint in his right front leg was arthritic from an injury to the bone. Racing 2-year-old horses is done to save the horse owners feed and upkeep money. Ruffian and Barbara were not the only horses to die. Sam was one of the bravest, strongest and most powerful horses I had ever ridden. He took off as though he'd been shot out of a cannon. If Sam had been able to win $60,000 with all those injuries, one has to wonder what kind of money Sam could have won if his original owner had waited until he was 3 to train him. Bet he would have been a million-dollar winner.

The woman who had purchased Sam when he was 5 had bought him guaranteed sound and wanted him for a jumper. When Sam came up lame, the vet took one look at Sam and told her that she should never jump him. She let him sit for a year. The worst thing you can do for a horse with arthritis is not exercise him. In that year of neglect he lost over 200 pounds.

Sam had never felt unconditional love. The first few times I worked on him in his stall while he was eating, he kept putting his ears back and looking at me. He was afraid that I was going to take his food away. For a bold horse, he was kind and gentle, but he was totally distrustful of humans. I worked with him on the touch points for bone, cartilage and muscle. I also rode him and taught him simple skills like stopping, bending when he turned, and to move away from my leg. Racehorse owners and trainers have it in their heads that because there is a slight turn to the left at the end of the race that a racehorse should only canter on his left lead. This would be the equivalent of a bowler or javelin thrower only developing the arm that they threw with. Modern exercise theory teaches us that both sides of body bodies are worked equally or there is a fundamental imbalance. The same is true for horses. There is no question in my mind that the first racehorse owner that stops looking at his or her horses as commodities only and begins treating his/her horses with love and regard will be truly blessed by the Creator. Sam worked for me because I gave him carrots, he felt love, and because his higher self wanted initiations into healing. By working with Sam and helping him to heal, it helped to heal my wounded heart.

For the **spine**, I am at the horse's right side. My right hand is just above the withers and my left hand moves as far down the spine as I can stretch. Jack, a 2-year-old gelding, couldn't walk without falling down. They felt that his problem was either wobbles, a central nervous system disorder, or trauma. As I felt the static in the aura above the spine, this was an indication that the problem was caused by an injury resulting in trauma. For Jack, I worked the spine points, the muscle points, and the **nerve** points (just below the horse's true knee, which looks like the top of the leg). As he could barely turn his head to the left, I massaged the neck muscles. Pulled off and drained misqualified energy, and then filled the area with Light and colors. Since I didn't start working on Jack until several weeks after the injury, he was able to trot and canter after the 4th healing.

For the **tendons**, I stand next to the horse's right right-front leg. My right hand lies on what looks from the front like the division between the leg and the chest. My left hand lies on the horse's true elbow joint and my fingertips lie across the humerus. Again, I let my etheric hand drop into the horse's body. I am looking for the point where the biceps and triceps become tendonous. It helps to have a good comparative anatomy book, or let Spirit do the work. If **cartilage** is involved, I ask the Angels to send energy to the joint. **People** may take 16 enzyme tablets taken water on an empty stomach to help heal connective tissue. (The idea is not to eat anything 4 hours before or 1 1/2 hours after taking the tablets.) When in season, cherries are good for connective tissue. (Fruit is also best eaten on an empty stomach. Wait before eating anything else.) The list of foods a horse is allergic to is long, and care must be taken before giving any herbs or supplements to horses.

An individual did not cause one of Abez's more dramatic injuries. One evening, I went to the barn and noticed a look of distress on my horse's face. After putting his halter on, I proceeded to walk him out of his stall. I walked out; he fell out. Why? Because he had dislocated his left hip; and rather than moving forward, his left leg swung out to the side. He could not have come in from the pasture in that condition! What probably happened was that he was rolling in his stall and became cast (stuck). In trying to free himself, he dislocated his left hip. I dropped the lead line and for well over an hour worked back and forth from the tendon/cartilage point to the injured hip. I also used the pain drain and pulled off misqualified energy. At the point of injury, I worked in the aura to reestablish the healed, normal pattern of a femur bone secure in the hip socket. Sometimes, I did place my hands on the area. Again, one of the very nice things about an injury is that if you can get to it right away, dramatic results are possible. When I was through, Abez appeared more relaxed and he was able to get back in his stall. The next day, the owner of the barn came out because he had heard about what had happened, but he couldn't understand why Abez was so active in his stall. We took Abez out and even trotted him a little bit. All I noticed was a slight hesitation at the left hip joint. Spirit told me to leave him in for a week and then let him build up his strength in the pasture for another week. Two weeks after his injury, much to the amazement of everyone, I was riding Abez. He easily cantered, did leg-yields (lateral movements) and could do turns on his haunches.

86

For the **muscles**, I stand to the side of a horse at one of his hind legs. Placing my hands on the insertion point of the gastrocnemius (page 88), right hand is on the left leg, left hand on the right leg. Or to be safer, go from side to side and work on one leg at a time. On the same side where the involvement is, the point will be sore. Rather than jumping right in at the rear end of an unfamiliar horse, I let him experience the energy first at his neck or ribs. Like Scotty, other horses may roll their eyes back to look at me while I am working on them because most of them have never felt anything like healing energy coming out of human hands. (Sometimes disbelieving people do as well.) When the horse figures out that the energy is making him feel better, he relaxes, oftentimes, slipping into a relaxed trance. In working with animals, as with people, I listen to the Angels as well as to the healee. My gut oftentimes tells me what to do. When an animal has had enough healing, s/he lets me know by moving restlessly about. Or the energy that flows through my hands slows down and then stops. Both of these things also occur when working with people.

Because they are work animals, and because horses are often worked too young, injuries are frequent problems. If there are other issues, I can adapt the same touch points I use on my human clients for my animal clients. In the case of a major **gland**, it would be both uncomfortable and unsafe for me to be half under a horse near his rear legs. On large animals, it is easier for me to work with another healer. If there are two other people present, I can have either the owner, or someone else who knows the animal well, touch the opposite side of the animal's body (the other stays at the head and reassures the animal). I visualize healing symbols coming into my assistant's crown and out of his/her hands. As with humans, I can also work directly over the affected area as well as with the touch points. With emotional issues on large animals and even smaller ones, it is easier to work on their back 2nd and 3rd chakras. **Fear** is held in the neck. The healer can massage the neck and then stroke the 'negative' emotion up and out. **Mental** issues may be addressed by placing the left hand over the 3rd eye and the right hand under the head.

Other problems and diseases do happen in animals. Abez and I were at Inez's stable when a valuable Arab stallion dropped dead unexpectedly. As he was insured, an autopsy was requested. Prior to coming to Inez's stable, the stallion had spent much of his life in a stall in another barn where automatic sprinklers sprayed pesticides periodically during the day to kill flies. The animal's body was so toxic from pesticide spraying that during the autopsy, the liver fell apart in the doctor's hands. Sometimes, our pets reflect problems or dis-ease within us. When we heal ourselves, we heal our animals as well. Whenever I do healings on animals, I like to have the owner present. More often than not, I end up working on them both. Sometimes, I work on the horse and the person feels the healing in his/her body as well. In the case of the Arab stallion's owner, her problem was deep-seated anger, which typically causes liver problems. She never asked me for my help.

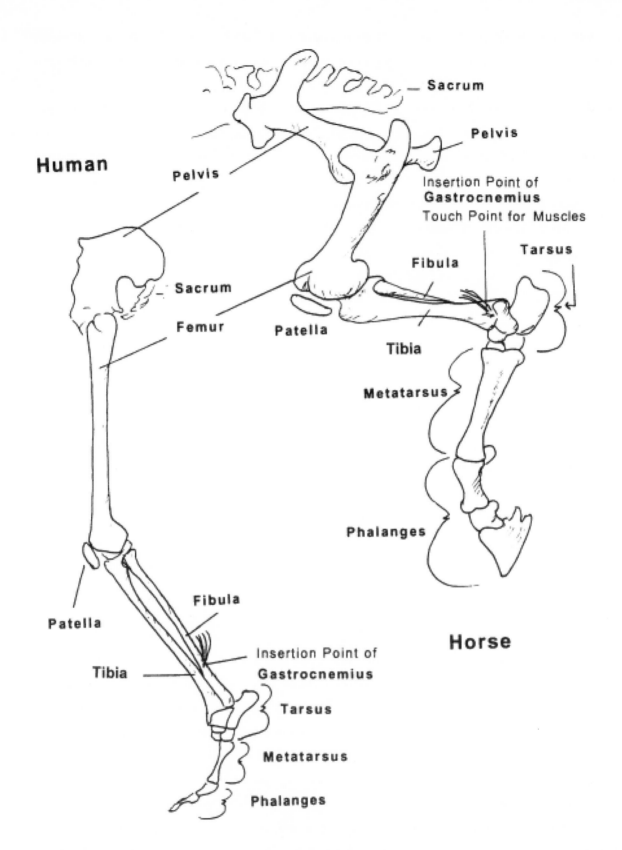

Human

Pelvis

Sacrum

Femur

Patella

Fibula

Tibia

Insertion Point of
Gastrocnemius

Tarsus

Metatarsus

Phalanges

Sacrum

Pelvis

Insertion Point of
Gastrocnemius
Touch Point for Muscles

Fibula

Tarsus

Tibia

Metatarsus

Phalanges

Horse

With animals as with humans, if they do not want to be healthy, if they are working out Karma through death, or if it is simply their time to go, the healing energy will help them with their transition. When my cat, Muffin, had to be put to sleep, I stayed with her to provide comfort, and companionship. People who channel healing energy help the soul to make an easy transition. Bodies feel different after the soul has left. Muffin's soul passed in front of me as she left her body and she gave me a gift. Your friends, relatives and pets will do this for you, too, after their passing. Newborns also bring in gifts for each of their parents. In order to receive these gifts, we do not have to be cognizant that they are coming; however, conscious awareness always helps. We do, however, have to be open and compassionate in order to receive. At exactly the same time I had to have Muffin put to sleep, Inez had a cat with failed kidneys. She let him die on his own, she did not want to spend the money and take him to a vet. It is likely to assume that her cat left her nothing.

As an act of compassion, I once attended the funeral of a client's father. Her family treated her miserably, and her psychologist also felt that she needed someone there for her. The wake for the family was held an hour before friends arrived. We wandered the funeral parlor looking for the right room and finally found a small door. Upon our entry, the casket was immediately in front of us, with the family looking on. As soon as they spotted us, every one turned their backs on us and walked to the other side of the room. Later at dinner, even her own son did not invite her to sit with the rest of the family. Sometimes, it is very difficult to stay out of judgment. While I couldn't see her father, I could feel that his spirit was very much present at the funeral, which was held immediately after the wake. Her father left my client a gift and he generously gave me one as well. I tuned into my client's sisters and brother to see if I could send them healing energy, and hopefully their attitude towards their sister might change. They were too closed to receive healing, or gifts.

Some individuals hold onto pets, friends and family members like a dog with a bone. Some healers doggedly insist on healing an individual regardless of whether or not they want it. Though well intended, these individuals interfere with the free will choice of others. There's another type of well intended meddling: After the cast came off my broken ankle, I went to a therapist in Arizona. He told me that years ago, his uncle suffered long from terminal cancer. One night, his aunt and uncle came over to his home for dinner. His uncle was in such a ghastly state that my therapist decided to intervene. My therapist was able to astral travel, and as he lay in bed that night, he consciously focused and willed his astral body out of his physical. He went to his uncle, who was also lying in bed. My therapist pulled his uncle out of his body and broke the silver cord. Shortly after the uncle's funeral, my therapist came down with a sudden and severe case of cancer, which he battled for a long time. He knew that because of his presumptive, well-intended actions, he had taken on Karma that his uncle had not worked out. *The road to hell is paved with good intentions!*

89

I was fortunate to learn to leave things in God's Hands early in life in life. After my grandmother fell and broke her hip, her leg became gangrene. The doctors were going to surgically remove it. She was in her seventies, and looked terrible. I wanted to pray for her, but wasn't sure how to go about it. Then it came to me to pray in this way, *God, if You are able to heal my grandmother in such a way that she will be able to walk again without pain, please do so. If it is her time to go, please forgive her sins and allow her to pass easily.* She died gently that night.

After his passage, Abez worked through me in my dreamtime. For several mornings in a row, I awoke with perfect recall of visiting and talking with Abez's former owners and the owners of stables I had described previously. Inez, the trainer, whose hand turned into a claw, stood in front of us dark and heavy with her head cast down. The man, who had beaten Abez unmercifully, appeared as a large, black form whose features were lost in his great bulk. I do not know if any of them accepted Abez's forgiveness; what I do know is that by releasing them all from their guilt, Abez freed himself. Those who are unable to accept forgiveness come back to experience the other side of the coin. A killer may identify with his/her victim to the point that in the killer's next lifetime, s/he may believe that s/he was the victim. S/he may even know the name and history of the individual whom s/he murdered in a past lifetime, but completely lacks the ability to feel the true character of the individual. The killer's perceptions contain too many erroneous facts or these memories are an empty facade. Could it be that people who are able to feel outside of themselves rarely committed crimes?

People have asked me if the grief I went through after Abez's passing was worth owning him. Some people say after losing a pet that they could never go through the pain of loss again. As for myself, I know and feel Abez's great joy and that he is still around helping me. I bless and thank Mother-Father God for the experience, which all of the money in the world couldn't buy. The time I had with Abez was more than worthwhile; it was unconditional love. While Dolores was doing the reading on Abez for me, she told me that Abez allowed her to touch his left rear leg and he said to her, "Feel for a moment what it was like when the two of us were one." Individuals who are unavailable, who are emotionally and mentally incapable of taking care of themselves, cannot be expected to take care of a pet or child. They need to find unconditional love for themselves.

Should we give up eating red meat? Not if you are going to be resentful, or if your body needs it. In the Golden Age it will be important to honor and connect to nature and God's creatures. God intended for us to be responsible stewards of His creation, Mother Earth, and God's creatures. Animals also serve mankind through their spiritual. When an animal works with an individual through a meditation called journeywork, Native Americans refer to these animals as power animals and the gifts they bring as animal medicine. The Bible says that God's Spirit is in everyone and everything.

Things That Go Bump in the Night!
& How to Clear Them

Earth, or Terra, as she has been called in other times, has been a three-dimensional world, where the Wholeness of the One is split. This produces the illusion of duality. The Jim Henson film, The Dark Crystal, explains this division. Through arrogance, two races of beings broke their master crystal. When the crystal split, they and their world tore apart as well. The master race disappeared, replaced by two other races. There were those who used strength, "their hard and twisted bodies, their harsh and twisted wills" to control those weaker than themselves and to ravage the land. Members of the second group were mystics. "Their ways were the gentle ways of natural wizards," those who work with, and have respect for the elemental forces. With love, but without power, they performed empty ceremonies, "numbly rehearsing the ancient ways in a blur of forgetfulness."

In high-vibrational planes thoughts produce reality; thus, missing the process of manifestation unfolding. In a three-dimensional reality, time is experienced moment by moment. Through the reincarnation cycle, it becomes clear that any actions we do onto others come back to us.

An individual who has a near-death experience is clinically dead. There is no brain activity! When life is restored to the body, many of these individuals are able to accurately describe events and conversations in the room where they died or far away places. Some tell of a wondrous journey through a loving vortex of Light. They came back because spiritual mediators or Angels explained to them that their work was not complete. If the soul asserts his/her free will and continues on, death of the physical body is permanent – there is no near-death experience. Some return even hours after a doctor has pronounced them dead. There is the story of the man who came back while his body lay in the morgue of a Catholic hospital. Wearing nothing but a toe tag, he wandered the halls looking for clothes, a blanket or someone to help him. The first person he met in the hall was a nun. The body and brain functioned hours after death because of Divine intervention.

Other people who have had near-death experiences hover around their bodies or visit distant places. Regardless, they are able to accurately recount events that occurred. While there are some people who have had near-death experiences and remember nothing, more often than not, near-death experiences bring about life-altering affects. Drugs, dreams and hallucinations do not induce consciousness-raising, life-altering experiences. Near-death testimonies are yet one more proof of the existence of other realities, and that consciousness exists outside of the brain. Some with dark souls have seen 'the devil' and returned to their bodies realizing that they had been given a second chance. It is not only people who work with black magic who have demonic attachments; evil deeds also open the door to demons. Releasing demons through contrition, right action and opening the heart is far easier to do while in the body than after death.

Messages brought back by the almost dearly departed suggest that love is a powerful force. Beauty and harmony are created on earth when humans become mediators between what Native Americans refer to as the power of the projective, masculine Upperworld and the loving, receptive, feminine Lowerworld. In the Holy Kabbalah, Hesed (love) joins with Gevurah (power) to form Tiferet (beauty and harmony). Regardless of which spiritual terminology is used, heaven is created on Earth whenever anyone's actions are heart centered. The heart is the fulcrum!

Intellect is an important, powerful tool. The mind also helps to create emotions. Worries, jealousy, mental torture chambers, etc. produce fear, anger and sorrow. There are also people whose physical body, heart, mind and higher consciousness are not in alignment. In both of these cases, the mind rules without love. *"We should take care not to make the intellect our god; it has, of course, powerful muscles, but no personality."* **Albert Einstein**

So that we might learn, spiritual guides and Angels travel with us on our earth walk. Those who consciously communicate with beings on other dimensions are called psychics or prophets. We are all supposed to have this ability. Jesus said, *"You will do greater things than I have done."* What did Jesus do? He healed! In some cases, he bent physical laws and created magic! And he was able to predict coming events! Supernatural events are beyond explanation within the vocabulary of known laws that govern a three-dimensional universe. Reality is dependant on location and time. Shamanic journeywork and dreams occur in another reality; Angels and the impossible become possible. In like manner, the Aquarian Age offers people a closer contact with spiritual dimensions.

Enmeshed in a three-dimensional reality, people often forgot to seek Wholeness, and created illusions in a veil of tears. "Let pain bring due reward of love and Light," may have been the motto of the Piscean Age. One Piscean high-drama is the story in the Old Testament of the fallen Angels luring man into the pits of hell. The good news is that God gave Lucifer and the third of the Angels who fell with him only a short time to tempt man and their time is ending now! In all great past civilizations there exists a common prophecy, the coming of a great Golden Age. The Australian Aborigines' calendar came to an end in August 1987, the month and year of the harmonic convergence, when all of the planets lined up. The Jewish 7,000-year calendar is ending as well. Aztec, Mayan, Egyptian and Incan calendars are coming to a close on **December 21, 2012**, when Earth's sun eclipses the center of our galaxy, or Galactic Rift. This conjunction occurs once every 26,000 years. 26,000 years ago signaled the end of the Ice Age, human's use of fire, end of Cro-

Magnum Man and beginning or Neanderthal Man, etc. Mankind took a giant leap forward. The Galactic Alignment always ushers in great change. Jesus said to look for signs in the heavens. Could powerful astrological signs be these signs? What else is up there? Spaceships?

The age of pain began its climactic descent on May 30, 2009. Healed, whole, youthful bodies will go into the Aquarian Age. Edgar Cayce foresaw this happening over sixty years ago. In his day, Edgar Cayce was called the Sleeping Prophet because he was able to go into trance and accurately answer health and other questions for individuals. He also gave other prophecies as well. For example, he predicted the crash of the financial and stock markets at this time.

As the higher vibrations of the Aquarian Age come into play, we come closer to the realms of the Otherworlds, which Shaman for millenniums have journeyed through. This may be why the astrological signs today and prophets from the past see new ideas, new ways of thinking, new technology and new creativity in the New Age. In order for people to vibrate at higher levels, it is important to heal the emotional and mental bodies. Physical bodies are more accurately reflecting who we are. The ever-persistent ghosts of the past, be they childhood pain or other traumas, continue to play out in the present until they are looked at, released and healed. To not do so is like watching a bad movie over and over again; we expect the past to recreate itself and it does. When personal demons are dealt with, doors of opportunity open; thus, offering a brand new reality.

Embrace change or choke in fear is a Hopi prophecy for this time. Masking fear or symptoms with drugs and surgery without getting to the core mental and emotional issues behind disease and pain prevents deep, sustainable healing. Releasing and healing mental blocks and dogmas prepares intellect for dramatic, upcoming changes. More people have had psychic experiences than one might imagine. Jesus said, "First the few, then the many."

The physical is wherever you are! John Edward and other mediums oftentimes communicate with spirits who do not know that they are dead because these spirits experience the reality of a body with form. In other realities form may become less dense and more easily manipulated. On the fourth dimension, beings may shape shift or alter their appearance more easily than you and I change clothes. In the age of darkness an interesting cast of characters exists on the fourth dimension. They include: Spirit guides, earthbound souls or what some call lost souls, nature spirits, Angels (both celestial and fallen), astral travelers, and extraterrestrials (both beneficent and malevolent). From a three-dimensional reality it is important to know who is being seen or heard. Lucifer is the "father of lies," and there is a very simple way to know the Truth. We are not supposed to blindly follow auditory psychic messages! This is not trust; this is insanity! If you hear a message

93

from another reality, ask **3 times**, "In the name of my Lord Jesus Christ, this is so?" Or ask, "In Divine Truth, this is so?" Or ask, "In the Light of Christ, this is so?" Or ask, "In the Love of Christ, this is so?" If you see a life form from another dimension, question it. Ask **3 times**, "You have come in the love of Christ?" Or ask, "You have come in Divine Truth?" Also, "Kadosh, Kadosh, Kadosh, Adonai Sebayoth," translated "Glory to God in the highest," sends negative thought forms running. Many names that by which God is called work! The Mayan name for God is Kunaku. Yes, that works! If the message or messenger is not in the Truth, then it or they have to go.

Dark, unconscious beings in and out of body know that the Golden Age is approaching, and they will hide behind the Light, and falsely present themselves. Also, just because a spirit says that s/he is a master, Archangel or famous person does not necessarily mean that it is so. Failure to check out messages and the messenger has gotten people into trouble. For example, initiations channeled to people by lower entities generate havoc in the astral body by creating blockages in the etheric channels and chakras, adversely affecting the physical body. Such initiations do not go back to God; they go back to the individual who made them up, who drains all initiates of his/her system of vital force energy. Manmade initiations are carried from lifetime to lifetime until they are cleared. (page 158) When manmade attunements are cleared, individuals may release major illnesses or pain, or feel more energized. Healers have more and clearer healing energy flowing through them.

Human bodies are electrical; the right brain controls the left side of the body, and visa versa. Scientists and doctors have failed to find the thinker behind our thoughts in the brain. The brain is like a computer, it receives thoughts Because of this it is possible to program the physical body. Dorothy Espiau's "The Gems of Excellence," self-programs a series of tap/touches using different number combinations on the body. For example, to clear: Start at the head of the fibula on the outside of the left leg, circle clockwise with coned fingers of the right hand and say 2-3. Move half way down the outside leg, circle and say 5-3. Move down to the ankle, circle and say 6-5. Repeat!

A **positive affirmation signal** may be programmed on your own body by asking for one in meditation either in a group or individually. Groups offer the added advantage of the power of the group effort. Facilitators serve to hold the energy and guide the experience. The advantage of working with a teacher who is already doing what you aspire to do, is that by working within the teacher's auric field, the student is able to process faster.

To begin, sit in a circle and do a clearing. If everyone is not clear, another simple exercise is to cone the fingers of the left hand and circle counterclockwise 3 times over the heart chakra (thymus) and say 3 times, "eight-seven-three-one-two to release horror." Then cone the fingers of the right hand and circle clockwise 3 times over the heart chakra and say 3 times, "eight-seven-three-one-two to integrate God's Love." In Sacred Geometry this might be called God's telephone number.

Positive affirmation signals are personal. The woman in Ireland, Ann Wood, who taught me this, has a positive affirmation signal whereby her head turns to her right side after she asks three times if the psychic message she received is in Truth. Other people have a vision in their third eye, or a twitch, or energy current. It is our own higher self and Angels who determine the best possible signal. If you do not get it on the first try, try again. Ask that it come in loud and clear. If you do not personally like the signal you get, then ask for another signal. We do have choices! After receiving the signal, ask three times, "In Divine Truth this is the best possible positive affirmation signal for me?" All that is written herein remains interesting ideas until it is experienced firsthand. Positive affirmation signals are additional evidence of the multidimensional aspects of reality.

For a **negative affirmation signal**, follow the same procedure. The advantage to having a negative affirmation signal is that after asking three times if the spirit or message is in Divine Truth, we have the confirmation of either yes or no. Ask that signals (answers) come in loud and clear.

Receiving **conflicting confirmations**; that is, it is 'yes' one time and 'no' the next, may be an indication that we are unclear. For example, lack of clarity happens when we are in judgment of others and we are caught up in their "stuff." To feel sorry for someone comes from the mind and is in fact a judgment; to have compassion comes from the heart. To stay out of judgment, simply view another's actions as being reprehensible rather than judging the individual to be a "jerk". Or see these people as having found a very interesting path or way to remember who s/he is. Unconditional love means loving people where they are, and accepting them for who they are. It is not up to us to give unsolicited advice or to try to change people who do not ask for help. Do we have the right to steal someone's lesson? If we do so, we are the ones who are wrong. Freewill is God's Gift to everyone. Morality is taught through example, not by preaching. This does not mean; however, that we should allow harmful behavior to be acted out in either our front or backyards. Calling a halt to destructive games around us is taking right action! Religious and political extremes keep us looking at everyone else in order to judge and control them. In reality, we are the ones who are being controlled and diverted from our primary task, which is to keep ourselves in Truth and maintain balance on the "Middle Road."

If we have questions we may **use the physical body to determine which path to take**. Take possibility A. Get it firmly into your head that this is what you will do. Then focus attention entirely on physical body and see how it feels. Clear the mind and do the same for all other possibilities.

Check dowsed messages verbally three times. Dowsing, kinesiology and affirmations using the physical body work because besides being electrical, the **physical body has a consciousness**. The best dowsers are 85% accurate because fears and self-interest may influence the physical body even when the brain has been put consciously into neutral. Because our bodies hold a consciousness, psychics who work with police departments on murder cases actually go into the morgue and touch the dead body to get psychic impressions that the body is still holding. For about 7 days after death, impressions last. To prevent their minds from getting in the way, these psychics typically do not want to know anything until after they have completed the initial reading.

In **dowsing or kinesiology**, questions are best put into the form of a specific statement. The pendulum or body decides the validity. Remember to ask about all of the alternatives. For example, you may get a 'yes' swing with the pendulum on possibility A, but you may get an even greater 'yes' swing with the pendulum on possibility B. All this said, the mind is more powerful than the body; thus, the mind can get in the way, jumping in to confirm either our fears or what we want to hear. Therefore, empty the mind of all thoughts. Put the brain into neutral!

Learning to dowse check to see that you and the pendulum are clear. Hold the pendulum with the thumb, index and middle fingers of either hand. Focus on the crystal. Ask out loud three times for your best possible Universal yes. When the pendulum begins to move, ask three times, "In Divine Truth, this is the best possible Universal yes for me." Do the same for no. My yes moves outwards from my body, back and forth; no moves from left to right. If there is confusion or the issue is unknown, my crystal moves in a circle. One woman's 'yes' is any movement of the pendulum, while her 'no' is no movement whatsoever. Another common movement of the crystal is clockwise for yes, and counterclockwise for no. If you use a crystal for dowsing, remember to clear it as you do your other crystals - either in sunlight, in coldwater, salt, or place it on a clear crystal cluster.

With **pendulums, Ouija Boards or table tipping**, keep checking to make certain that the messenger, the message and the object you are using are clear. Again, you do this by repeating 3 times, "Have you have come in the name of Jesus?" when the pendulum, Ouija or table starts moving. After each and every question, ask, "In the name of Jesus, this is so?" If the board is not clear, you will receive conflicting answers. Once you start clearing, keep clearing. The advice is don't start unless you are committed to clearing. Give underlings the opportunity to go to the Light. Do not send them to a black hole; they are already there. The Hosanna clearing is on pages 129 to 130.

How to provide a way for earthbound or negative spirits to return to the Light: When I end up doing exorcisms or clearings, underlings are given the choice of leaving the planet or going to the Light. Many do not want to go to the Light. I cannot force anyone or anything to be subjugated to my will, even if my intentions are the very best. If I do so, I must suffer the consequences.

It takes Universal healing energy to release black magic and demons. Angels may send these entities to the central fire for transformation, off the planet, or through the surrogate and back to the original black magician. If the healee murdered that soul in this or another lifetime, then that entity feels it has a right to inflict pain and suffering on the healee. I explain to the earthbound spirit that s/he is imposing as much harm on him/herself as on his/her victim. In New York, I worked on a friend of Charlotte's who felt that she had a fallen Angel attached to her. While mocking me for over an hour, my spirit guides untangled the entity from her. I told him that Mother-Father God had forgiven him long ago. He continued to ridicule me, claiming he wasn't interested and that I was a fraud. My guides said he was frightened. So I asked him if it was true? With that he broke down in tears and fell into the arms of Jesus, who said, "I have been waiting a long time for your return, brother." The Angels asked him to drop his old robes, which reeked of a vile odor. They were burned. He was dressed in clean garments, and went to the Light. Once this process or an exorcism begins, the healer is committed to stay with it until the spirit or demon is released.

Open the vortex of Light by asking the Celestial Angels to do so. Invite exorcised demons, lost, or earthbound souls to take the hand of an Angel and step into the Light. Then chant the following in a monotone, using the names of higher beings that you are comfortable with. *You are loved, blessed, healed and forgiven. You are loved, blessed, healed and forgiven. You are loved, blessed, healed and forgiven. You are one with your own higher self. Take the hand of an Angel. Go now! Go with Jesus, go with Mary, go with Buddha, go with Quan Yen, go with Krishna, go with Kahli, go to God! Go now! Go with the Great White Brotherhood, the Brotherhood of Light, go with the saints, go with the Angels, go with the Bodhisattvas, go with the Titans! Go now! Go to heaven! Go to Nirvana! Go Now! Go to love, light, peace, forgiveness, joy, enlightenment, healing! Go now!* Repeat the invocation until all who want to go have made the transition. The vortex of Light is the same channel that those who have had a near-death experience describe. As soon as it is completed, the Angels will close access to the vortex. Ask the Angels to fill in any voids with love.

When entities will not leave under the circumstances described above, stronger methods are required. The longer a fourth-dimensional underling and its messages go unchecked, the more powerful the hold it has. In the cases of demonic possession the Catholic Church used to do **exorcisms**. The Exorcist was based on a true story of a young boy in Chicago, who did not know to or know how to check out messages or messengers. In order for the exorcism to happen, the healee must be willing to let go of the attachment. Some people will not let go; they enjoy the power.

I have been asked to do exorcisms on buildings, but am rarely asked to facilitate an exorcism. A few people have called and asked for an exorcism on the telephone. This I will not do! On occasion during a healing session, it becomes obvious that the healee is possessed. This typically comes up during the **emotional healing** because my left hand is on the healee's solar plexus, which is the will center. People who are possessed have given away their will to the will of demonic beings. Keeping the left hand on the solar plexus causes entities, which are attached, to become extremely agitated! I do not say anything about any of this to the healee, but continue holding my hand on the solar plexus, knowing that this may take a while. The entity may move around in the body, and my right hand follows the awareness or pain that is in the healee. After attempting the methods mentioned previously, I call in the Angels of Exorcism and Release. Tibetan monks for exorcisms use the symbol, MOTOR ZANON (page 126). The symbols, JOHRE (page 125), CHRIST LIGHT and MARIA (page 128 & 129) work well together to move things along. The symbol, RELEASE, is on the cover of my book, Becoming a Shaman: It's Never Too Late To Be Who You Were Meant To Be, and may be seen by going to my website and clicking on BOOKS, or checking out amazon.com. There is also an ancient exorcism technique in this book in the chapter on Ama Deus or Katimbo, a Shamanic divination and healing system from the jungles of Brazil.

Entities find their own way out. The more Universal healing energy that the healer is able to channel the more uncomfortable the entity will become, until it is literally forced out of the body. Oftentimes, the entity will leave out of the healee's mouth. The healer may use his/her right hand in the healee's aura to stroke the entity out. When the healer's right hand is above the healee's mouth, the healer grabs a hold and pulls up. Eventually, the healer pulls it out. Even at this point, I will ask demons if they wish to go to the Light. God's Forgiveness is available to everyone.

Some people come to healers with tales of having been abducted by spacemen. Refusing to accept their experience as valid does not help! **Angels work in a healee's reality.** Victims say that the Grays told them that their kidnapping and violation was something that they agreed to before they were born as part of their life's plan. However, in an effort to help the victim gain a different perspective, healers might ask, how did the Grays know your personal agreements with God?

The story of the Grays would make a popular science fiction movie! They are gray in color with large heads and eyes, emaciated limbs, and small mouths. Gray is actually the color of their space suit. Their brains are insect-like and their skin is scaled like a reptile. They have suction-type disks on the tips of their fingers like an insect and they leave behind a sticky substance on whatever they touch. A flaw in the cloning process partially manifests in the inability of a clone's ring and little fingers to fully function. These 2 fingers lie over the palm when the other 3 are extended. The second (creative) chakra is shut down. Devoid of emotions themselves, they take pleasure in another's fear and pain. In this manner, they literally suck the life out of a planet and then move onto another. The Grays fit Andrew Vaachs' definition of evil like a glove. Their heart chakras are shut, so there is no heart love energy. (Interestingly, people who have heart problems often have a gray pallor to their skin.) The Gray's choice of spacesuit color is an interesting reflection.

The Grays come from a twin star system where the suns are so closely together that early in creation, life forms in each solar system began to telecommunicate. Their psychic abilities advanced, as did their civilization. They perfectly understood that with psychic and technical knowledge comes power, which they used to subjugate others to their will. What they missed was that knowledge is not finite; the process of creation is ongoing. In cutting themselves off from The Creator and formulating a god to suit their own selfish purposes, they closed themselves off to the real God.

Eons ago, the Grays were more humanoid, very much resembling us. Initially, the Grays' decision to reproduce by cloning served the dual purpose of convenience and control. This and their distorted thought forms brought about physical deformity, and reproduction became neither loving nor natural. This further evolved into an inability to reproduce naturally. Their demise was predicted 2,000 years ago in the <u>Apocalypse</u>, for the Grays are the beasts that the 7-headed beast (the seven Illuminati families) worshiped as gods.

Some people work with the Grays and demons. In the case of black magicians, they do it knowingly. Without question, all of these people know at some point that whom they are working with and what they are doing is wrong. Those who choose to ignore the warning either do not care or justify their actions. Whenever something has to be justified, it is usually false. Unfortunately for these individuals, the end never justifies the means. Just as black magicians are slowly taken over by the demons they conjure, the Grays increasingly controlled people who worked with them. People who summon demons are increasingly controlled by the demons that they summon. The same is true for those who worked with the Grays. If there is no change of heart, if the individual has never prayed to God for forgiveness and help, there comes a point when those who work with evil become slaves to the dark. Those who try to use good for evil incur God's Wrath.

It is possible for an individual to lose his or her soul. Thousands of opportunities throughout many, many hundreds of lifetimes offer each lost soul the possibility to begin the journey home to the Light. When a soul continuously chooses to close his/her heart, the eyes, which are the window to the soul, become a lifeless black void. Once, the Angels showed me a group of black magicians. In the image, each black magician was a thin line drawing on and even thinner piece of

99

yellowed rice paper. All wore ancient ceremonial garb, as an indication that they had practiced black magic in countless lifetimes. The drawings were devoid of emotion. Jesus spoke of the separation of the wheat from the chaff in these times. For these black magicians, the Angels have shown that personality will not survive death; they face total annihilation. Their greatest offense was to use good to create evil. More than 2,000 years ago, they stole the remains of a great and good man. There is a black magic ritual that uses a recently dead body or its parts to capture the essence of soul. Afterwards, they use the bones or remains as a base for black magic.   The problem for black magicians who do so is that this is a crutch. When the crutch is gone, their psychic abilities and power also disappear. The Angels told me that the particular black magicians they showed me had reincarnated over and over again in the same land, using the power of the bones to do black magic arts. They found other good and turned it to evil, and in the process they lost their souls. The bones of the holy man were cleared during one of the Wednesday night 8:00 pm clearings. As soon as the bones were cleared, the energy of the holy man left the bones, and the powerful black magicians were left completely powerless.

With each energy shift Earth's vibration goes up, and more and more people make a transition. As Earth adjusts to the new energy vibrations, the death rate slows. Granted, for many who are leaving at this time, it is simply their time to go. Those who have unfinished lessons to work out will reincarnate on a three-dimensional planet elsewhere in the universe. As the transition from the age of darkness into the Aquarian Age continues, **it will be increasingly easier to see people for who they are**. Secrets, what is hidden, and the unconscious are all surfacing.

Visualizing or asking the Angels for color cobalt blue before going to sleep at night stops abductions. Egyptians and Mayans painted the ceilings of their temples blue to keep unwanted influences out, not to imitate the color of the sky. The temple floors were not painted brown or green to duplicate the ground. Cobalt blue calms, thereby dispelling fear. Cobalt blue also protects the mind and thoughts.

Knowing how to be safe is important before developing psychic abilities. **Meditation develops psychic abilities**. One meditation method is to **go within the Silence**, to be the silent observer, and achieve a state of Beingness. In meditation gently push thoughts out as they come in. When the brain is devoid of chatter and silent, try focusing on the third eye. Go back to the silence. If thoughts come in, gently breathe them away. At some point, it will be possible to transcend ordinary consciousness. Attention will automatically be brought to the heart, as it opens to joy. Through joy one is able to step into the surrounding space. It is through this space that each individual is able to make his/her own connection to God. It is then that the individual is able to align to his/her life's purpose. Through acceptance, it is possible to become **self-realized**. The same events occur in the lives of both individuals stuck in fear-based personalities, and those who are self-realized. The difference is that the first group is stuck in the pleasure-pain wheel, and they miss the joy and passion of life. The key is in how life's situations and opportunities are handled. Fear naturally comes up in new situations, be they opportunities or challenges. The first group clutches or flees. The second group recognizes fear in change, walks through the fear, and looks for the adventure in living life moment by moment. Life's journey may be experienced step by step, by being joyful and attentive in the moment, which allows the future to evolve. In other words, to live!

There are three kinds of fear: Fear that warns us, fear that is instilled through abuse or trauma, and fear of change. The latter two stagnate growth unless healed. Without growth there is no sense of direction, which provides meaning and an inner knowing that life's journey will bring success. Dick Roberts has aided people in career/life transformations by helping them to discover their true passion, hidden talents, and life/career purpose. Depression, anxiety and addiction occur when people live outside their potential. Whenever fear presents itself, try asking the Angels or God for the answer. *Is this fear warning me to stop? Is this fear something for me to go through?*

Erhart Vogel, author of Self-Healing Through Awareness of Being, is one of many instructors who teach self-realization through meditation. Both Vogel and Osho (Ragneesh) taught **heart-centered meditation**. The heart is the gateway to the upper chakras; it is where we listen to God, and know right from wrong. The heart is the avenue through which affluence flows. Without an open heart, there is a tendency to either hoard wealth or fear that there will not be enough. So as love flows, wealth must also flow. Otherwise, at some point in the current life or a future reincarnation the soul will experience poverty. Many former millionaires are born in the streets of India. When people do not believe me, I suggest that they tune in (get into a meditative state) and ask for themselves. Typically, people are surprised at the answer they receive.

To dispel those who wish harm by releasing hooks inside of us that serve as magnets that draw heavy, dark energies: Get into a slight meditative state and call in one at a time those who wish harm. Say to them, *Thank you! You have made me strong. I respect you and I respect the path that you have chosen for yourself. Now it is time for you to leave.* Calling in a general assemblage of people or groups who take issue with you, or whom you judge works. This simple act releases hooks inside of us, which serve as magnets for heavy, dark energies. Then release any hooks we have left in others. Call in people (known and unknown) whom you've harmed and ask for **forgiveness**. Tell these individuals, *I am sorry! I release any hooks that I may have left in you.*

Black serves as a vessel to hold the Light. Black is the color of The Great Mystery and The Womb of Creation. Each color has its darker side; for example, red represents grounding and power. Nasty shades of red represent outrageous anger or misuse of power. Black magicians, to conceal their magic so that those of consciousness will not dispel it, use the hidden aspect of the color black. One task on a 3-dimensional planet is **to reconcile our love and our power**. We do this by looking at our own dark side, those lifetimes where we might have even been black magicians, and events in this lifetime that we all have that we are not particularly proud of. We don't know what's lurking in our hearts until we open up and look in. Alec Baldwin in The Shadow says, "I cannot forgive myself for the evil I have done." However, we cannot be whole until we do so. At the end of the movie, The Dark Crystal, the master crystal is made whole again. The two races rejoin and are made whole as well. "What was sundered and undone shall be whole, the two made one."

Initially, I put the story of Anne Boleyn in this book because I thought that if I could admit that I was an unpopular character in history that others might look at lifetimes when they didn't get it either. Too many people refuse to look at their issues. Interestingly enough, through the healing of Anne Boleyn, she has become increasingly understood and popular.

The **dawning of the Age of Aquarius** was dramatically ushered in with the powerful astrological aspects on February 14, 2009. On May 30, 2009, God turned the page from the Dark Age to the Golden Age of the Return of the Angels. The age of pain is being replaced with one of joy. The song is becoming a reality. Goddess and God are joined together on Earth.

Ramona Kirk asked me in August 2008, if we could do clearings once a week. We began with handful of Tera Mai healers from around the world. We agreed upon Wednesday night at 8:00 pm, wherever we happened to be. Because we all lived in different time zones, in order to connect with one another at 8:00 pm, we asked the Angels, *Please connect me to the Tera Mai healers who are doing the clearings.* This short phrase has become the key to connecting to the group and to the energy of the **Wednesday night 8:00 pm (20:00 hours) clearings**. Because people saw positive results, they told others. By the end of 2008, a million people were participating. By June 2009, over three million people took part. Our ranks include groups of chanting Buddhists and Catholics praying the rosary. Anyone may join by doing clearings, meditating, praying, sending healing, chanting, or holding the energy. If 8:00 pm does not work out, simply begin at the top of any hour on Wednesday, and ask the Angels to connect you to wherever it is 8:00 pm on Earth and to the Tera Mai healers who are doing the clearings. Then you are free to do as you wish. Whenever you are finished, ask that the healing wave continue through the following Wednesday.

It is a good idea for all healers to clear any of the healee's negativity from them after a healing session. As Earth has become much clearer since the Wednesday Night Clearings, go outside and stand on the ground. (Concrete does not count.) Call upon God / Goddess to clear you of anyone else's 'stuff', and send it into the ground. You will feel a downward pull. You may also get down on your hands and knees and place the palms of your hands upon the ground and do the same. Afterwards, ask the Angels to give you an angelic shower or fill in voids with gold. In the etheric level gold light repels demonic and evil beings. **Ramona Kirk, New York**

Call upon God/Goddess, Holy Spirits and Angels to create a **Circle of Protection and Purification** around you or that which you wish to clear. Then pray, *into this circle of protection and purification, which surrounds and permeates me; please bring Pure Energy from Source. Create a sphere of protection and purification to surround and permeate me.* Then ask for Violet Fire to fill the sphere of protection and purification and say the following three times, *I am one with my higher self. I am a being of Violet Fire. I am the purity God desires.* In the same manner ask for White Fire and say three times, *I am one with my higher self. I am a being of White Fire. I am the purity God desires.* Then ask for Pure White Light and say three times, *I am one with my higher self. I am a being of Pure White Light. I am the purity God desires.* Ask for Golden Light and say three times, *I am one with my higher self. I am a being of Golden Light. I am the purity God desires.* Ask for Silver Light and say three times, *I am one with my higher self. I am a being of Violet Fire. I am the purity God desires.* Call upon Archangel Chamuel to create an outer circle of pink love and compassion. Ask Archangel Michael to build a second outer circle of cobalt blue protection and cleansing. Then ask for mirrors of protection, reflection and attraction to be placed on the outer circle facing outwards. (Based upon the work of the Summit Lighthouse with the Violet Flame.)

It is possible to **use white magic to dispel black magic**. Call upon God and His Chosen Angels to return any and all black magic back to the original perpetrator with love. If you know the individual's name, speak it. Then repeat the following 3 times, *thrice around the circle bound, send all evil to the ground.* Then say, *so mote it be!* (So must it be.) Ask for Violet Flames of Transformation to burn the evil. To go a step further, call upon Saint Michael the Archangel. *Thrust your sword into the earth in such a way that it pierces this evil. Continue until the tip of the sword touches the very center of the core of this planet, drawing fire into the sword to balance the core, burn the evil, and create a way for evil and darkness to go down to the central fire for transmutation. Please fill in all of the voids with Violet Flames of Transformation and the protective color of gold.*

Dispelling evil through the Universe's desire for balance. Call upon God /Goddess and in the blanks speak the name of the individual who wishes you evil. *I acknowledge that it is*

103

_____'s free-will choice to send harm. However, _____'s actions are interfering with my free-will choice. Thus, it is my free-will choice to reject all harm that is sent to me, and ask it be sent immediately down to the central fire for transformation. Please fill in all of the voids with Violet Flames of Transformation and the protective color of gold._ **Cathy Towle, New York**

To bind or block someone who is sending evil to you call upon the Angels of Exorcism. If you know who it is, name the individual in the blanks. Because they are interfering with your free-will choice, you have the right to do this. The angelic binding material that the Angels use looks like Egyptian burial mummy cloth. _Go to _____ and bind him (or her) so that he (or she) may not harm himself (or herself) or others._ Then repeat the following 3 times while you circle your right hand and arm clockwise. _I bind thee, _____, so you may not harm yourself or others._ Healers who are channeling Universal healing energy may do this for people who come to them for clearing.

To clear the timeline for yourself, others or Mother Earth, get into a meditative state. Ask the Angels to show you the timeline. Begin with the present. Send clearing, healing and/or prayers to the present. If negativity comes up, ask the Angels what to do with it. Ask that all negativity that is known or unknown, seen or unseen be removed. Angels may take the stuff down to the central fire for transformation, into God's Hands, back to the individual who sent it or somewhere off the planet. Fill in the voids with healing, love, joy, peace, prosperity, enlightenment, inspiration, etc.

Then do the same for the past. Ask that the core issues of any blocks, evil, etc. be uprooted. If one or both of your parents were abusive or emotional absent, when you get to either the moment of conception or birth, ask the Angels if it is appropriate to cut cords, chains, ties and attachments. Call upon Saint Michael to do so. Fill in the voids with healing. Go back to the present, and then onto the future. Send clearing, healing and/or prayers to the future. Ask the Angels to open the vortex and send lost souls from your past to the Light. Pat Osborn of Vermont saw that locks had been removed along the entire timeline for one woman who had been cleared in this manner. This clearing may have to be repeated, especially if the clearing is for Earth, as her history is long and involved. It is always possible to drain evil and send it down to the central fire; it is not possible to release anyone of Karma that s/he has not worked out.

Psychic Abilities in the Aquarian Age

The energy of the Aquarian Age is coming closer to the realms of other realities. More people are becoming intuitive or having psychic impressions. At some point very soon, the reality of the Dark Age will be gone, replaced by a more joyful one. Along with this, it will be easier to access new energies, beings in higher dimensions and new technologies. For example, manned space missions beyond the Moon are not possible using three-dimensional knowledge and atomic or fossil fuel. Trashing Earth and re-locating to Mars or the Moon, which are dead and have no eco systems, is the height of arrogance, and absolutely improbable. There is no usable water. There is little in the way of an atmosphere, which not only makes breathing difficult, but makes being hit by a meteor or solar flares likely; especially the part about solar flares on Mars. There is a prediction that the United States will join the Galactic Confederation, these are the 'good guys', not the Grays. The technology for space travel of this kind is found in the dimension that Earth is headed for, the Aquarian Age. What is impossible in the Piscean Age is looming as a promise in the Aquarian Age. We are about to discover for ourselves that there is more to be told than what is found in meager philosophies.

In North Carolina I get phone calls from born-again-Christians. One frequently asked question is, "We are taught that we are here on Earth, and that those who have passed on are either in Heaven or Hell. How come John Edward is able to speak to the dead?" The answer is that not everyone who dies is able to go to Heaven or is destined for Hell. They exist on another dimension and do not think of themselves as being dead because their astral body is very real to them, as real as the physical body was when they were alive on Earth. Some earthbound spirits are able to communicate with a psychic who has the gift to see beyond the veil. There are also Angels and spirit guides, who exist on the same dimension, but are not as easily accessible.

When healers or psychic readers, who are channeling Universal-healing energies, use their inner vision, they may contact higher beings, who are on yet another dimension. As with dreams, what the healer or psychic sees may appear real or earthly, or as visual metaphors? Somehow Universal healing energy works with the power of the mind's eye to bring about healing and accurate information. It is important for the healer or reader not to manipulate the imagery, but to watch and ask questions. The key is not to force the imagery. Images from these Otherworlds may also be found in an altered state of deep meditation.

One of the really great things about going into the Aquarian Age is that low-vibrational entities are not going. Parasites and pain will be a thing of the past. Until then it is essential to understand what is going on now.

105

Along with each of the physical five senses (seeing, feeling, hearing, tasting, and smelling), there is a corresponding sense that perceives on other dimensions. We lose what we do not use. In the Age of Aquarius these abilities are important. The best way to do this is through meditation. Focused, concentrated attention is required, however, the paradox is that forcing or willfulness actually shuts down these psychic centers. What is required is gentle, loving, persistent attention.

There are as many ways to meditate, as there are groups that promote it. **Meditation** has long been an important aspect of spiritual practice and soul growth. The Catholic clergy, popes, sisters and brothers alike, meditate. It is best, but not necessary, to do meditation when the stomach is not full. Prior to meditating, **focus and breathe into stretch exercises** or those that open joints (shoulders, elbows, wrists, hips, knees, and ankles). Remember to do any movement exercises in both directions for balance. Some do **eye exercises** as well; that is, rolling the eyes clockwise and counterclockwise, moving them back and forth, and up and down. This is good for the physical eyes as well. My Aunt June did this and never needed glasses. She died in her 80's.

After exercising and before meditating, or before doing healing work, I **call in Spirit**. On page 35, there is one way to do this. You may also call in the energies beginning by whatever name you call Divine God and Divine Goddess. Then add the names of any higher beings, Angels, Archangels or saints that you are attracted to. Native Americans recognized that God's Holy Spirit was in everything; actually, the Bible says this as well. Native Americans called in the energies by using the *Twenty Count*, which included plants, 4-legged, winged, etc. I add the names of higher beings that I have encountered. Asking to be surrounded by cobalt blue and gold is protective. Intentions should be clear, yet at the same time allowing Mother-Father God to take care of the details. **Ground** before meditating! See or feel the etheric feet or the root chakra going deeply into the earth like tree roots. **To further open the third eye** and crown chakra, before beginning, slowly tilt the head back for less than a minute. *You may want to check with your doctor first before trying.* Once in a meditative state, **go into deeper levels** by taking a slow, deep breath, exhaling slowly and relax. Focus behind the eyes. If there are outside noises, use them to go deeper. Excess energy may be moved down to a center that is roughly 1-1/2 to 2 inches below the navel where it can be stored; this can be done through visualization or feeling. When through, **giving thanks and gratitude** completes the cycle and opens the way for Angels and other higher beings to return. The strongest force in all this universe is love; close on its heels is that of gratitude.

Silently repeating a **mantra**, which may be meaningless, works. Om, and Amen (pronounced ah-men) are popular. Effortless repetition occupies the left brain. With a corresponding slowing down of the breath, the intuitive right brain becomes active, which leads us to the **silent observer**

within. If other thoughts can come in, and the mantra is no longer being repeated, gently go back to repeating the mantra. If the mantra alters on its own, go with the flow until it feels right to go back to the original mantra. When entering the silence of the Great Mystery within, remain with a silent mind as long as possible. If a pain comes up in the body, repeat the mantra into the discomfort. Relax and breathe into the center of pain to move through it, or blow it away. This technique also works for other things, such as, fear. Move through fear in order to see what is on the other side. Repeating the mantra into other 'negative' emotions works as well. If visuals come in, enjoy them without trying to figure them out with the left brain, or ask the Angels questions.

Silva Method utilizes both visualizations and in some cases, corresponding body movements. It is very much like **Shamanic journeywork** in that the meditator focuses on a visual image of him/herself. The original name for this workshop was Silva Mind Control, which conjured visions of brainwashing. What the word 'control' was meant to convey was that we are supposed to be in control of our thoughts that we might literally change our lives. Beginning with Silva or journeywork will lay a foundation for all psychic work that you do. Completion with Silva or journeywork will tie everything else together. Silva Method and journeywork have aspects of self-hypnosis. One of my students, Roxanne Louise Miller, wrote Your Unlimited Potential, a full self-hypnosis course and guide to creating yourself and your life through use of your mind. Teri Mahaney, Ph.D., author of Change Your Mind/Life, teaches people how to create their own meditation tapes. Lots of methods work!

Arhat is a word for the consciousness of ascended beings. **Arhatic Yoga** utilizes the breath in combination with different mantras and visualizations in meditation. In Taoism, the word Tao means God. However, God is not a noun, but rather an active verb - a creative, dynamic, thinking, invincible force. The Taoist's Microcosmic Orbit also combines both the breath and visuals in meditation. The more advanced meditation includes mantras at each of the chakras as well.

East Indian gurus teach several meditation techniques. One is by **focusing on the chakras.** The mantra is similar to the sound the breath makes. On every inhale silently say, "So", and on every exhale say, "Hum". In meditation sit with the spine erect. Relax and let thoughts go. Allow the breath to naturally slow down. Begin repeating the mantra, **"So-Hum"**, by focusing at the crown at least 3 times. Feel the prana or Universal energy being drawn into the chakra on every inhale; expulsion of used energy within the body released on every exhale. Be aware of the silence at the top of the inhale and bottom of the exhale where there is no breath, where there is no mantra.

A **vertical energy line** or channel, which originates from Source, runs down through the crown and out the root chakra, grounding into a chakra that is located about 12 inches below the feet. The crown chakra spirals upward; the root chakra spirals downward! Other major chakras are connected both front and back to the vertical energy line. At the point of connection, the diameter of the chakra is quite small; the chakra increases in size as it spirals outwards towards the surface of the physical body and into the aura. These chakras are at the mind's eye and the back of the head, front and back throat chakras, front and back heart chakras, front and back solar plexus chakras, navel chakra and one at the small of the back, and front and back creative chakras.

After the crown, "So-Hum" is repeated down each front chakra to the root chakra and then up the chakras on the spine. Maintain focused concentrated attention. Become aware that the chakra is breathing along with your breath, and of the silence at the top and the bottom of the breath. At the crown pause and visualize Light. Repeat the process. To either cleanse the chakras or to slow down the energy, work down the spine and up the front. It is important to begin and end with the energy moving down the front and up the spine.

If you would rather say another mantra, Amen (pronounced ah-men) or K'in (Mayan word for Sun pronounced key-yin) works well. Many people simply say Ohm. Ohm is the mantra I began with before I took the meditation class at the Meditation Institute in Milwaukee. Repeating a mantra, allowing it to take its own form apart from the breath, is yet another meditation method.

An **advanced meditation** is to sit in meditative silence with no mind, no thoughts, for at least one minute. When there are no thoughts, the heart opens to joy. When the heart opens to joy, we are able to go through the heart to see that the emptiness around us has energy. The goal is to make our own connection to God through The Great Silence. One way to do this is by starting with a mantra and gently allowing it to become or not become what it will be. Another technique is to hold one visual image for one minute with no other thought. For those who take my Shamanic class and are having difficulty seeing him/herself, I suggest to these students that they try the bathroom exercise. That is, during a break or lunch, stand in front of a mirror for one minute just looking at him/herself. Close the eyes and try to hold the vision. When the image goes, repeat the exercise.

With meditation and working on personal issues the **kundalini, the energy of the root chakra**, will begin to rise. Jesus taught that the mind, heart and emotions must be clear before going into the Great Silence. That is why teachers, including Master Choa Kok Sui, say that the kundalini awakens from the crown downward, not the root chakra upward. When the kundalini rises, fire rises and reaches the brain. Three things are possible when the fire reaches the brain - insanity, death or enlightenment. We want door number 3. If issues have been dealt with and the lower chakras are cleared first, enlightenment is possible. For this and other reasons, it is vitally important to breathe away mental issues in meditation or a healing session. Once a man, who was ready to commit suicide because of ringing in his ears, came for a healing session. During the session, he got very little out of it. Then I saw an image of a black man and asked him what it meant. He told me that he was a racist, and he had no intention of changing. Then an image of a rightwing radio talk show host came into my mind's eye. When I asked the man about it, he said that he listened to the program all of the time. Then he received an insight, which was the only thing he got out of the session. He realized that every time he listened to the show, the ringing in his ears got a little worse. I asked him if he was going to stop listening, and he answered, No! Meditation, initiations and healing sessions are not enough; there has to be willingness to look at issues, and let go. If we want something different in our lives, we have to be willing to try something new.

Master Mantak Chia and Taoist Masters teach how to **circulate energy** up the spine and down the front central meridian, like the "So-Hum" meditation. This is NOT the energy of the kundalini. Mantak Chia calls this circulation the Microcosmic Orbit Mantras (chants) and mudras (hand positions) that may be incorporated into the meditation. An example of a mudra would be the thumb touching the little finger. Jesus is sometimes depicted holding his thumb to his middle finger. While meditating you may wish to touch the thumbs to different fingers and feel different energy patterns.

Good teachers are a good investment. Along with proper instruction, students are working and studying in the aura of an individual who is already doing what they want to do. Quantum leaps are possible. Go beyond the written hype; check teachers and classes out before taking the class. Our guts tell us, if we would only listen to our instincts. Any organization or person, who claims to be the only one with the answers, doesn't! Jesus taught his disciples to heal, and sent them out to heal and teach others how to heal. That piece of information is still in the New Testament. For those who say, "that was then and this is now," does that mean that people get to pick and choose which of Jesus' teachings they wish to follow? Healing was a major aspect of Jesus' teachings.

Another meditation would be to maintain focused concentrated attention on the **crystals** in your hand. Crystals have their own type of consciousness. Native Americans were aware of the teaching qualities of stones and the mountains, and referred to this consciousness as 'the stone people'. In Medieval Europe Kings still understood the power of certain rocks and crystals. (See Richard III: White Boar)

Visuals in meditation are helpful, but there are consequences if visuals are used to manipulate the freewill choice of others. For example, salesmen have been taught to visualize a particular individual or business buying their goods or service. This interferes with another individual's right of choice. Later, the salesman wonders why the sale didn't hold, or the commission didn't come through as promised, or their job is lost, etc. The true use of the third eye is to pray with the heart for a specific thing without tying God or spirit down to particulars. For example, if we need a place to live, ask for the best possible home, not your neighbor's villa. Then in silent meditation, watch with the third eye and wait for the answer. Give God the opportunity to surprise.

This is not to say, however, that you cannot use particular visual techniques. For example, before going out on a job interview, send blue color to the building and room in which you will be interviewed. If this is the best employment for you and you are meant to get the job, you will get it. If there is something better for you, you will be saved a whole lot of time and trouble. There are other non-manipulative techniques. A simple check is, "Would I want somebody doing this to me?"

Visuals may or may not address the core of the problem. For example, visualizing fat cells burning up, or fat being wrung out of the muscles is helpful. However, if the emotional issue behind the unwanted fat is not healed, the subconscious or super-conscious will either recreate the fat or create something else to call attention to the problem. Visualization is neither a substitute for exercise nor for eating properly.

Shamanic journeywork utilizes visuals and the Shaman's drum. It is the rapid, pulsating, non-varying beat of 205 to 220 beats per minute that quiets the active left brain and sends the Shaman into altered states of consciousness. The overtone of the drumming harmonizes and balances the two hemispheres of the brain, and may be the reason why we feel dissociated from our bodies and participate fully in the imagery. It is more powerful than virtual reality. Visualizing ourselves activates the holographic mind, and a Shaman who is channeling sufficient Elemental Universal Energy may effectively bring about changes in the hologram simply by altering his/her piece of the hologram. It is helpful to learn in a group situation with such a Shaman.

The brain is a computer; awareness resides in the seat of consciousness. The thinker behind our thoughts is in the aura, above the head. Scientists and doctors have unsuccessfully tried to find it in the brain. It's not there! Sleeptime is the soul's awake-time! While the brain sleeps, the subconscious travels with the astral body. At night, the astral body, which is only part of the soul, leaves through the crown chakra and travels outside of our body, connected by a silver cord, which is mentioned in many different mysticisms and spiritual texts. It is this aspect of self that journeys with the drum. The Shaman is always in control and may return to the three-dimensional world at any time. With spirit guides and helpers, s/he is always protected. We hear about "body-mind connection." In Shamanism, the missing element, "spirit", completes the formula, "body-mind-spirit

110

connection". Before beginning journeywork, one traditionally honors the 4 directions and 4 elements, and calls in higher forces, spirit helpers, power animals and guides. A goal or an intention is set before beginning. Goals may be as simple as finding a power animal or spirit helpers, and exploring aspects of nonordinary reality, or for healing, knowledge, strength, creative inspiration prosperity, etc.

We use different **states of consciousness** during our waking day. Speaking with a friend, testifying in court, or computer work require different states of mind. Just as there are various levels of awareness and concentration in ordinary life, there are also multidimensional levels of awareness in nonordinary reality. In general, there are three worlds that Shamans from different cultures around the world travel to: The Lowerworld of power animals and nature spirits; the Upperworld of the Angels; and the Middleworld, which is something like the astral body of Earth. Michael Harner in The Way of the Shaman refers to what is beyond our ordinary perception, as nonordinary reality. The idea is to pay attention to the physical, but also be able to shift. To our greater self, this realm is real reality. The hero experiences another realities when, with super awareness, s/he follows an inner knowing courageously, without doubt, and does whatever is required in the moment. Nonordinary feats of bravery and daring are accomplished in altered states, where the senses are heightened in what is described as a peak experience. Another example is when audiences are drawn into other realities while engrossed in a well-orchestrated play, concert or sports event. When actors, musicians or players skillfully draw our attention in, we focus intently on the event, our awareness heightens and ordinary physical reality disappears. As Earth's vibration rises in the Aquarian Age, our ordinary reality is becoming more akin to the nonordinary reality of the Shaman.

Nothing but self-fears and negative thoughts may cause harm in nonordinary reality. Nothing! Spirit helpers, guides and Angels are there to assist. Negative energies are easily sent away. Other's fearful projections may be banished through laughter. Drug-induced trances rarely, if ever, reach higher states of reality, and the would-be journeyer is always at the mercy of the drug. Street drugs, as well as harmful pharmaceutical combinations, are becoming increasingly toxic.

Once in New York, two men came to me, desperate to learn Reiki and other rays of touch healing. One man told me that he used to do drugs on a regular basis until he had one extraordinary experience; he went into the higher realms with the real Celestial Angels. He stopped doing drugs, turning instead to advanced meditation techniques, attempting to recreate the experience. They took my classes and initiations, and were supposed to pay me when they returned to Germany. They didn't. Most people who have extraordinary experiences become more responsible. Either the man lied, or he's only looking to recreate an experience and missed the lesson. Jesus said, "If you cannot be trusted with the small things of this earth, how can you be trusted with the keys to heaven?" I let the loss go, and moved on.

Effectiveness in non-ordinary reality or meditation/visualization is dependent upon how much spiritual, psychic or healing energy the individual has. To attain strength and powerful spirit helpers, Native Americans would go on vision quests, whereby they would stop eating and drinking water, and exercise vigorously for days until they collapsed. They could have a stroke, die, pass out, or go consciously into the Otherworlds. The objective was to meet a higher being, who would bestow a Gift of the Spirit, which would be clearly demonstrated in the physical reality. Going through personal trials, living and speaking Truth regardless of how difficult or impossible it appears at the time; right action and conduct, experiencing love and other virtues, meditation and traveling to places of power are yet other ways to grow in spirit. Receiving Universal initiations of healing are only tools; receiving Gifts of the Spirit is not the final goal. Gifts of the Spirit may be taken away if misused.

Clairsentience is the ability to feel on other levels and enters through the solar plexus. It is experienced when the Truth is spoken and every hair on the body stands on end, or chills run up the spine. It is sometimes said that our skin has eyes because of its ability to perceive.

Using the to third eye to visualize may be learned by anyone. **Clairvoyance** means to see clearly. Visions within the mind's eye corresponds to the third eye chakra, which is comprised of two chakras, one between the eyebrows and another at the forehead. One very old exercise is to hold a simple object like a pencil or crystal in front of you, close your eyes, and hold the image as long as you can. When you lose it, look again. Close your eyes and try to hold more of the details. Maintain focused attention. When you lose it, look again. Try to hold the image longer. Do this for 5 minutes a day. It takes 21 to 30 **consecutive** days to build a new skill or change a habit. At the end of 30 days, work with another object and you will find that it does not take as long. Then sit with a mirror and try to hold the image of yourself in your mind's eye. An old Wiccan method for opening the third eye is to stare at a burning candle flame for one minute and then hold the image in the third eye. If this causes headaches, stop using the candle or meditate on the candle for a shorter period of time.

One way to develop psychic hearing on other dimensions or **clairaudience** is to listen to the tone carried after ringing a Tibetan bell. Or listen after striking an ordinary bell. If you wake up early in the morning, listen to the wind. It can be a powerful experience. The Holy Inquisition burned people alive for this act alone. Remember to check out messages! Auditory messages come in about an inch and a half above the ears at the temple bone. In meditation, ask that these centers be cleared and then watch. Give yourself permission to see and hear on other levels of reality.

Preconceptions or mental blockages interfere with psychic messages or intuition. **Inner knowing** comes in through the solar plexus; it is a knowing experienced within the body and is more reliable than psychic messages. **Psychic messages** may come into the pituitary gland and then into the brain where they are translated into language. That is why the sound seems to be inside the head. However, the voice is so quiet that the mind must be free of the incessant chatter and clutter. Freedom from negative, worn-out, internal CDs, mental torture chambers, judgments, worries and reruns of 'old bad movies' brings peace of mind and the ability to listen. A quiet mind and listening skills improves perceptions on all levels – physical hearing, clairaudience, and inner knowing.

Gut feelings come in through the solar plexus. This sensation in the pit of the stomach is familiar to many people. When we don't act on our gut feelings, things always go wrong. In this manner we learn to trust our gut. If gut feelings are continuously ignored, they will go away. Sometimes before somebody dies a friend or relative may feel sourness only in the pit of the stomach. It seems to be a way for spirit to prepare the living. Another aspect of the solar plexus' ability to help us make choices is clairsentient awareness. This is when the skin feels or perceives, like when we get goose bumps, or a chill down the spine when the Truth is spoken. Individuals who force their will and are unable to surrender themselves to God's Will block their solar plexus.

Psychic centers may be opened by meditating on the points mentioned previously - crown, pituitary, solar plexus and third eye. The Taoists understood the healing power of smiling into the organs. It is also possible to smile into the chakras. Opening the heart to love and allowing love to flow into these centers in meditation is yet another way. Pray to God and ask that psychic abilities be opened safely, and for the gift of discernment. It is important to **check out all messages and messengers three times**. "In Divine Truth, this is so?" or "You have come in the Light of Christ?" To trust means to follow the heart and inner knowing, not to blindly follow auditory messages.

To see past lives stand in front of a mirror; a cobalt blue background is best. Place a small candle in between you and the mirror. Be aware of the consciousness above your head and look at your eyes, and then watch your own past lives flip before you. Einstein proved that time and space does not exist the way we perceive them. We are vibrating and everything is happening simultaneously. If you have a group of people, a fun parlor game is to have someone stand against a blank wall and dim the lights. Focus your attention on the individual's eyes and watch as the past lives flip in front of you. Initially, you may have to half-close your eyes. As you get better and better, you will begin to see in lighter environments. At first, you will see the face changing. As your skill develops, you will see costume changes. If people verbalize what they are seeing it somehow helps others in the group to see as well.

If there is a healer(s) in the group, other things and healings will happen. People who are flipping rapidly may be integrating past lives or experiences. When a form persists, it is coming up for healing. Past beauty is gone if negative thought forms are present, faces and bodies will look sickly or have some kind of distortion. Sometimes, death wounds are visible, or there is a weapon. At an Angel conference, which was featured on **CBS's *Eye to Eye*** with Connie Chung, after doing the third eye initiation for a group, we practiced seeing the past lives of one another. One of the women present was one of my students who had done this exercise on Long Island almost 2 years previously. On Long Island, a Native American brave with half of his face blown away appeared. She personally was not in any kind of pain, although the past life was angry, distressed and in obvious discomfort. At the Angel conference, the brave reappeared; however, much healing had transpired since his initial appearance. The form was more illuminated, stronger, and his face was completely restored. Not everyone in the group sees with the same definition, clarity and completeness; for example, not everyone sees the body and clothes change. Many of the people present at this particular session saw the brave complete with colored war paint on both sides of his face. From head to foot, another individual turned into a muscular caveman. Connie Chung's producer nearly flipped out.

If an individual is too heavily burdened with negative thoughts, guilt, etc., the soul is unable to go to the Light within the 3-day time period after death. He or she remains earthbound, even if the anger is justified. This is what had happened to the brave mentioned above. With their mystical and spiritual practices, Native American nations or tribes had at their disposal the means of defeating the white man, even though the Europeans had guns. Loathing and contempt interfered with spiritual abilities and practices. Native American deaths, however, were not in vain; the shedding of their blood into the land insured that this nation would always be spiritual. Native American prophecies had foretold of the near annihilation of the great Nations. It was also prophesized that there would be signs when the time of darkness would end. They include: When the eagle lands on the moon. When the eagle and condor meet. When a white buffalo calf is born. When large, wild animals enter the cities. When trees die from the tops down. All of these things have come about! The Goddess is here and the Golden Age is coming into being. All over the world there is fallout as the Dark Age crumbles under its own weight of greed and corruption. There is only one more prophecy that is not Native American, which is waiting to be fulfilled. That is, that the Golden Age will commence when all of the men who fought in the Great War (World War I) had passed. As of July 2009, there were five.

Traumatic deaths may result in the soul's immediate reincarnation. Because time and space do not exist the way we understand them, it is possible for anguished souls to reincarnate at a time that they were still alive in the first lifetime birth. These souls may bring into the second life memory and characteristics from the first. There was a woman who claimed to be the daughter of the assassinated Russian Tsar. Observers claimed that not one member of the royal family could have escaped. Yet, this woman, while unable to speak Russian, was able to recount things to her grandmother that she couldn't possibly have known unless she was a member of the royal family. She was the Tsar's daughter, the reincarnation of the Tsar's daughter. Men, who are killed in battle are oftentimes unable to move through trauma to go to the Light, and may immediately reincarnate.

Misqualified energy or unresolved thought forms from past lives may appear in the present life in the form of pain, disease, fear or anxiety. **When the past life is healed**, the current lifetime receives healing. This may mean the healing of more than one lifetime. When I facilitated the third eye initiation at Ishpiming, a New Age retreat center in northern Wisconsin, one man kept flipping between Native American lives and those of white European settlers. While his clothes kept changing, his bone structure and features were always similar to his present incarnation. By reincarnating back and forth between two clashing groups, by walking in another's moccasins or boots, the soul sees through perceived differences and learns to love. In his present life as a white male practicing Native American ways, he is resolving and harmonizing past conflicts.

One man I used to date had alternate lifetimes between being a black slave and being a slave trader. He told me that in pictures taken of him in his youth during the summer, he was so tan that he looked like a little black boy. Others have gone back and forth between being burned as a witch, and being clergy of the not-so-Holy Inquisition. In the Middle East, many souls go back and forth between being Israeli and Palestinian. In India souls alternate from Buddhism to Hinduism. Understandably, many people do not want to see this! We do not like to look at lifetimes that are in discord with who we are now. However, by embracing all aspects of ourselves, accepting and healing our dark sides, and cultivating and integrating love, we become whole. In each lifetime we are only able to do what we are capable of. The story of *Sleeping Beauty* is a tale of reincarnation. The prince walks through the forest and he sees skeletal remains of men who tried and failed before him. These are all former reincarnations of himself, each one getting closer to Sleeping Beauty. Each lifetime gave him skills and strength, which now enable the prince to accomplish his goal.

While watching past lives, healers in the group may ask **to see the internal physiology of the body** (skeletal system, cardiovascular system, etc.). To do this, keep awareness above head and focus your concentration between the eyebrows while visualizing. If asking to see on higher levels, concentrate on your forehead. When using both the eyebrow and forehead centers together, forms will begin to have more dimension and more color than those objects and people that are seen in a three-dimensional reality using the physical eyes.

115

Distress occurs hen the **subconscious mind is in conflict with present reality**. Many people think that intuition or the subconscious is illogical. The subconscious is as logical as a computer. First, problems arise when old inner programs do not fit changed perspectives. For example, childhood or adolescent sexual abuse oftentimes results in thinking that love has to hurt; if it isn't painful, it isn't love. This conflicts with achieving satisfying, loving sex and relationships. Meditation may help in the process of releasing past harm and in reprogramming new constructs. Secondly, problems arise when the mind is given conflicting paradigms or contradictory programs. For example, we are told that we live in an abundant universe; yet, we see lack and limitation daily. Many people have stopped watching the nightly news. Meditation helps to not 'buy into' negative programming. Thirdly, the super-conscious may come in and reprogram the subconscious as life goals change. Meditation helps individuals to switch gears. Fourthly, mediation can help sort through muddled confusion, get to the truth and correct subconsciously filed inversions, omissions, distortions, misunderstandings, substitutions, and misfilings. They are found in inner sanctuaries.

Inner sanctuary in the Silva Method consists of a laboratory. The individual works with a male and female guide. Inner sanctuary in Shamanic Journeywork is a beautiful place in nature. The individual works with power animals, nature spirits and Angels. Individuals may create an inner sanctuary of their own; a place to meet with Angels, guides and the higher self. It is in the inner sanctuary where inversions may be found. For example, we are inundated with information stating that mother and love are equivalent. But if mom was abusive or emotionally absent, there is a subconscious belief that love is hate or distant. Thus, the conscious mind may desire love, but the subconscious draws in harmful relationships. Seeing reverse forms of logic for what they are, helps to reprogram the subconscious during meditation.

Sorting out the truth helps the mental and emotional state, and quiets the mind. This enhances psychic abilities. Without the confusion and the constant chatter, there comes an ability to be observant. As all psychic observations are viewed through preconceptions and feelings, quiet clears the channels or receivers and psychic impressions are more accurate. The ability to receive clear psychic information aids the healer in facilitating the healing process.

Visuals given by spirit guides are oftentimes influenced by their previous incarnations. For example, visuals Abez's sends me are very much horse-oriented. Once I saw a woman's past life in which she was a man, who was blocked. Abez was near me, so I asked him, "How is he blocked?" *(Yes, ask questions about information received in the moment*.) Abez showed me tangled bridles. Again, I asked, "What does this mean?" I was told that this man had a twisted perception of control and that he had misused power. If I see visuals, and I neither hear nor know what the meaning of the visual is, I simply tell my client what it is I see. Thus, keeping my left brain out of it. I give this same advice to students who take my Shamanic class, or the second degree of Tera Mai Reiki or Tera Mai Seichem. When visuals are personal, go deeper within or problem-solve in the dreamstate.

It is **the healee's task** to <u>verify objectively</u> and/or <u>ask for confirmation</u> on psychic information that is brought into the session. Good psychics go to Source or focus upwards for answers; they do not read the individual. Individuals may ask that psychic impressions be corroborated. For example, when Dolores Arechavala did the reading for me on Abez, she suddenly looked quite startled. Having learned to pay attention, I asked her what it was that she saw. She hesitated and then said, "You and Abez were once wild horses together. It is what he loved, freedom." I immediately saw myself as a white mare, and without telling Dolores, I asked her what color horse I was. She answered, "White." I asked God for further confirmation. A week later, I was in New York. Late at night, lying in bed, I was neither asleep nor awake. Something energetic but tangible moved inside of my chest from the center to the right. Too amazed to speak in this in-between state, my arms lengthened and my shoulder blades shifted around to the side of my body. There was a sensation of being able to use my front limbs to move forward. Then a worry came regarding slipping on Charlotte's highly polished tile floors. With awareness came analysis; with thought, came consciousness. My body shifted back. It was a long time before I could fall asleep.

For protection, healing and to begin to develop or further enhance psychic abilities you may want to try the **White Gold Alchemy Meditation**. *(Source unknown)*

Get into a meditative state. Focus behind physical eyes. Go deep within. Release all thoughts. Be in silence. Bring awareness to the brow and then to an inch behind the bridge of the nose. You have found the mind's eye or third eye. Focus your breath on third eye. Breathe in and out of the third eye. Feel the third eye being energized and opened. Look into this space.

Breathe in and visualize **Gold Light** from the Sun coming into the third eye. Gold goes backwards to the center of the head, and into pituitary gland and then the pineal gland. Exhale, allowing Gold energy to circulate through the brain and then down the spine to the root chakra.

Breathe in and visualize **Silver Light** from the Moon coming into the third eye. Silver goes backwards to the center of the head, and into pituitary gland and then the pineal gland. Exhale, allowing Silver energy to circulate through the brain and then down the spine to the root chakra.

Breathe in and visualize both **Gold & Silver** coming into the third eye. Gold and silver go backwards to the center of the head, and into pituitary gland and then the pineal gland. The Gold and Silver combine and are transformed into White Gold. Exhale, allowing White Gold to circulate through the brain and then down the spine to the root chakra. **Repeat two more times** and go on to do the World Alchemy Meditation.

World Alchemy Meditation (*Source unknown*)

Shift awareness to the Earth. Visualize and connect to the Earth. See the Gold Sun energy and the Silver Moon energy in the space around Earth. Focus on this space.

Breathe in both the energies of the Sun and Moon. Visualize the Gold & Silver Light meeting above the **North Pole** where they are transformed into White Gold. Draw White Gold through the North Pole into the center of the Earth. Exhale and breathe White Gold throughout Earth.

Breathe in both the energies of the Sun and Moon. Visualize the Gold & Silver Light meeting above the **South Pole** where they are transformed into White Gold. Draw White Gold through the South Pole into the center of the Earth. Exhale and breathe White Gold throughout Earth.

Breathe in both the energies of the Sun and Moon into both the **North Pole & South Poles** where they are transformed into White Gold. Exhale and breathe White Gold into the center of the Earth. **Repeat this two more times and begin over again.**

Taking care of the physical body is important. Nerves carry psychic and healing energy, and potassium is good for nerves. If muscle pain originates with the nerves, it may be beneficial to find a combination of Lemon Balm (Melissa), Skullcap, Ashwagandha and Reishi at the health food store. Thyroid is a part of the immune system. Kelp and minerals are beneficial for all of the glands, keeping in mind that trace minerals should be taken in small quantities.

Kidney stones and bone spurs are not an indication that the body is getting too much calcium; they are signs that the body is not getting enough calcium. Or that magnesium and Vitamin D are not being taken with calcium. **Joel Wallach** was a veterinarian before he became a medical doctor. He is an author, and in 1991 he was nominated for the Nobel Prize. He applied the agricultural health care system (preventing and curing diseases in animals with nutrition) to his human patients. In the early 1960's, he was hired through a 7.5 million-dollar government program to do autopsies on zoo animals who died of natural causes. In approximately 17,500 autopsies, Dr. Wallach found that these natural deaths were in fact due to nutritional deficiencies. The physical body gives signs when there is a mineral deficiency. These signs include, animals licking the ground or cribbing (gnaw on the wood in their stalls) in animals. Human signs include continually crave sweets or chocolate. The average life expectancy of a medical doctor (the majority of whom do not believe in vitamin and mineral supplements) in the United States is 58 years. Joel Wallach states that many doctors die from diseases that farm animals, who do have a supplemented diet, would not die from. Dr. Wallach took up a hobby while speaking around the country; that is, collecting obituaries of doctors and lawyers. These obituaries back up his statements. Dr. Wallach has an audiotape and book, <u>Dead Doctors Don't Lie</u>.

If a change is made on one level (even the physical), other levels are able to follow. Physical exercise buffs may develop other aspects or extraordinary abilities. Japanese Samari were both adept soldiers and psychics.

Using Symbols

Symbols are the conscious communication of subconscious minds. Long used in both magic and divination, symbols work for a variety of reasons. God is The Great Mathematician; symbols in part work within mathematical constructs. Typically, the effectiveness and energy of symbols depends upon how much healing and/or psychic energy the user is channeling. Some symbols are very old and carry energy (be it 'good' or 'bad') because they have been used so many times. Other symbols work because an Ascended Being gave them to an individual, as is with the case of HARTH, ZONAR an HALU. These particular symbols tend to work better for people who have been properly initiated into them, but others might use them as well. Altering the way in which symbols are drawn will change the energy pattern. This is not necessarily bad, unless the symbols are used in initiations. Any alteration in an initiation inexorably changes the energy of the initiation and what is passed onto the initiate. Universal initiations are the same for everyone. For more information go to www.kathleenmilner.com and click on TERA MAI SYMBOLS.

As with the ancient art of hands-on healing, one does not necessarily have to believe in the power behind symbols to have them work. If believing is a requirement for healing to occur, then why does hands-on healing and symbols work on babies and animals? The effectiveness of symbols depends on how much healing and/or psychic energy the user is channeling. We begin collecting symbols from the time we are born, and we all have the ability to work with symbols. Traditionally, three symbols were taught in Reiki II – Say Hay Key, Cho Ku Ray and Hon Sha Za Sho Nen.

Since my consciousness-raising experience with Buddha, Tera Mai Reiki Masters have reinitiated and taught Reiki Masters from all Reiki associations and branches thereof. Galina Molodtsova of Russia reinitiated many European Reiki Masters, as well as first-degree and second-degree Russians, before her death. What Galina and others found out rather quickly was that there is no core body of information concerning original Reiki symbols, even within the same Reiki organizations. The symbols' definitions, function, strength, and how symbols work was entirely dependent upon the Reiki Master who taught the second and even third-level Reiki.

Ascended Masters do not think in terms of what is. What I am about to share with you is knowledge that Buddha gave to me, and what my students and I have learned from working with symbols. Information about how to use Reiki symbols is applicable to other symbols, so, I have included examples of these as well. There are healing systems such as Angeliclight and the Order of Melchizedek for which there are NO symbols! Like aromatherapy, Angeliclight works with vibrations in an altogether different manner than Reiki, Sakara or Sophi-El do.

119

Further **empowering symbols** is possible. First, rather than using just the index finger to draw, cone the fingers. Thus, using all of the fingertip chakras, and the palm chakra as well. Second, try drawing with both hands; either draw the same symbol simultaneously with each hand, or put the fingertips of both hands next to one another and draw one symbol. Third, while drawing a symbol, name it three times, the number of creation. Fourth, Eileen Gurhy found that punching (poking the symbol after it has been drawn with coned fingers) further empowers it.

The two spiral symbols are both called **Cho Ku Ray**. Draw the clockwise Cho Ku Ray with the left hand, and simultaneously draw the counterclockwise Cho Ku Ray with the right hand. Clockwise connects to the heavens, or what the Native Americans call the projective masculine energy. Counterclockwise connects to the earth, or the receptive feminine energy. Together, balanced Cho Ku Rays work to energize all other symbols. They may be drawn in front of a symbol, after a symbol, or a symbol may be sandwiched in between two sets of Cho Ku Rays. My Reiki Master, Margarette Shelton, gave me the knowledge of both Cho Ku Rays. In looking through the many books on Reiki, Tera Mai is the only Reiki system that includes Margarette Shelton in its lineage (see page 134).

Say Hay Key is a traditional Reiki II symbol and is good for mental healing. It looks like a horse's head. From the top, draw the face. Then draw the back of the neck and then the mane. Clearing and changing thoughts, perceptions, or change the way we think, alters our whole lives. Quieting the mind creates peace of mind, and the ability to live in the present moment. Being here and present opens the heart to joy, and through the heart we enter The Unmanifested Potential and beyond this to The Creator. (Eckhart Tolle The Power of Now.)

Zonar was the first symbol Buddha gave to me. Draw the "Z" first, come up and draw infinity three complete times. Zonar works well with past life and karmic issues. Valerie Weaver was given that infinity is a Reiki symbol that works on emotional issues. Cells can carry the memory of trauma, both the shock of our own individual experiences and those of the mass consciousness. This holds true for all holocausts, as well as all individual crimes. What we do to another, we do to ourselves. The nature of a holographic universe is that each part contains within it the consciousness of the whole. Scientists have discovered an energy that permeates this universe. Could this be The Creator? Interestingly, Zonar is also the symbol used by a secret metaphysical society called the "Z's" at the University of Virginia. Benjamin Franklin, who wrote Poor Richard's Almanac (which is based on astrology) and Thomas Jefferson were both deeply interested and involved in metaphysics. Thomas Jefferson designed the architecture for the University of Virginia.

Cho Ku Ray   **Say Hay Key**   **Zonar**

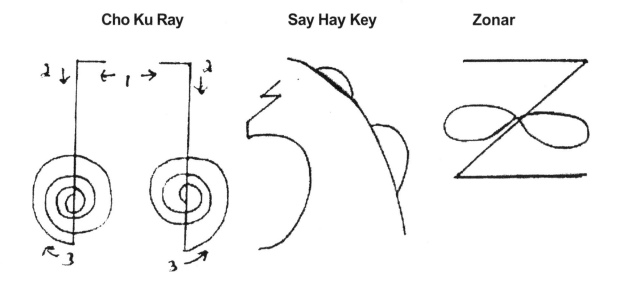

Harth is the second symbol Buddha gave to me. For many people, this is their favorite symbol. It heals emotional issues, childhood issues and the heart. Before sending Harth as an absentee symbol, energize Cho Ku Rays and Harth. See yourself in your mind's eye, by meditating deeper and deeper behind your physical eyes. When you see yourself, ask the Angels to take you to the Harth you just energized. You may see a three-dimensional pyramid constructed to scale rotating in front of you. Try going into the symbol, or see Harth going into you heart or inner child. *(Going into a symbol may be done in meditation with other symbols as well.)*

One of my New Jersey students, Aaron Sapiro, met a Japanese American who as a young boy left Japan with his family just prior to World War II. He said his family had worked with some of the men Mikao Usui had trained as teachers. They were given a symbol with a pyramid in the middle of it. It is a real shame that there are no Japanese adults alive who worked with Makio Usui.

Mara is an elemental earth symbol, which connects and grounds. Draw each 'check mark' towards the center, and the spirals from top to bottom. Kellie Ray Marine was given Rama during one of my classes. Buddha changed the name to Mara because the intonation, Mara, connects more powerfully to the Earth, and that this symbol should be used to initiate the feet in the second degrees of Tera Mai Reiki and Tera Mai Seichem. The initiation opens the chakras in the soles of the feet, which further opens the initiate to the electromagnetic, cobalt blue healing energy of Mother Earth. Cobalt blue and the golden energy of TM Reiki combine to form a third green healing ray.

The 5 spirals represent the 4 directions and 4 elements. The spiral in the center represents oneself, specifically the heart. The heart is like the center of the medicine wheel, the center of the circle. The 2 "V's" are drawn towards the center, representing the masculine and feminine aspects of

121

God and Goddess. Mara helps people, who have no earth in their astrology charts, ground.   As it is of the Earth, it is also a symbol for prosperity and healing of the physical body.

Shanti (Peace) is a symbol channeled by Pat Courtney of Milwaukee, Wisconsin after taking my Reiki Mastership class.   Shanti heals the past, which heals the present and the future, free of worries and expectations.   Shanti thus helps to manifest the best possible.   It may also be used to heal the physical body.   To heal and open closed chakras, Maria Rawlins of Ireland energizes and puts Johre into closed chakras.   The next time, Maria uses Shanti in the same manner.

Mara   **Harth**   **Shanti**

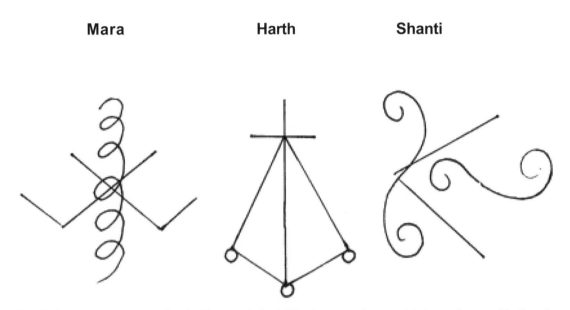

Symbols were so secret that in the past that Tibetan monks would draw them with the tips of their tongues on the roofs of their mouths when doing healings in public.   Teachers might draw symbols for students, but all paper was burned after each and every lesson.   Some of Takata's Alliance Reiki Masters never drew the symbols on paper or chalkboard.   As we go into the Golden Age, everything including sacred texts and sacred symbols are coming into the Light to be examined and evaluated.   I have energized all of the symbols drawn in this book.   If you would like to feel their energy and use them in your own self-healing, simply place your palms on the symbols.   To further activate the energy, get into a meditative state and direct healing to wherever it is that you need it. The symbols will keep working no matter how many times you use them.   Remember to thank all of the higher beings who work with you and the symbols you use.

Each initiation into an elemental healing ray opens the initiate further into the energy.   Each elemental ray of healing has as a **Dai Koo Mio**, which is given in the last initiation.   This symbol, when used in correct combination with other specific symbols, is used by the master or teacher to open the initiate to the full expanse of the energy.   An individual who has been initiated, who knows the initiation procedures, and is able to bring down, hold and transfer the full expanse of the ray makes the energy transfer on the breath. As the initiation comes into the teacher before the transfer is made, people who change initiations for their students are stymied as well. It is important to remember that a teacher is unable to initiate anyone into something that s/he does not have!

Takata gave out only two Dai Koo Mios. The hard-edged Dai Koo Mio, not the gesture drawing (which has the same number of strokes), "holds the key" to full empowerment into the earth elemental healing ray. From reinitiating Reiki Masters from other associations, we consistently found that while Hon Sha Za Sho Nen was a theme in variation, those Reiki Masters who had the hard-edged Dai Koo Mio all had the same identical symbol, stroke for stroke. Susan Peterson Siegler worked with a Tibetan monk in the early 1970's before he returned to Tibet and was subsequently murdered by Chinese Communists. He told Susan that the hard-edged version was the stronger of the two. In one-way or another, I receive confirmation on all of the information Buddha and the Higher Beings gave to me. As a further affirmation, Susan's monk showed up for her initiation.

All of the Reiki Masters knew that they could not do the same healings that Takata could do. They all knew that something had been left out. Some altered the Dai Koo Mio in an attempt to raise the energy. One Reiki Master gave out a different Dai Koo Mio every time he taught. Another Reiki Master gave out a symbol that he found on a stone in New Grange, Ireland as Dai Koo Mio. There are many symbols at New Grange, and as this particular Reiki Master told people for years that he was not psychic, what was he doing? Another Reiki Master used a symbol retrieved from a Japanese restaurant. Yet another Reiki Master translated Dai Koo Mio into Japanese characters, not realizing that the symbol, like the energy, comes from God, not Japan, Tibet or Jupiter! For whatever the reason, everything has served a purpose. However, when people change Universal initiations they inexorably change the energy. Many manmade initiations are becoming increasingly toxic.

What are manmade initiations? Almost 2,000 years ago, popes and cardinals began changing Church initiations; some dating back to the Old Testament, others were initiations Jesus gave to his disciples. They did this so that they would have more power than the clergy. Thus, anyone who has had a former lifetime as a nun or priest received a manmade initiation. Anyone who belonged to a black magic group received a manmade initiation that was channeled to a human by a demon. These initiations are also manmade initiations, whereby the individual gives away his/her power to a demon. The initiation called The Death of Compassion given at Owl Lake is one example. Manmade initiations do not go away, they are carried from lifetime to lifetime until they are removed. Because manmade initiations go back to an individual who made them up and not to God, that individual literally drains those who have been initiated. (How to remove them – page 158.)

Richard Bennett and Joel Pfeiffer were given the same message simultaneously during their Reiki Mastership initiation. That is, the **Dai Koo Mio** is only to be used for initiation, not healing. It does and will work in healing; however, the healer then assumes responsibility for the healee's healing. We have enough just being responsible for ourselves. Many psychics around the world have confirmed this information as being the Truth.

Hon Sha Za Sho Nen, along with Say Hay Key and the counterclockwise Cho Ku Ray that gets smaller, were the three symbols taught in most second-degree Reiki classes. Hon Sha Za Sho Nen is considered the absentee-healing symbol. However, while Takata gave out two versions of Dai Koo Mio, the master symbol, she gave out approximately 15 different versions of Hon Sha Za Sho Nen. Within each one of the versions there are variances. Buddha told me that Takata had made up the symbol and that it was a combination of Buddhism and Hawaiian Shamanism.

When a Buddhist monk took my class, he told me that there was a Buddhist chant, "Hon Sha Za Sha Nen", to help release Karma. Interesting! It may be that because the symbol Hon Sha Za Sho Nen has been intoned thousands of times by Reiki initiates that it has become a healing symbol in its own right. The particular version of Hon Sha Za Sho Nen on the following page encircles the individual or the issue and brings up the root cause by squeezing it out. It is also possible to chant "Hon Sha Za Sha Nen" and send the vibration absentee. This chant may also be used in hands-on healing; however, it is always desirable to ask the healee's permission beforehand.

Johre means White Light. It is drawn from the top down, and comes from Iris Ishikuro, who was one of the 21 or 22 original Alliance Reiki Masters whom Takata initiated. (Alliance Reiki was the only Reiki system taught by Takata.) Before her death, Iris made Reiki Mastership available and affordable. This Johre is not the Japanese calligraphy Johre. The calligraphy Johre was brought in 100 years ago, which was about the same time that Mahikari and Reiki also appeared in Japan. Sometimes, a particular place pulls in a specific energy in a given period of time. An example of this is rock music from England in the 1960's. Johre works well to release blockages. When it is combined with Christ Light and Maria, an etheric vacuum is created that pulls negativity out.

Fire Dragon is a Yoga symbol. It is indirectly a symbol for the kundalini in that the seven swirls represent the seven chakras. It is always drawn from the top down. Works well with spinal injuries. Moves energy in the spine and through the chakras by addressing issues and removing blockages associated with each chakra. For example, in the second chakra, Fire Dragon can aid women and men who have gone through, or who are going through menopause. It is not advisable to draw Fire Dragon from bottom to top, as this could open the kundalini before it is ready to rise.

124

Hon Sha Za Sho Nen	Johre	Fire Dragon

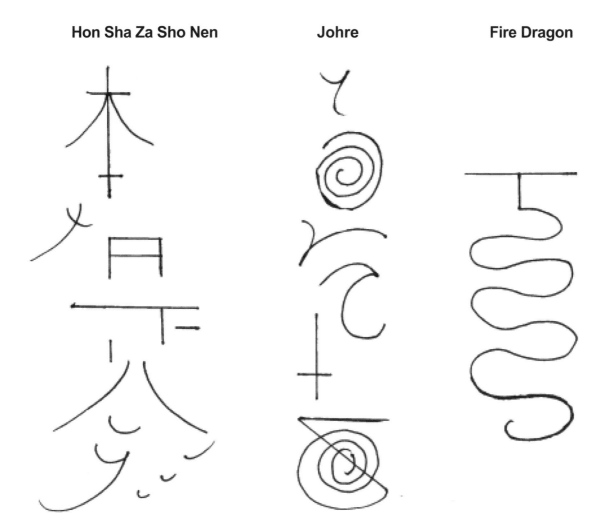

Halu is the third Reiki symbol that Buddha gave to me, which has typically been given out in TM Reiki III classes. It is included herein because it was never intended that any of Buddha's symbols be sold for large sums of money. Halu is Zonar intensified. The tall pyramid is for mental healing. The so-called tall, pointed dunce caps that they used to put on mentally slow children actually worked. However, by referring to both the hats and the children as dunces, much beneficial energy was negated. This symbol may be sent to meditation rooms before meditating. Halu may be used within other healing combinations. Begin drawing Zonar, saying Zonar 3 times while drawing the infinity symbol 3 times. Lifting the finger, close the "Z" from top to middle and then from bottom to middle. Beginning in the upper left hand corner of the "Z", raw the tall pyramid and say Halu 3 times. Draw the counterclockwise circle at the top, which represents the capstone of the pyramid.

Kadoish and **Samaran** are water crystals. Kadoish heals feminine issues and helps to open nurturing, compassion and creativity. Samaran heals masculine issues and helps to open up the teacher, consoler and the warrior who protects within us. While the spark of creation is found within the Masculine Aspect of God, the power to regenerate is found within the Feminine Aspect of God. The Goddess is here. We are moving into balance, so these symbols might be used for regeneration. They bring up emotional barriers, which prevent physical bodies from regenerating. Together, they help to open and integrate the personality, and heal deep-seated emotional issues from childhood or past lives. You may visualize them before going to sleep and/or repeat a mantra of "Kadoish, Kadoish, Kadoish! Samaran, Samaran, Samaran!" <u>While Cho Ku Rays are energizers of other symbols, if you use them to energize these or other symbols before you go to sleep, the energy may keep you awake.</u>

Halu   **Motor-Zanon**   **Kadoish** & **Samaran**

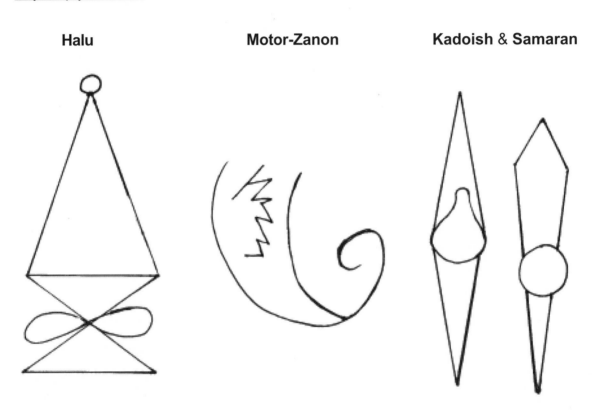

Motor-Zanon is a minor Sanskrit symbol that at least one Tibetan monk uses for exorcisms. Motor-Zanon has two names and works to release viruses in this manner: Energize the symbol with Cho Ku Rays and intone "Motor" three times. Motor goes into the body, and the little squiggle in the middle rotates on the horizontal line, catching the virus. To change the symbol's polarity, draw and energize the same symbol, and call it "Zanon" three times. The symbol reverses polarity, leaves the body and takes the virus with it. This symbol, as well as <u>The Master Cleanser</u> by Stanley *Burroughs (fresh- squeezed lemons, Cayenne Pepper & grade B, pure maple sugar),* works on the AIDS virus. However, core issues behind any disease or pain must be addressed first before real healing takes place. The root problem with AIDS is often extremely low self-esteem and self-hatred. There are other individuals who love their pain or the attention it brings. For them the question is, "Why are you doing this to yourself?" Finding aspects within, which may be built upon establishes a true sense of self-worth. Breathe destructive thought patterns away and down to Earth's central fire. Some people need the help of a healer or somebody who has successfully accomplished stepping away from disparaging thoughts. Worries or fears, wishing to redo the past, or living in the past block healing.

Universal Wisdom & Light   **Midas Star**   **Trinity**

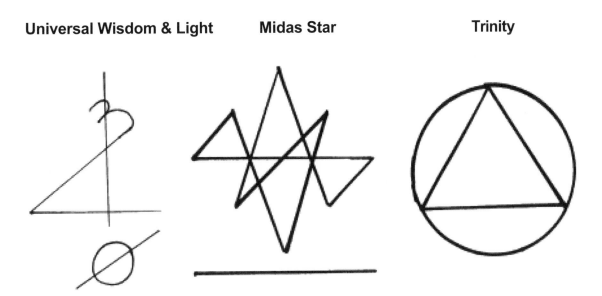

Katherine Szedenik, another of my students, was given **Universal Wisdom & Light**. Katherine draws it on the crown and third eye to open these chakras. It may be toned "OMRA".

    Midas Star is a symbol for affluence, not just money. There is a Cree Indian saying, "Only after the last tree has been cut down. Only after the last river has been poisoned. Only after the last fish has been caught. Only then will you find that money cannot be eaten." Money is supposed to be an expression of our power and a vehicle for us to be able to do the things we need and want to do. Using numbers from the Bible and the Holy Kabbalah, Bert Goldman, a Silva instructor, connected them and found Midas Star within the points. Drawing a red line over the bottom horizontal line under the star increases and grounds the energy. I invite you to try it.

    There are two ways in which to draw **Trinity**. To release blockages, cone the fingers of your left hand and draw the triangle three times counterclockwise beginning in the lower left-hand corner. You might redraw the triangle two more times. Then circle counterclockwise three times, or the circling motion may be continued as the blockage is drawn out of the body and up to the Light for transformation. To put energy in, cone the fingers of your right hand and draw the circle clockwise three times. Then draw the triangle clockwise three times, starting at the top of the triangle. Then lay your hands over the affected area or touch point. Susan Peterson Siegler, under guidance, has added a five-pointed blue star in the center of this triangle which she meditates on. Her guides call it the stillpoint, which is a point of inner balance. If you are sending this or another symbol to someone, you may energize it with Cho Ku Rays and then watch the symbol to see what happens. Watching the symbol to see what happens keeps the healer's personality out of the healing process.

The swirl in **Mary** or **Maria** is an energizer; the open "M" represents feminine power, present in all women. Men may also benefit from this symbol, as it opens their nurturing, creative, healing nature. To use it, pray to the Mother aspect of God for aid in whatever our need is. This symbol, like all others, may be energized with Cho Ku Rays. Call upon **Mary**'s name three times while drawing the "M." Then send her the symbols, asking her to further empower them and to send energy back for healing. Other masters, saints and Angels will help with self-healing, planetary healing or in the healing of others in the same manner. It is also possible to draw this symbol or other healing symbols in the sand or earth with coned fingers.

Christ Light may draw cancer of the spirit into the point where all of the lines converge, where energy is transformed. Draw the long line first, and then the two V's. For personal use, focus above the crown. Visualize the symbol, Christ Light and love coming into the crown. The high vibration is subtle but powerful. See it lighting all of the dark corners and secret closets where hidden skeletons lie. This symbol can be energized with Cho Ku Rays and sent to the Crystalline White Light. Then pray to God for help. The energy may return immediately, or be experienced later. Like most symbols, Mary and Christ Light are not initiation symbols.

Valerie Weaver, M.D. was given **Gratitude**, a symbol for thanks. It may also be used to end a ceremony. We begin disconnecting from Source when we take, but forget to give thanks. For example, many of the vortexes in Sedona were losing their energy because people come, take and do not give back. Some readers of my books have gone to Sedona to clear and send energy back to the earth through these vortexes. The strongest force is love, but close on its heels is gratitude. Giving thanks completes the cycle so that more may be given to us. Forgetting to give thanks stops the cycle. **Gratitude** is the symbolic representation of the universal gesture of thanks with the arms crossed over the chest. Circles represent the elbows and closed fists.

Justice and Compassion is a symbol that came to me at Ground Zero in New York City, where over a thousand souls were waiting to go to the Light. For some it had been difficult to go on because they died in great fear and pain. Others were held back by black magic that was used to create 9/11, or because black magicians had used the energy after the tragedy to perform other black magic. Sometimes, people make it very difficult for me to stay out of judgment. The best I am able to do is to look at their actions as being despicable, rather than judging them as loathsome. It may seem to be a subtle difference, but for the people I have suggested this to, it has made a big difference in their lives. They say that they attract less darkness or negativity into their lives. At Ground Zero, Angels asked me to do a clearing first – especially in clearing black magic staying out of judgment is mandatory! Some souls did not go to the Light; they wanted justice. Those responsible for the tragedy had left the door open for their deeds to come back to them. As justice should be tempered with compassion, Angels gave me this symbol for the souls to take with them. When they were ready, I told them that I would be available to help them go to the Light.

Maria   **Christ Light**   **Gratitude**   **Justice & Compassion**

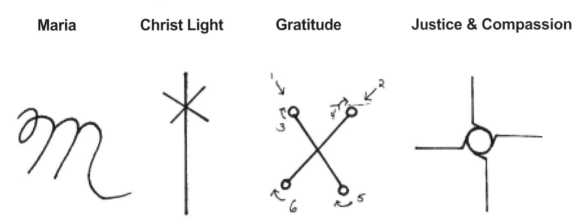

Hosanna is used for clearing. Eileen Gurhy channeled it shortly before I came to New York City in 1992. It is drawn in two continuous lines. Begin in the upper right hand corner and draw down, across, up and spiral. Say, "Hosanna, Hosanna, Hosanna." The second line begins in the lower left-hand corner. Draw up, across, down and spiral. Say, "Hosanna, Hosanna, Hosanna." Then punch the triangles in the middle. The first Hosanna radiates clearing energy outwards. The second Hosanna focuses on specific issues. In the blank lines on the Hosanna Clearing place the names of 2 people who are bound 'unhealthily' to one another. For example, "between Mary and John, and John and Mary". This may also be used for planetary healing.

Hosanna Clearing: Draw the symbols for the clearing by sandwiching Cho Ku Rays between the two Hosannas. Give the symbols to the Angels and ask them to fill the Hosannas with Violet Flames of Transformation, energies of exorcism and release, cleansing, purification and healing. Ask the Angels to multiply and intensify the energy times infinity to the 21st power. Then chant, "Saint Michael the Archangel. Saint Michael the Archangel. Saint Michael the Archangel, with your legions of Angels and power animals, by your flaming swords, jaws, talons, claws cut and release any ties, any cords not of God's Desire between _____ and _____. Cut free, cut free by your flaming sword. Release, release by your flaming sword. Cut free, cut free by your flaming sword. Release, release by your flaming sword. Cut free, cut free by your flaming sword. Release, release by your red flaming sword." Visualize the symbols and simply watch.

Draw and energize Hosannas as described previously and chant, "Angels of the Violet Fire, Angels of the Violet Fire, Angels of the Violet Fire, take any debris that Michael and his legions are cutting free by their flaming swords, jaws, talons and claws between _____ and _____. And release, release to the Violet Fire. Consume, consume by Violet Fire. Transform, transform by Violet Fire any ties. Transmute, transmute by Violet Fire." Visualize symbols and simply watch to see what happens!

Repeat the process and chant, "Saint Germain, Saint Germain, Saint Germain, master of transformation I invoke your name. Quan Yen, Quan Yen, Quan Yen, keeper of the Violet Flame, I invoke your name. Take any psychic debris that the Angels of the Violet Fire are bringing to thee that Michael and his legions are cutting free by their flaming swords, jaws, talons and claws between _____ and _____. Release, release to the Light for sanctification, purification, healing and release." Repeat and visualize!

Immediately fill the void: "I call forth the great celestial Angels and Archangels to fill any voids with colors, tones, symbols, flower remedies, and herbs that are needed for perfect and divine healing. (If specific colors, crystals, etc. are seen, name them.) Father-Mother God, please give a very special blessing to those beings who have helped with this clearing and healing, and let their blessing be now, dear Father-Mother God, please let it be now."

Michael's sword may be blue, or red, the color of Christ Consciousness, or another color. Knowledge cuts through shackles of ignorance that keeps us unconscious. Some healers use Aura-Soma Essences of the Masters in the aura of the healee. They may also place it on their own hands and wrists before beginning a session. In this system, Christ Consciousness is red. Katherine Ettmayer and I were given the following colors for commonly known Archangels: Michael comes in on a crimson red ray. Uriel (feminine presence) is a soft yellow. Gabriel's color is a soft pink (again a feminine presence). Raphael brings various shades of healing green. This is not to say that each Archangel works with only one color, or always comes in on the same color. Angels and Archangels, like humans, are multidimensional.

When I was in Normandy, France in 2007, we were guided to clear the megaliths with Hosannas and then energize them with Christ Light, Cho Ku Rays and Maria. Afterwards, we asked the Celestial Angels to reprogram them so that the megaliths would take the darkness off this planet to the Light for transmutation, clearing, healing and balancing. We asked God/Goddess to transform evil into good, great evil into great good, and the Dark Age into the Golden Age of the Return of the Angels. The Celestial Angels also reprogrammed the megaliths to bring Light into Mother Earth.

Other healers around the world have used this process on other megaliths, stone circles, and even whole mountains. Since the Catholic Church built many churches over energy vortexes, where Wise Women and other Shaman practiced healing and other metaphysical work, healers have also used this process on church towers.

Hosanna　　　**Hosanna**　　　**Planetary Healing**　　　**Iava**

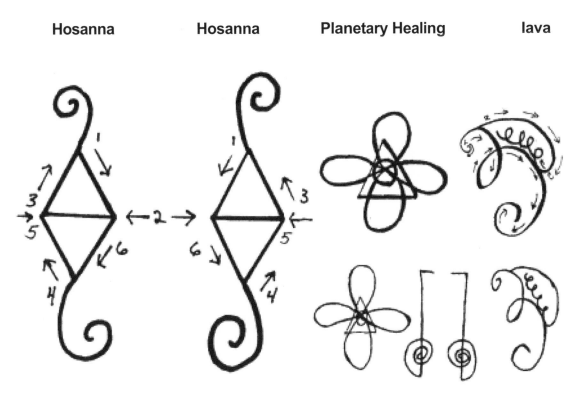

Iava (pronounced EE-AH-VAH) was given to Catherine Mills Bellamont of Ireland shortly after taking my Reiki Mastership class. Catherine was told that Iava was only to be used for planetary healing only. The first line represents the cosmic wave. The four loops of the second line represent the elements and are to be intoned, "earth, water, wind, fire" while they are being drawn. **Planetary Healing and Enlightenment** was given to Marla Abraham of Long Island while she was taking my Reiki Mastership class. It is easy to see how this symbol might have evolved into the symbol for the Violet Flame. Thus, this symbol might well be healing for the Earth though transformation.

In **hands-on healing** draw symbols on healees only <u>after</u> asking for their permission. One reason is that many black magicians place symbols (typically incorporating a square) onto people without asking. After drawing symbols, simply watch to see what happens. In **absentee healing it is not necessary to ask people if you may send them healing.** Why? Because in absentee healing individuals have the free-will choice of accepting or rejecting the healing. However, if the individual rejects the healing do NOT send it again unless they either ask for absentee healing or there has been an extremely noticeable character change. (However, it is always possible to pray for

131

someone.) When symbols are just drawn directly on the body or in the aura, the healee has lost his/her option of saying, no. Some healers arrange a time in advance with a client, where the client meditates and the healer visualizes and sends symbols. Some people make a list of individuals who ask for healing and send symbols to the list. Healing symbols may be drawn on the local telephone book, asking that healing be sent to those who are open. Many possibilities exist! It is possible to do some initiations over the telephone, because the telephone establishes a direct connection between the initiator and initiated. Cell phones are OK to use. The Internet is a portal through which anything is able to come through, and is NOT suitable. **Without a physical connection, an absentee initiation is only an absentee healing at best.**

In **sending healing symbols,** several things are happening. By concentrating on the symbol, the healer holds the consciousness of that symbol. Since the healer and healee are both a part of the Oneness of All There Is, in a very real sense, the healee and the healing symbols are present with the healer ethereally. Albert Einstein proved that time and space does not exist the way we understand them on this three-dimensional plane.

Books on spirituality often mention the fact that the left side of the body is the receiving side; the right side is the sending side. In Reiki both hands may be used to either send healing energy or pull off misqualified energy. Typically, the left hand is more effective in drawing or receiving; the right hand is more powerful in sending. Healing may be sent over the telephone wire, with or without the symbols. The healer holds onto the telephone with his/her right hand; the healee holds onto the telephone with his/her left hand. After my daughter, Jennifer, had ear surgery, she could feel the pounding in her ear leaving her ear and going into her cell phone. In any healing situation, using psychic abilities, working with Holy Spirit, and communicating with the healee are all important.

In sending healing symbols, close the eyes either while drawing or right after drawing the symbols. Watch the symbols and see what occurs. This helps with psychic development. Symbols may also be drawn in the palms of either the healer's of healee's hands *(with their permission)*. In absentee healing, healers may turn the palms of the hands so that they are facing one another and visualize the individual between the hands. If it is known where the pain or symptoms are, the healer may place his/her hands on his/her body either on the appropriate touch point(s), or on the involved area. It is not as important to visual the healee as it is to focus upwards and watch the visuals and other information that come. Many Reiki classes teach the student to visualize the thigh of their leg as being the individual lying down, with one leg being the front, the other the back. Many methods work. The same healing techniques used in hands-on healing may be used in distant healing. For example, pull or lift off misqualified energy, drain the area and then fill the voids by asking the Angels what is required. Sometimes, the symbols change. Sometimes, the individual is seen as they are in life; other times, the astral body or a past life is seen. Yet, other times, the individual or problem may be seen as visual metaphors. Healing is interesting!

If I am working with a group of healers, or if I am teaching a second-degree Reiki class, we sit in a circle. We can send energy to world events, situations, places, or even to one another, but I like to begin with people that we know so that information received during the healing might be verified. Each person takes a turn speaking only the first name only of an individual who comes to mind. We then all draw the same healing symbols, saying the name of each symbol 3 times, and then say, "To (first name of individual)." After the healing, each person in the circle shares what s/he saw, heard or felt. The individual who placed the name in the circle goes last and may provide confirmation or clarification. It's a good way to teach individuals how to do psychic readings. Sometimes, everyone in the circle is working on a different issue on the same individual; sometimes, several healers are working on the same issue, but receive different visual metaphors.

In these group situations, sometimes, Angels will give me similar metaphors every time energy is sent. Once, I saw everyone as a dog. The type of dog related to their personality; and the injury or disease I saw in the dog's body paralleled the body part that the healee had issues with. Even the ages correlated; I saw young children as puppies and elderly people as dogs with traces of gray hair. One time in New York, my angelic theme for the evening was flowers. We were sending healing to one of Sean Grealy's friends in Ireland when I saw a carpet of flowers. Frustrated, I asked, "Now what does this mean?" Immediately, the blanket of flowers fell to the ground, revealing a coffin. The woman next to me saw his upcoming death, but with a different visual metaphor - an empty hospital bed. The sheets were fresh and there was a clean nightshirt lying on top of the bed. The lights were turned down. Sean's friend died two weeks later. Perhaps the healing energy helped him in his transition? Sometimes, the body is too far-gone or it is that individual's time to transcend.

Robert Wachsberger of California put a glass of water in the center of the circle. We all sent energy to the water while the healer who put the name into the circle concentrated on the individual. Afterwards, that same healer drank the water. If the individual was open, s/he received the healing.

Crystals come from the earth and are connected to electromagnetic energy. They may be programmed with healing symbols and healing. You may lock in the program and give the instructions that you are the only one who can change or alter the programming. Crystals or programmed crystals may be used for hands-on or distant healing work. Crystals should be cleared in coldwater, cold salt water, salt or in the sunshine after using them. If crystals are not cleared or if someone has tried to misuse them, crystals can become cloudy and eventually lose all of their vital force energy. Crystals also have the ability to shut down if they fall into the wrong hands.

Cho Ku Ray

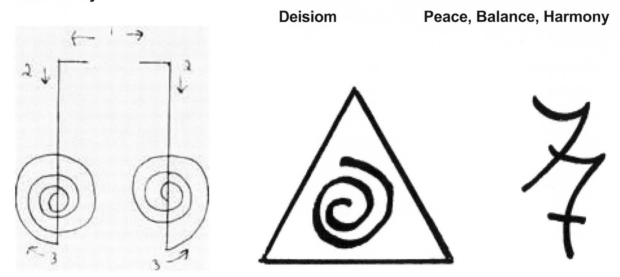

Deisiom   Peace, Balance, Harmony

Peace, Balance, Harmony was given to Beth Dennehy of Ireland. Visualize it during discomforting situations to clear. It may also be sent to situations or people to bring about harmony.

The Golden Buddha in April 2008 gave **Deisiom** and four other golden symbols to Franky the day after I facilitated a group healing session at Zewenkerken in Bruges, Belgium. Deisiom works to heal the physical body; gold is a color of protection. More information on Deisiom and four other golden symbols may be found by clicking on TERA MAI SYMBOLS on www.kathleenmilner.com.

The **Cho Ku Ray**s that are on this page get smaller; they focus in on the issue. The Cho Ku Rays that get bigger see the whole picture. They may be used separately. If they are used together, the Cho Ku Rays that get smaller go before the Cho Ku Rays that get bigger.

A healing circle may be created when healers draw symbols and then send the symbols to the Angels. The Angels are then asked to multiply the symbols and the energies they represent and return them to the circle. Everyone feels and/or visualizes the energy coming back in through the crown, out the right hand to the individual on the right. The energy goes around the circle and comes back into the left hand. Process may be repeated. Sending energy out the left hand and back into the right creates a double circle. When ready, the group works together to send healing to people in the group, others or the Earth. Any of the healing techniques discussed herein may be used. The Celestial Angels may be called upon to create a vortex of Light, with which to send lost souls to the Light (page 97).   The power of the group intensifies all of the healings.

After the **Rune Masters** drew their symbols, they extended their left arm straight upwards; wrist and elbow unbent. The right arm held straight down at the side, but with the right palm parallel to the earth. This drew creation into the left arm and hand, and grounded it or gave it earth form through the right. This is the way the magician stands in the Tarot, and also the way Hitler stood. All of the Nazis misused metaphysics, including Rune symbols. Even their philosophy was a hoax. After Hitler became Chancellor, he sent the S.S. into Austria to murder his own relatives and others who knew that he was 1/4 Jewish. I was told this by people in Austria when I visited there. These symbols have been cleared and are safe to use now. However, because of hundreds of years of abuse, the energy that was once in the symbols has been greatly depleted.

Universal energy may be used with or without drawing symbols, which is one reason why people who study Tai Chi and other martial arts take Reiki. The following **healing technique** may be done with or without drawing healing symbols: Stretch the left arm upwards, and with wrist and elbow unbent, pull in life force energy into the left hand. At the same time, hold a washcloth in the right hand. The cloth may be dry or rinsed in hot or coldwater beforehand. If there are large areas of discomfort or for areas difficult to reach, a scarf may be used. Afterwards, place the cloth on the pain. This process may also be used with herbs, or to charge amulets or crystals with Universal energy.

Archetypal universal **symbols from Egypt** may be used for healing. Cartouche is the name of the oval within which the hieroglyphs are drawn. The Way of Cartouche by Murry Hope does an excellent job of explaining 25 fundamental symbols. Most people are very familiar with some of these symbols. The Caduceus, the winged staff with two intertwining snakes, is the symbol adopted by the American Medical Association. In Egyptian lore, the Caduceus is the symbol of Thoth, patron of healers. Some early Ascended Masters found their way into mythology by ancient storytellers. Pyramid, a powerful symbol for grounding and healing, is found on the back of the U. S. dollar bill. The Mayan high priests used to sit in lotus position (which is the human body imitating the pyramid) on top of the pyramids. They would then visualize the sun's energy coming into their crowns, going down through the pyramid, and out onto the land for the benefit of all the people. Crook and Flail is the symbol of the Pharaoh's power and authority. Royalty has come to be seen as fearful powers, to which humanity is subservient. Rather, those who would be king, high priestess, etc. serve the people. True authority comes from the people through respect, in part because authority figures are aligned with, not demolishing the forces of nature.

Initiation into Egyptian symbols brings about a state of heightened awareness of universal concepts - to see What Is and past external allusions. **How did these symbols become empowered?** The Book of Genesis contains many variations of Egyptian stories, which are

135

variations of many Sumerian stories. The evidence is more than compelling; it is overwhelming, that the Sumerians passed their stories to the Egyptians, and the Egyptians to the Jews. The Egyptians and Jews each adapted the stories, which taught fundamental principles, to fit their particular culture. The characters and principles of these stories became bigger than life. In Egypt designated values of these stories were represented through symbols. For thousands of years, powerful Egyptian priests and priestesses used many of these symbols in magic and in healing. If perchance, these symbols initially didn't hold consciousness, by intention and repeated use they began to.

Psychics, regardless of whether they read tarot cards, do astrology readings, or other types of readings, who are initiated into the Egyptian symbols, receive more and clearer information. Universal concepts remain the same, regardless if the shape of the symbol is a Rune, Egyptian hieroglyph, or astrological sign. The catch is that because the energies are both high and subtle, the initiate must have a quiet mind and clear conscience to use the energy. I initiated Aaron Sapiro into the Egyptian. Here's what Aaron had to say, *"I woke up at 4:00 am with an absolutely clear understanding of the 24 Runes and of the order in which they usually appear in the arrangement called the Elder Futhark. What this means to me is that I can now read them syntactically, in whatever order they occur. Apparently the Cartouche initiation worked!"* He used the same initiation procedure and initiated his wife, using the symbols from the Runes. It worked, which would strongly suggest that the Runes were based upon these Egyptian symbols, and that Aaron was a Rune Master in another lifetime. *"The next day she could understand the complex relationships among the Tarot cards, as well as the connection between the Tarot and the Kabbalah."*

After Cocorah received the Egyptian initiations she asked Jake, who channels through her, what the effects of the initiation were. Jake answered that he could see more clearly, and that he was able to bring in more in-depth information. **In healing the Egyptian symbols** help by providing information concerning the healee. The awareness of where the healee's pain, source of the issue or blockages are may be felt in the healer's body as a three-dimenssional awareness. It can be an odd sensation to suddenly clearly feel the dimensions of ones own spleen. The healer might also call upon or visualize Egyptian symbols that represent aspects of healing. For example, Bast may be called upon for mental protection, mental healing or the healing of the brain. Bast may also be called upon to protect ones thoughts. Eye of Horus aids in healing the eyes and family issues. Eye of Horus also represents artisty. Isis helps with general healing or healing of feminine issues. Mirror of Hathor is also for feminine issues, and, like other mirrors, it is protective in nature. Ptath is used for masculine issues and thought constructs. Thoth is used for general healing, and may be called upon to release any Karma that has been worked through, or to send the sins of the ancestors back to the original perpetrator (with love). Osiris may be called upon for protection.

136

Using Elemental Forces in Feng Shui

Tao is God in action; Taoism is a way of living life in harmony with God and nature. Native American mystics were aware that everything is part of a Divine Plan. Mayans saw astrology as understanding The Mind of God and God's Plan for Earth. Three different expressions of spiritualism; three different names for God! All three honored nature and the cosmos as a manifestation of God. They all expressed this in ceremony and in acts of conscious living.

Taoist philosophy began in China twenty-five hundred years ago when Lao-Tzu, a gifted philosopher and scholar, wrote Tao Te Ching. Taoism covers all aspects of one's life on earth, with different disciplines found within the philosophy. For example, Qi Gong Masters moved energy through the human body to chase out evil, hot winds (blockages) and bring in healthy Chi (energy). Feng Shui Masters worked with the same elemental Universal energy, but they moved energy within the living environment (homes, businesses or landscape) for the purpose of facilitating change.

Taoism uses five elements rather than four. Because Feng Shui operates on Universal principles, it works. For example, in western astrology, my sun sign is Pisces and my moon and ascendant are both Capricorn; in eastern or Jyotish astrology (which is the original), I am an Aquarian with a Sagittarian moon and ascendant. Because both are based on Universal concepts, I am told basically the same things about myself in either reading. However, it doesn't work to mix apples and oranges. For example, Barbara purchased Horoscopes of the Western Hemisphere by Marc Penfield so that she could compare her birth chart with the birth charts of different states and cities in order to find the ideal place for her to live. After all, we are all supposed to be the star of our own life. Initially, she compared her eastern Jyotish chart to all of the state and city western charts. Things were not making sense. When she discovered her error, she went back and used her western chart. *(If you are contemplating doing this, compare your birth chart to each astrological chart of the city and state you are thinking about moving to as if you had been born in that city.)* The difference may be why someone might be successful in one state, and struggling in another.

Shamanism, magic, astrology and Feng Shui survived the test of time because they work and are practical. The energy that Qi Gong Masters and Feng Shui Masters channeled and the knowledge they possessed brought about profound changes. Good Feng Shui Masters literally tip the scales of fortune. Good Qi Gong masters bring about healing.

Feng Shui is the Chinese art of placement, within which there is an underlying respect for nature. There are different sects of Feng Shui, but two fundamental schools - compass and location.

Both schools work around a schematic frame, or Ba-Gua, which describes the house and eight qualities making up a successful life. The eight categories or corners are: Career, Knowledge & Self-cultivation, Health & Family, Money & Power, Fame & Reputation, Marriage & Partnership, Children & Inspiration, and Travel & Helpful People. Compass school is based on a land topography that is particular to China, and the Ba-Gua rotates every year, so the Feng Shui Master must return each year to re-Feng Shui the home or business. In the location school, which is the original Feng Shui, the front door determines how the Ba-Gua is laid out.

Interior Design With Feng Shui by Sarah Rossbach is based on a sect within the location school. There are easy things that anyone may do to initiate change by implementing cures for what is out of balance. In simple acts, statements are made to God when one is ready for improvements, and God listens. I do have a few suggestions; many people, after reading the book or taking a Feng Shui class, activate their Money Corner and their Marriage and Partnership Corner only. Without Helpful People, nothing is going to happen. It is highly beneficial if all eight areas of one's life are activated and balanced. My primary intent in this particular chapter is not to replicate a perfectly good book, but rather to **address the elemental forces within the location school of Feng Shui**.

First, find the architectural front doorway, even if the front door is not used. However, if the doorway is blocked, energy is blocked. Stand outside of the house, building or office and then apply what I am about to explain to the interior. (See Positive Cycle page 139.) If you live in an apartment, your architectural front doorway is not the entrance to the building, but rather your own front door. The front outside wall is where the front door is located; here is found the element **water** - black represents water. The outside wall to your left represents the element **wood** – green represents wood. The back outside wall represents the element **fire** – red represents fire. The center of the building is represented by the element **earth** – yellow represents earth. Outside wall to your right represents the element **metal** – white represents metal. Beginning with water, follow the arrows on the **Positive Creative Cycle of the 5 Elements**: Water produces wood, wood produces fire, fire produces earth, earth produces metal, and metal produces water. Arrows show the flow of energy.

Look at the **Destructive Cycle**. (page 139) Earth is where water should be - earth destroys (absorbs) water. Fire is where metal should be - fire destroys (melts) metal. Wood is where earth should be - wood destroys (absorbs) earth. Water is where fire should be - water destroys (puts out) fire. Metal is where wood should be – metal destroys (cuts) wood. The solution to the problem is to use the arrows on the Destructive Cycle to find the cure, which is the missing element. The missing element is found between the arrows. Let's say trees (wood) are in an atrium in the middle of the house. Because Earth belongs in the center, look at the Destructive Cycle to find out where earth is on the Destructive Cycle diagram. Between wood and earth is the element fire – fire is the missing element. The cure is to put something red in the middle of the house.

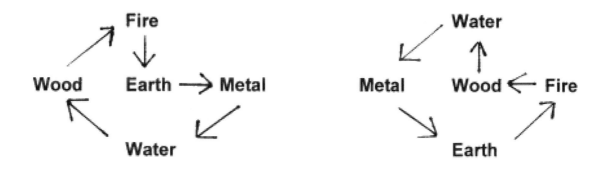

Positive Creative Cycle of 5 Elements   ## Destructive Cycle

Elements on or near the wall or corner may also be either beneficial or harmful. For example, a water fountain in the front of the house brings good fortune; an outdoor pool close to the back wall causes problems. Water along or near the back wall causes setbacks as Fame and Reputation lies along the back wall of the house. Water puts out fire; it also puts out the fires of fame or throws water on your reputation. This particular problem may also adversely affect the eyes. The cure is not to get a plumber and move the fixtures, or fill in the backyard pool with cement, but rather to supply the missing element. Look at the Destructive Cycle and you will find that between water and fire lies wood. Wood is the missing element along the back wall. The cure is to put up something green or wooden over the sink, or whatever fixture is running or holding water. Or paint the wall green. In India the toilet is located on the back wall in the farthest left-had corner from the front door (the Money Corner). A bowl of rice, which may be disguised by placing potpourri over it, should be placed on the back of a toilet, thus, preventing money from going down the toilet.

Metal on or within the wall to the left of the front door may cause feet problems. (metal destroys wood) As this is the Health and Family wall, there could be other health issues or family disruption. The missing element is water, as it lies between metal and wood. The cure is something black, or the element water, such as a fish tank. A photograph or painting of water will also work if the picture conveys strongly the energy of water.

Earth destroys water. If there are potted plants along the front wall, or if the front wall is stone, it can be harmful to both career and to the ears. Between earth and water is metal. Either the missing element, metal, or the color white along the front wall is required for the cure.

139

Fire destroys metal. If the kitchen stove or fireplace is on the wall to your right, this may also adversely affect children or inspiration. Mouth problems are also possible. The missing element is earth, as it lies between fire and metal. Rocks, plants or the color yellow will provide the cure.

In astrology earth and water are considered feminine, while fire and air are masculine. In addition, **each elemental force is related to one of the 5 planets**: Wood with Jupiter. Fire with Mars. Earth with Saturn. Metal with Venus. Water with Mercury. Both mountains and buildings, by their shapes, exhibit characteristics of the elements and their corresponding planets. Whenever you have natural or man-made shapes that are next to one another and exhibit the qualities of two elements that are in a destructive phase, the missing element needs to be added.

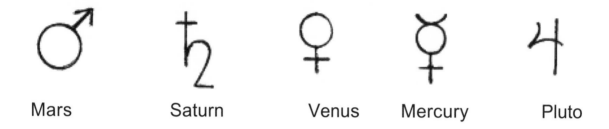

Mars   Saturn   Venus   Mercury   Pluto

Fire and Mars-type structures: Bold mountains with straight peaks running out to a sharp point. Tall, pointed buildings. Best businesses in these buildings are those dealing with energy.

Earth and Saturn-type structures: Mountains with extensive plateaus. Older, heavy buildings, especially those built of stone, marble and other earth materials. Big colonial homes and structures with flat roofs. Most businesses do well in these kinds of buildings.

Metal and Venus-type structures: Mountains with softly rounded peaks. Churches with crosses and softly rounded domes. Also buildings that are rich and ornate. Best businesses in Venus-type buildings are big business and banks.

Water and Mercury-type structures: Mountains with a cupola-shaped top. Buildings with scalloped or projecting roofs. School and libraries, as well as transportation and communication business thrive in Mercury-type buildings.

Wood and Jupiter-type structures: Bold mountains with straight peaks, where the top is broken off (flat and narrow). Jupiter-type buildings are tall and straight with a flat top. Best businesses in these buildings are schools, bookstores and those dealing with philosophy.

If **natural objects or buildings**, which are next to one another, exhibit characteristics that are destructive a cure is required. For example, <u>Metal destroys wood.</u> If two buildings are in close proximity and one is characteristically metal-Venus and the other wood-Jupiter, the missing element is water. A water fountain or the color black between the buildings is required for the cure.

<u>Wood destroys earth</u>. If one building is wood-Jupiter and the other earth-Saturn in construction, the missing element is fire. Torches may not be possible; the color red is probable.

<u>Earth destroys water</u>. If one adjacent building is earth-Saturn and the other is water-Mercury, the missing element is metal. A bronze statue or the color white will provide the cure.

<u>Water destroys fire</u>. One building is a water-Mercury type, the other a fire-Mars type. The missing element is wood and the cure is something green and wooden, such as, planting trees. Very effective and easy to do, and also brings in positively the forces of nature.

<u>Fire destroys metal</u>. A fire-Mars building is next to a metal-Venus building. Missing element is earth. Plant a flower garden behind a rock wall, a large rock display or the color yellow.

Feng Shui deals with energy in other ways. **Outdoors**, any lines (roads or waterways) that run off in straight lines, or that are steep or sharply angled create dangerous energy. It is especially dangerous when long lines point towards a building. When Chi runs too fast, it becomes Sha. Homes at the end of a road frequently change occupants; a large water fountain in the front lawn helps. If the problem is on another side of the house, plant trees. Living over an underground river also creates Sha in the home; large quartz crystals on the floor may help. Gentle, graceful curves, natural settings and elevations are the best locations. Beautifying and bringing nature back into cities results in an advantageous boom to business. Productive cities, like New York and Paris, are often famous for their beautiful parks.

Indoors, long hallways, or a series of 3 or more doors will cause energy to run too fast. Hang multifaceted crystals from the ceiling. After it had been remodeled, a home I rented had two such energy patterns, which ran perpendicular to one another. The home had literally thrown people out of it, including the owners. I signed the lease anyway. As the lengths of the passageways were long, I hung several crystals from the ceiling, and placed a crystal cluster on the fireplace mantel.

In using both natural structures, and in the construction of holy places and shrines, Feng Shui venerates and utilizes the forces of nature. There are two types of ley lines, which the Chinese

141

called the dragon and the tiger. Interestingly enough, in both Celtic and Chinese traditions, the dead were buried in relationship to these energy lines. In both cultures this was considered an important way for the ancestors to benefit the living. In this way, the spirit of the land and the ancestors brought about good Karma and beneficial results. On the other hand, if the energy patterns were negative, or spirits were unfriendly, Feng Shui Masters **used the energy of the elemental forces and physical reconstruction to change the energy**. What we might call underlings, earthbound souls, black souls or demons were also released through clearings and prayers. Native Americans smudged with sage to clear, and brought in new, benevolent energies with cedar. An old Christian exorcism consists of going to every window and door; one person holds a burning white candle, the other person dips his/her hand in the holy water and makes the sign of the cross in front of the door, window or other opening. Both individuals pray the complete *Our Father*.

What is not typically taught in Feng Shui is to **look for thought forms and energy behind objects** within and around the home or office. For example, a mask of Medusa in the Marriage and Partnership Corner may well serve the purpose of keeping likely suitors away, even though it may have all the right colors - pink, red and white. One of my clients in Chicago had a painting of red, black and green in his Money Corner. All of the right colors, however, it was a painting of a hobo. Even though he was a doctor, he was headed for bankruptcy. The picture of the hobo was pitched out immediately after I explained the Feng Shui reasoning behind the picture of a hobo in his Money Corner! On the other hand, lucky objects, which are not normally considered to be Feng Shui activators, may bring in positive energy or complete a missing section of the Ba-Gua. Typical Feng Shui activators consist of objects, such as, mirrors, mobiles, multi-faceted crystals and electricity, or placing something that has the correct color or the element itself along the wall or in the corner. For another object to bring about the cure, the energy within the talisman, painting, picture, crystal cluster, etc. should be positive and strong. Objects may be religious; however, one woman in Phoenix had so overdone her religious displays that she created clutter, which blocked the flow of energy. A woman in Chicago had a missing corner, which meant that there was a missing aspect to her life. However, when I dowsed, it was not missing even though there was no mirror to bring in the energy of the missing corner. Instead, she had a painting of a Native American on the wall that was pulling in the missing aspect. No other cure was required.

A woman in Milwaukee who was having an affair on her husband also had a missing Marriage and Partnership Corner. Feng Shui was evident through the entire house - upstairs and down. However, no mirror was placed to bring in the missing corner, and she did not want one. Interestingly enough, the doctor whom she was having an affair with kept her tangling, and really had no plans of leaving his wife. **In order for Feng Shui to work, people must desire change.**

Correct Use of Ceremonies and Magic

Magic occurs around us. When something major happens we call it a miracle. Doctors refer to healing miracles as spontaneous remissions. Most people are familiar with only black magic, but have little idea about the large number of people who practice black magic. Should you find this incredulous, go to one of the big bookstores and look at the rather large shelf of books on black magic. Though I wouldn't advise picking one up. Black magic is a part of the culture for many people living in India. Voodoo is not the only metaphysical practice that involves both white and black magic. Besides the fact that such individuals belong to neither the Light nor the dark, there are two other problems. For one, there are the Laws of Karma. Two, as the Light separates from the dark, Voodoo practitioners and everyone else who is sitting on the fence are being torn until they make a choice. Interestingly enough black magicians are some of the biggest opponents to white magic. Hitler had perfect past-life recall of being one of the leaders of the Holy Inquisition. In that same lifetime, he was also an adept black magician. Trevors Ravenscroft describes this in detail in The Spear of Destiny.

Magic that is manipulative is black magic. Black represents that which is hidden and unseen; white is that which is known and seen. Black magicians cloak their magic in black because secretiveness makes their spells more effective. The black that they use is not the velvet black of the womb of the Goddess or The Great Mystery; rather black magic is a dull, dense color. Like extreme politics, black magicians hold others suspect, seeking control of even the most trivial of actions. In The Spear of Destiny, which inspired the movie, Indiana Jones, Trevors Ravenscroft documents how Nazis practiced black magic, which involved more than a mere handful of officers in the inner circle.

To learn how to dispel black magic, it helps to understand it. Black magicians work with forces of evil; those who call themselves the Illuminati think they are working with an evil god. The misunderstanding dates back to Constantine (see page 55). Destructive, negative emotions may be built up for a week or even more before a spell is cast. They repeat spells that utilize some of the foulest things you would probably never in your wildest imagination think of. While they stand in the middle of a pentagram for protection, they call up demons and underlings to carry out their Luciferian pacts. The pentagram is upside-down, and the bottom point of the star is elongated.

In magic, the circumference of the circle of the pentagram represents what the Hindus call Brahman, what metaphysics might refer to as Absolute Consciousness. Contained within the circle is a five-pointed star, the star of the ancients. The five points represent the four elements and spirit. It is a tool for manifestation. Pentagrams are a symbol of protection, but symbols have limitations.

Black magicians invoke demons! From the first time demons are summoned, they begin forming attachments to the person who beckoned them. Black magicians are given the illusion that they are powerful and controlling, but it is they who are controlled by the dark. When the black magician dies, the pentagram is gone. The demons, however, are carried from lifetime to lifetime until Karma has been worked out, the heart opens to love and forgiveness, and the demons are exorcised.

How to break black magic spells. First, the exorcist asks the Angels to surround him/her with golden light, and God The Father Almighty's Shield of Protection. Higher beings and powerful energies of the Light are called in as well. Secondly, mirrors or the Egyptian Mirror of Hathor is visualized facing outwards in the exorcist's aura. Third, ask that all black magic be returned to the black magician with love and repeat the Thrice Around the Circle Bound. (page 103 & 104) Fourth, the black magician may have powerful protection surrounding him/her. Ask the Angels to contain the black magician and his/her black magic in golden cubes. Then pray to God, *I accept that it is other people free-will choice to create and send black magic, it is my free-will choice to ask that it be returned immediately or sent to the Earth's central fire for transformation.* Repeat Thrice Around the Circle Bound. Fifth, ask the Angels, *please drive Saint Michael's sword into the Earth and through the evil in such a way that the sword continues going into the Earth until the tip of the sword touches the very center of the core. Draw fire into the sword to balance the core, burn the evil and to create a way for all of the evil to go down to the central fire for transformation. Please fill all voids with pink love. Divine God, Divine Goddess, I place these individuals in Your Hands.* If there is Karma that has not yet been worked out, that will not budge, but it is possible to remove evil.

Dispelling black magic through Shamanic journeywork is also possible. Ask the Angels to place a silver cloak of invisibility over you, and to set up a divergence. Then keep asking the Angels where to go and what to do. For several years, in my mind's eye I would see myself as Snow White and the Angels as the Seven Dwarfs. It was completely unexpected the first time it happened; in fact, it continued to startle me whenever I began such a journey. After the initial impact of seeing myself as Snow White, I simply participated in the imagery by asking the Angels (or in this case the Seven Dwarfs) where to go, how to dispel and what to do next. When something out-of-the-blue occurs, the individual who is in a Shamanic journey knows that it is not his/her imagination. Something is happening on another dimension that is or will impact the physical reality. (Additional information in <u>Becoming a Shaman: It's Never Too Late To Be Who You Might Have Been</u>.)

Clearing a place or building is similar to breaking black magic spells. After protecting him/herself and calling upon Spirit, the exorcist asks the Angels to completely surround the structure and/or grounds with golden light – above, below and all around. This completely contains evil; dark

144

entities are unable to go through golden light. Ask the Angels to begin filling the space with golden light. This causes dark entities to become extremely agitated and willing to leave. Ask the Angels to construct an etheric vacuum tube, which leads from the structure and/or area to the central fire. Ask the Angels to pull out evil and darkness and send it down to the central fire for transformation. Ask the Angels to put all demons in golden cubes. Ask the Angels to pull out any demonic beings and send them to 'behind the doors' or release them to God. Ask the Angels to keep filling in the voids with golden light and violet flames. To keep the vacuum tubes unblocked and flowing, pray to God, *I accept that it is others free-will choice to block these vacuum tubes, it is my free-will choice to ask that they be cleared immediately afterwards.* It is possible to use any of the above techniques, or to use symbols to help the clearing along.

Clearing implants: Lightworkers or would-be lightworkers have been targeted by demonic beings, which have implanted painful devices. If a pain bounces around in the physical body, and there is no medical reason why, try the following if you are channeling Universal energies. Ask the Angels to remove any shadows (page 9). This makes it easier to see the implants with the 3rd eye. The implant may look like a black disk, black box or black circle. It is likely to be encased in a sphere, which has a spin to it. This allows the implant to float, and cause pain wherever it happens to land. Call upon the power animals, crocodile and alligator, to unbind and reverse the spin until it comes to a stop. Ask the Angels to cut open the sphere, pull it apart and send it down to the central fire for transformation. Ask the Angels to cut apart the demonic implant. It won't go down to the central fire; God has determined that these devices are going back to the original perpetrators.

If there is difficulty getting it free, look for etheric chains, bolts, anchors, etc., by which the implants are attached. Ask the Angels to cut them free! To get to the root or core attachment, use the symbol. Release, which may be found on www.kathleenmilner.com under the click on TERA MAI SYMBOLS. (Additional information in Becoming a Shaman: It's Never Too Late To Be Who You Might Have Been.) Send attachments down to the central fire. The exercise, Thrice Around the Circle Bound, also helps (page 103 & 104). Fill in the voids with cobalt and aqua blue, and gold. While the healer is doing all that, healee dredges up, feels and releases any anger, fear, sorrow, worries and other emotional and mental garbage.

Light brings deceptions up to the surface because lies, unlike the Truth, have no weight or substance to them. One has to keep telling more lies to keep the original lie down. The pieces of the tale do not fit together. A fabricated story becomes elaborate; the Truth is always simple. A good example of this is the assassination of John F. Kennedy. It won't go away!

Black magicians have spread other lies. Ram is <u>not</u> the symbol of the devil. The devil has neither regard for, nor wishes to emulate nature. Nature is a manifestation of God, Whom the devil holds in contempt. Kay Gloege's spirit guides told her Ram is "striking force." It is energy that sends the magic off. Black is the color of the Great Void, Great Mystery. Raven is magic; crow is shape shifting. The half-man/half-goat figure is not the devil, but Pan. Pan is neither a drunkard nor a rapist; he is symbolic of our connectedness to nature. Stories are told of Atlantean scientists who abused animals and conducted unnatural experiments, creating half-man and half-beast beings. Through a fatal flaw, they eventually died off. While they lived, they were subjected to humiliation and abuse. Many souls, including reincarnations of the scientists who were responsible, evolved and worked through their Karma in these forms. Chiron, half man/half horse, is the wounded healer.

To dispel black magic you might include the pentagram. Draw the counterclockwise pentagram to clear. Draw the clockwise pentagram in gold to purify and protect.

<u>Dispelling & Releasing</u>   <u>Manifesting & Protective</u>

There always have been nuns, priests and other church officials who compassionately worked for humanity. And not all popes were privy to the original doctrines of Jesus. As a young girl, what I learned from the Church was that a personality of a saint survived death, and it was possible ask him or her for help from beyond the veil. The old Latin Mass involved ceremonial ritual. Each year began another predictable liturgical calendar, honoring specific times and events.

In much the same way, mysticisms honoring The Goddess use simple **ceremonies** and simple things of earth. Eye of Newt and other horrific-sounding ingredients were code names for herbs that wise women used. In this way, witches bravely protected knowledge so that their torturers would not obtain and abuse these herbs in black magic ceremonies. White magic, like Shamanism, utilizes the power of the four directions, four elemental forces, and is particularly effective when done in conjunction with lunar phases, or when there is fog or lightening outside. (It is not recommended or necessary to go outdoors during thunder and lightening.)

Utilizing the power of the moon for expansive magic, such as the accumulation of wealth for an intended purpose, is best begun under the new moon. This allows the power of the growing, waxing moon to help. While the full moon is a time for fulfillment, magic that is decreasing in nature, such as losing a bad habit, disease or extra pounds, is best begun under the full moon. Thus allowing the waning moon to assist us in diminishing unwanted traits or energies. Utilizing seasonal changes and planetary aspects further increases the energy and results of white magic.

Have clear intentions and leave the details to God. Purposes for performing white magic can be for getting new guides, healing, resources, or psychically obtained information or divination. The root word of divination is Divine. Divination is knowledge obtained from Divine Sources. Secondly, create an altar honoring the four directions and four elements. One way to do this is to find a red cloth *(red to ground and aid physical manifestation)*.

Different native tribes, different mystical cults have different placements for the four elemental forces. **To cast a circle**, the following placement of the elements is the same used by the great Iroquois and Sioux Nations. Interestingly enough, the elements in the wisewomen's circle were all shifted 90 degrees, as if to protect esoteric knowledge and keep it away from the Inquisition. Fire belongs in the East. All mysticisms recognize the rising sun in the east as a sign of spiritual illumination. Illumination is a quality of fire.

East wind brings spiritual illumination, healing, transformation, creativity and passion; all being qualities of the element, **fire**. Place a candle in the east. White is the most popular; however, color may be adjusted to need. If you dress a candle with oil (the oil's qualities may add to the magic), begin in the middle and rub the oil up to the wick. Then go back to the middle and apply the oil downwards. Symbols may also be etched into the candle specific to intent. Light the candle by slowly making a full arch with your arm. Name the candle as you light it, a name that is appropriate to the magic being performed. For example, to create abundance, on or within 3 days after the dark moon, anoint a green candle with frankincense, and draw the symbols Cho Ku Rays and Mara on it. Place it in the east. While lighting the candle say something like, *I name you Prosperity and I call upon the Angels and higher spiritual forces to assist me.* If the planet Jupiter is also making nice aspects in the heavens, the magic will increase, as Jupiter is energy of expansion, manifestation and wealth. Blowing out candles will cause you to lose about 40% of the energy. When the ceremony is completely over, either snuff out or allow all candles to burn out in a safe place.

Porcupine (innocence) or coyote (laughter) typically sit in the **South** of the medicine wheel. It is the place of **water** and emotions. Water's qualities are love, compassion, psychic development,

147

healing and specifically emotional healing. Place a glass of spring or ocean water in the south. Then invoke the energies.

Oftentimes, bear (deep hibernation suggests meditative reflection) or horse (power and grounding) resides in the west, which is the place of **Earth**. Attributes of earth are grounding and foundation, prosperity, introspection, prayer, and physical healing. Prosperity is a viable tool, but it is not an end in itself. Generosity and working from the heart allows wealth to flow. Failure to do so blocks the flow. Place a stone, crystal or both in the **west**. Some people place a clay vessel of earth here. Invoke the energies.

Buffalo, specifically white buffalo, (wisdom) is found in the **North**. North wind brings the element of **air** - wisdom and knowledge, communication (telepathic included), gratitude, clarity and peace of mind, and mental healing. Place a knife (preferably one with a white handle) in the north. As feathers cut through air, a feather will work as well. Invoke the energies.

With clear intentions call in Angels, personal power animals, ancestors, etc. Call upon The Goddess – the energy comes up from the earth, and God The Father Almighty – the energy comes from above. From the center, we pull in the energies and qualities of the invisible world. Energies are called in verbally, with a drum, or a combination of both. Michael Drake's audiotape has nice drumming patterns, specifically designed and intended to invoke the 4 elements, which are also in the directions described above. Chanting in a monotone creates a droning tone, like the drum.

Worldwide, the elements remain in the same place; however, the qualities of the winds change. In the Midwest of the United States, the East Wind is dazzling and fresh. South Wind is hot and fiery. West Wind is bountiful and buoyant. North Wind is cold and mighty. In Argentina and Australia, the South Wind is cold and the North Wind warm.

The amount of Universal energy held by the individual who is doing the magic will determine the impact of the magic. As elemental healing energy is utilized in Feng Shui, so too, it is used in magic. The leader, who holds the ceremony, uses Universal elemental energy to create a space for spiritual helpers they call in. Powerful energy brings in powerful Spirits and Angels, who are able to accomplish more. During the ritual positive forces work on everyone present and carry out the magic.

After doing magic, like a psychic reading, it is best to let the energy go and allow it to do its own thing. Talking about it takes away from the energy of manifestation, and magic may take a grosser physical form or not physically happen at all.

148

After ceremony, give thanks and dismiss the elementals and other spirits so that they may go about and do the work asked of them. Ask God/Goddess to bless them. Dr. Valerie Weaver was given the message that when we forget to give thanks and gratitude, we slip away from Source and into the illusion of three-dimensional reality. Egos become inflated and there is no room for God. For example, I was unable to help one woman whose fortunes were failing, even though through Feng Shui I had helped her sell her empty penthouse apartment, which looked over Central Park, years earlier. It had been on the market for years. After Feng Shui magic, it sold in less than two weeks. Afterwards, she did not give me any kind of donation. I just dismissed it, knowing that God would provide for me in other ways. Only recently, out-of-the-blue, Spirit gave me a message. That is, that she knew at the time that she should give me money for what I had done for her, but she chose to ignore her conscience. From that moment, whatever stopped her from honoring my help also stopped her flow of wealth, and there was nothing that either I or anyone else was able to do for her.

There are many books out on ceremonies that may be used. My personal preference is for those that deal with white magic only. For this reason, I use Scott Cunningham's books. The Enchanted Tarot by Amy Zerner and Monte Farber is also a nice place to begin. While there are few guarantees in this world, the magic of the Wheel of Fortune card works. By doing magic, an individual learns which enchantments or spells work best. Incantations that rhyme are particularly effective. Knot magic is so powerful that it was banned in Europe in the Dark Ages, and women were burned at the stake for simply whispering into the wind. Even though white magic oftentimes takes longer, there really is something to this. Magic, which is non-manipulative and does not cause harm, does not create bad Karma.

During magic or shortly afterwards, nature may provide a sign, indicating that something is happening. For example, when I burn pieces of paper and herbs during a ceremony the smoke will reach a certain height, usually about 3 feet off the floor, and then disappear. The smoke is literally carrying petitions and prayers into another dimension. Particularly when I'm in Ireland, a rainbow appears or the clouds open at an auspicious moment during the magic. Magic works!

After Abez was put down, I cut and then wove some of the hair from his tail. I did this. After Dolores did the reading for me on Abez, we went outside so that she could cut my hair. Abez told Dolores, "Now it's your turn, Kathleen."

After awhile, Dolores said, "I don't know where your hair is going? By all rights, the ground around us should be filled with it." Looking around, I saw tiny whirlwinds. We both watched one off to the side of us with bits of my hair shining in the sun. About 3 feet above the sidewalk, like watching an etheric vacuum cleaner, my hair disappeared into another dimension.

Abez told Dolores that he wanted something of me where he was, and that my hair reminded him of the rainbows that he loved so dearly. Just before he died, I had asked Jesus to make Abez a Cahokia Master. Dolores tuned in; yes, Jesus had fulfilled my last request for him, which was also Abez's. Now, Abez was performing magic in front of our eyes.

Besides performing ceremony, wisewomen in Europe did Shamanic journeywork. Like Edgar Cayce, they would search for answers (Divination) and do healing work. While Native American Shamans travel through openings into the earth, the witch would lie on the hearth next to the fire, which kept her warm, and spiritually she would travel up the chimney. If you go into Saint Bridget's Kitchen in Ireland, you will see the stone hearth worn in such a way as to better accommodate the physical form. The torturers-questioners of the Holy Inquisition altered the imagery of the wisewomen's journey and put ugly, evil women on brooms. Many were beautiful young witches, like Joan of Arc. However, wisewomen also revered the spirituality and wisdom, which age brings, and these women were lovingly and respectfully called crones. It is estimated that the Catholic Church burned 9 million people during the burning times. Most were women, but children and Essenes were included. Whole towns were burned. Many historians say that the number 9 million is too low.

In South America, ceremonies began in the south. In North America, they began in the east. When you drum or rattle, it is important to call in the energies that you want to be there. Otherwise, it is like going to the corner bar and saying, "party at my house."

The following is a version of a journey performed at the time of the full moon in South America called the **"Transformational Fire Ceremony."** Each person brings an offering to burn, hoping that the fire will transform or manifest something. If everyone states his/her intent before beginning, a group consciousness is also created. That is, that the intentions of any individual are available for transformation or manifestation by group members. The object that is brought to the fire may represent in some way the goal to be manifested, or the habit or disease that is in need of transformation. The intent could also be written on a piece of paper, or the participant may simply take a log lying next to the fire and throw that in when it is their turn.

Begin by having participants stand in a circle or cast a circle. Then build a safe, friendly fire outside or in the fireplace. Build a friendly fire by adding a few drops of scented oil, or a combination of sage and cedar, or other herbs. Chant, "Wichi - Ti - Ti - Enui - Aurinicka - Aurinicka - Ohhh - Whi."

If you prefer, chant another invocation; or sing old Bible hymns. Sacred Sounds subtitled Transformation through Music & Word by Ted Andrews, and Circle of Song: Songs, Chants and Dances for Ritual and Celebration compiled by Kate Marks are excellent sources. Everyone stares into and meditates on the fire, concentrating on their particular need. The individual leading the meditation guides the others:

"In the south, see the snake. (Pause) What are you releasing? (Pause) See it being released as a snake sheds its skin." Meditate!

"In the west, see the jaguar. (Pause) Look into the mouth and the eyes of the jaguar. (Pause) See jaguar's sharp claws. (Pause) Die to the old aspect of yourself. See it dying." Meditate!

"In the north, see horse or buffalo. (Pause) Climb on the back of the animal. (Pause) He takes you to the crystal cave where a master sits. (Pause) Be with the master. He can answer your questions." Meditate!

"In the east, see the Eagle or Condor. (Pause) What vision is the bird showing you?" Meditate!

While everyone continues to concentrate, one person at a time brings up the object s/he has brought to be burned. S/he cleanses him/herself before the fire, and places the object in the fire while everyone chants, drums or rattles if they wish. The next day, the completely cooled ashes are buried in the earth.

The following is a variation of a North American ceremony, **"Morning Star"** (Our Sun), which is performed as the sun is rising or in the morning. Set up your altar as described above. In addition, place the following candles on your altar: Yellow in the east, green in the south, red in the west, white in the north and a pink candle in the center. Call in spiritual energy, "Oh Great Spirit, Mother Earth, Father Sky, the power of the 4 directions, the power of the 4 elements, all my totem animals, all my ancestors, all my spirit guides and helpers, be here with me now!"

Begin in the east. Light the yellow candle saying, "With the lighting of this yellow candle in the east, I call forth the energies of the great Archangel Uriel, the energies of fire, the energies of clarity and purification. Here I honor the life force that keeps this planet green." Burn sage and cedar and address Great Spirit (God/Goddess) in this fashion, "You were there when I needed You. You stood above all the rest. With Your Strength, You guided me. To You I offer my love, my being and all that I am."

Face the south. Light the green candle and say, "With the lighting of this green candle in the south, I call forth the energies of the great Archangel Raphael, the energies of water, the energies of

151

healing and the awakening of my psychic abilities. Here I honor the plant kingdom and blessed herbs." Burn sage and cedar and address Great Spirit in this fashion, "You were there when I needed you. You stood above all the rest. With your strength, you guided me. To you I offer my love, my being and all that I am."

Face the west. Light the red candle and say, "With the lighting of the red candle in the west, I call forth the energies of the great Archangel Michael, the energies of earth, the energies of grounding, prosperity and prayer. This is the place of the sun trail and the carving out of paths. Here I honor my ancestors, those who have come before me." Burn sage and cedar and address Great Spirit in this fashion, "You were there when I needed you. You stood above all the rest. With your strength, you guided me. To you I offer my love, my being and all that I am."

Face the north. Light the white candle saying, "With the lighting of this white candle in the north, I call upon the Holy Angelic Host, the energies of air, the energies of wisdom, communication and gratitude. It is here that I come full circle and I offer prayers of thanks to All There Is. It is here that I honor the Great Mystery." Burn sage and cedar and address Great Spirit in this fashion, "You were there when I needed you. You stood above all the rest. With your strength, you guided me. To you I offer my love, my being and all that I am."

Meditate! Feel yellow color coming into the crown from Father Sky, flowing down, through and out the root chakra and feet, and into Mother Earth. Feel cobalt blue color coming into the root chakra from Mother Earth, flowing up, through and out the top of the head and into Father Sky. Feel the uniting of Mother-Father God in the heart. When finished, light the pink candle in the center of the altar. "With the lighting of this pink candle, I call forth the energies of the great Archangel Gabriel, the energies of love and compassion. I ask that my heart might become the center of the medicine wheel, that I might be connected to the Circle of Life, that my life might be a reflection of Your Love and Your Strength, God/Goddess, so that beauty and harmony might flow through me." Meditate again, feel the love from God/Goddess, and the love connection between the third eye and heart chakras. Feel energy in the navel.

Whether praying, or performing rituals or magic, come from a place of strength rather than being "needy". For example, say, "I choose love" rather than "I need love". Needy people pull in other needy people. Decide is another word many people stay away from as its ending is the same as pesticide, homicide, suicide, etc. Choice comes from a place of power. It allows us the freedom or the choice to change our minds. If we don't make our choices, life makes them for us, and the outcome is not as good. If choices are made from the heart, we can live with them.

152

Shamanic Use of Colors in Healing

On the first day of the Shamanic I class, I call in Spirit and hold the energy so that students may explore the Otherworlds (Spirit worlds) of the Shaman. In between journeys students receive initiations into The Order of Melchizedek (see page 60), Seven Rays (which opens the chakras in the fingertips, and the heart to the 7 directions), YOD (which opens a channel whereby information from Spirit comes into consciousness, but the initiate must have a quiet brain), Violet Flame (healing through transformation) and the first Enochian Magic Initiation (see page 161). The three Enochian Magic attunements were taught to me by one of my students, who learned them from a former cleric, and date back to the early Church. They have nothing to do with Aleistor Crowley or the black magic system brought in by Dr. John Dee and Edward Kelley, two of Queen Elisabeth I's advisors. We end the first day with Death of a Shaman, whereby students die to old fears.

It difficult to plan a day when everyone who had received the first Enochian Magic initiation is available to take a Shamanic II class and receive the next Enochian Magic initiation. It was simpler to invite those who wanted to receive the second and third initiations to simply repeat the Shamanic I class. Other Otherworld experiences were put into 2 one-day workshops. In both workshops we work on quieting the mind so that students are able to think in the three-dimensional world, journey successfully and go into The Great Silence. In the first one-day workshop, we connect with *The Goddess & Nature Spirits* for purposes of healing, ceremony, and discovery that there is more to this world and God's Creation than that which is perceived by the five senses. Using the energy of the earth and simple, natural things we create magic. As my horses are fully initiated and I have worked with them for many years in healing, students journey with them one at a time. In the *Shamanic One-Day Workshop* we develop the sixth sense of feeling, Shakti Pac, journey with Celtic power animals, heal in groups of 3, and work with Katimbo (Ama Deus), which was brought to the United States by a Brazilian, Alberto Aguas. It is found in Becoming a Shaman and Tera, My Journey Home. Since the publication of those books, Debora Kichen of Holland and her students have found that the symbols, Christ Light and Mary, work with Katimbo. To open this Shamanic system they begin by saying Ama Deus 3 times, and then Katimbo 3 times. They also found that by asking to be connected to the original Guarni Shaman and the original Guarani Shamanic system that the energy became stronger.

In the afternoon of the second day, we do the fun stuff: Power animal retrieval and, because they have received initiations into healing, soul retrieval. We also do healings and readings from the Otherworlds. In the morning of the second day, I connect the students to colors, a place in nature where the colors are found, and ascended masters. After each color, I stop drumming. I suggest a chakra where by the color comes in, and give them a few minutes to integrate the color. I begin by

153

saying, "When I begin beating the drum, you will see yourself clearly in your minds eye, standing in a beautiful place in nature. You will journey to . . . "

Cobalt blue: Journey to the cobalt blue heart of Mother Earth and to the guardian, Hava, the mother of all living. Blue is healing, cleansing and protective. Helps connect our front to our back. *(Return to your body and pull the color blue into the soles of the feet and root chakra.)*

Emerald green: Journey to the leaf of a plant or tree. Become very small and explore. Find Pan and the fairies. Green is healing and helps to facilitate new growth. *(Return to your body and pull the color blue into your front & back heart chakras.)*

Blue-green: Journey to the sea. Find Neptune and ask him to help you find lost knowledge. Kelp is a good herb to take before the initiation into the colors because it, too, is regenerative. *(Soles of the feet and into the mouth. Initiates oftentimes taste the salt of the sea.)*

Indigo: Journey to the in-between time of dusk, when it is neither night nor day. Go to the indigo color of the first evening sky. Find Saint Martin and Bast. Indigo aids intuition and second sight. *(Return to your body and pull the color indigo into the third eye and back of head.)*

Pink: Journey to the in-between time of dawn, to the eastern sky. The sun is still below the horizon. Connect to the Archangels. Pink is love, forgiveness and compassion. *(Return to your body and pull the color pink into the front and back heart chakras)*

Violet: Journey to Mount Shasta. Find an opening into the mountain, and locate the Violet Flame, Saint Germain (a master of transformation) and Quan Yen, the Chinese goddess of Mercy. Violet is expansive and transformational. *(Return to your body and pull the color violet into the Crown)*

Silver: Ride on Pegasus to the moon. Find Athena and Master Mary. Silver is psychic energy and is also the color of invisibility. *(Feel a silver cloak being placed over your shoulders, and the silver entering the psychic centers.)*

Yellow & Gold: Journey with Mercury on his chariot to the sun. Find the Archangels Metatron and Sandlephon. Yellow is masculine, spontaneous, carefree energy. Mental healing! *(Solar plexus)*

Orange: Journey to the Earth's core or to an active volcano. Find Buddha and Babaji. Orange was the first healing color on planet earth and is a color of manifestation. *(Return to your body and pull the color orange into the front and back second chakras.)*

Ruby Red: When Atlantis sank, the majority of the continent sank below the horizon and became Antarctica. Journey to Antarctica and either go into the depths of the sea or find an opening through the ice. Find the large Atlantian ruby, which Atlantian emperors used for regeneration. Red is the color of Christ Consciousness, and has elements of love and passion. Connect with Jesus, the color ruby red and Christ Consciousness. Red is grounding and the power to manifest. *(Root chakra)*

Crystalline White: Journey to a white flower - a lily, apple blossom or white rose. White represents The Oneness, which has been missing from this planet. In healing the healer focuses on crystalline white, while the healee meditates, focusing behind the eyes. *(Return to your body and pull the color white into all of the chakras.)*

Black: Represents The Hidden Mystery, which is within us and draws us to the knowledge of The One. We cannot draw upon something that draws us; we can only bring it forth. Thus, the focal point is in the pituitary gland, the master gland for the physical body. Auditory and visual messages from other dimensions are processed through the pituitary. Black is unlimited energy, and it is an absorber of misqualified energy. It is NOT negative in itself but, like so many things on this Earth, it has been misused. A Shaman keeps focusing back behind his/her eyes until s/he sees him/herself. To use black in healing, keep focusing behind the eyes without asking to see anything. Sometimes when you are doing this, you will come to what seems like a cliff. The idea is to let go.

Why Universal Initiations Work

Physically, mentally and emotionally demanding initiations that the Mayans, Egyptians and Native Americans endured prepared the initiate. Today, that is not necessary, as the knowledge of Universal initiations is being made available. However, after any initiation it is up to the individual to own the initiation. If an initiate disavows the energy or the initiation because his or her ego is inflated with unprecedented self-worth the energy does go away. Here are initiations given in Tera Mai.

Shaktipat is an energy transfer to the initiate's spine. (Nerves carry psychic energy.) Everyone does not receive the same gift or the same amount of energy. This initiation is something like sitting at a roulette table in Las Vegas. Spirit determines what each initiate gets, not the initiator!

Tera Mai™ Reiki initiations were brought in through a series of consciousness-raising experiences. Buddha did not give me healing energy, he added onto the original Alliance Reiki attunements that Takata passed on. Buddha established the Tera Mai standards so that everyone receives the same initiation and the same energy. With each of the three **Tera Mai Reiki** initiations, the crown chakra is expanded to receive more elemental earth healing energy, which comes directly from Source. If an initiator does not know the correct procedure, or has not been properly attuned, or is channeling manmade attunements, then the full energy transfer does not occur. If an initiator changes the initiation, the altered initiation comes into him/her before s/he passes it on to the initiate. This further alters the energy of the attunement until the energy of Tera Mai disappears entirely.

Each initiation into an elemental healing ray sets off a crucial 21-day cleansing cycle, beginning at the root chakra and lasting for a full 24 hours. The second day, the energy moves to the second chakra, where that chakra is cleared for 24 hours. By the seventh day, the energy is at the crown, and at the eighth day, back at the root chakra. Thus, there are three clearings of the seven major chakras. The initiate is wide open and it is an excellent opportunity to release 'stuff'. Jane Rijgersberg in Holland found that those who hold on to their 'stuff' only attract more 'stuff'. For example, one man had lost all of the fillings in his teeth. At the fifth day, the energy reached his throat and mouth and went no further because he could not look at the issues behind his dental problems. The initiation did not take!

Tera Mai Seichem initiations were given to me by Buddha and are based on the Tera Mai Reiki initiations. That is why the Tera Mai Reiki initiations are within the Tera Mai Seichem initiations. That is why the Tera Mai Seichem lineage is the same as the Tera Mai Reiki lineage. Besides the three Tera Mai Reiki attunements, Tera Mai Seichem includes the beginnings of the elemental

155

healing energies of fire, air and water. The Seichem initiations that Phoenix made up after taking Patrick Zeigler's Shamanic-type workshop contained extremely unstable fire energy. The unstable fire energy is no longer within these particular Seichem initiations. However, anyone who was attuned to these initiations or any manmade fire initiation might consider being cleared of them.

Universal healing energy is neither the master-teacher's energy, nor does it come from Japan, Tibet or the planet Jupiter. You would be amazed at the stories that have been told! Universal elemental healing energy is found within rays emanating from Source. Each initiation carries its own particular vibration. For many initiates, the first initiation into **Sakara** (fire) is memorable, as if hot liquid gold was poured into their crown. Protection of the nerves is a part of any Universal fire initiation and continues throughout the 21-day cleansing period. Manmade fire initiations, or changing Tera Mai Seichem initiations alters or eliminates this protection. If any fire energy is passed on in the initiation procedure, it is volatile and destructive. One such initiate emailed to say that he had uncomfortable fire sensations in his body, and that his wife avoided him.

The complete list of qualified instructors, who are able to pass on the Sakara, Sophi-El, and Angeliclight attunements, are on www.kathleenmilner.com under FIND INSTRUCTOR. In this way, the initiations are kept standardized, as opposed to the free-for-all attunement methods that have been the signature of most Reiki and Seichem systems. For some reason, many people feel that they have the right to change initiations, oftentimes, not telling their students.

Dousing the chakras is easy once an individual has learned how to use the pendulum to obtain a universal yes (page 96). The healee lies down on a massage table, and the healer begins by holding the pendulum in the soul star chakra, which is 12 inches above the head. When the direction of the spin of the chakra is determined, the healer douses the crown. The healer continues down the body, dousing each chakra in turn by holding the pendulum in the aura above the 3rd eye, heart, solar plexus, 2nd or creative chakra and root chakra. If only a chair is available for the healee, after the healer douses the soul star and crown chakras, the healer places his/her left hand in the aura of the 3rd eye and holds the pendulum in front of him/her. After the spin is determined, the healer moves down to the next chakra. Chakras are wheels of energy, they are part of the etheric body, and they do spin both ways. Counterclockwise spin releases spent chi or energy, clockwise brings in chi or universal energy. However, in dousing for the health of a chakra the pendulum will spin clockwise in a perfect circle if the chakra is healthy. If an individual is balanced, all of the chakras will be relatively the same size. The degree to which the pendulum is off course is an indication of what the issue might be. For example, a small circle over the 3rd eye may indicate that the individual does not dream in color. Counterclockwise may show that the chakra is not clear.

Erratic movement may reflect trauma in the body. If the pendulum swings back and forth in a straight line, the chakra is closed. Manmade attunements that initiate the soul star chakra will close that chakra, and all of the other major chakras. Unstable fire initiations will produce the same effect.

To clear unstable fire initiations, a healer who is channeling stable Universal fire energy, and who has facilitated a number of clearings begins by clearing manmade initiations (page 158). When that is completed, the healer uses the douser to clear out the unstable fire energy at each chakra, beginning at the soul star chakra above the head. Clearing fire initiations is like the clearing for Lou Gehrig's Disease (page 63). The healer holds his/her left hand in the aura of the soul star chakra, and holds a douser in the right hand. The right arm is straight down. *(Like the pain drain on pages 33 & 34.)* The douser automatically spins counterclockwise, sometimes, wildly. As the initiation is being released, the douser slows and then comes to a stop. The healer continues on with the crown, third eye, throat, heart, solar plexus, creative and root chakras. And then clears the chakra that is 12 inches below the soles of the feet.

What is considered to be a manmade initiation is discussed on page 122. Manmade initiations are often developed out of greed, ego and ignorance. The **consequence of manmade initiations** is that they block etheric channels. If they are not removed they cause corresponding problems in the physical body. When I was in Argentina I cleared several people of manmade attunements that they had received in this or other lifetimes. One opera singer was able to sing again, and a woman with liver cancer had a spontaneous remission. In Arizona a woman drove down to Paradise Valley from Sedona. She had a skin infection from 'hell', and she was unable to bend most of her fingers. Basically, she drove the car with the palms of her hands. (Sure glad I wasn't in the car!) After clearing away the manmade attunements, the skin infection left and she was able to bend all but one finger. Most people, however, experience a weight being pulled from them and afterwards, energy flowing within them or a sense of being unstuck. Stephen Buck saw that in addition, people who receive manmade attunements actually give their own energy back to the originator of the initiations. Many people who make up or change initiations are not born healers or psychics; they themselves were initiated into something that worked, like the original Alliance Reiki initiations, and then try to take that energy and use it for the initiations they make up. When initiations are changed, the energy is inexorably altered! Just because there is energy it does not necessarily follow that that energy can be used for healing! Unconscious, dark forces can produce a lot of energy. Manmade attunements may be given fancy or misleading names. Usui Reiki is not the original Reiki and the Usui Reiki attunements have nothing left in them of the original Reiki Alliance initiations. Tibetan Reiki does not come from Tibet!

Anyone channeling Universal healing energy has the ability to **remove manmade attunements**. The healer stands in front of the individual and asks, "Would you like me to remove any and all manmade attunements?" If the individual says, yes, the healer proceeds to circle his left hand counterclockwise and his right hand clockwise in the aura over the chest. The healer says, "Take a deep breath!" The healer grabs a hold of the misqualified energy. The healer says, "Exhale!" And as the individual exhales, the healer pulls the manmade attunements off, and throws them down to the central fire. (Manmade initiations will not go to the Light for transformation.) Then the healer walks around to the back and repeats the same procedure but over the back heart chakra. I have only had one person tell me that they did not want manmade attunements removed.

Removing demonic initiations given during black magic rituals is more complicated. Before reading further, please know that many people have been freed of these initiations, and that the forces of evil have lost most of their power during the Wednesday Night 8:00 pm Clearings/Healings. If you wish, skip these paragraphs and move onto **initiations into elemental rays**.

How do I know about black magic initiations? From students who have worked with people to release these initiations and attachments, from Pat Osborn's vivid past life recall, and through the clearing of such initiations that I have facilitated! Why do I include this information? So that people will think twice before getting in above their heads, and so that a healer will have some idea of what s/he is dealing with! A black magic initiation ceremony involves the death of a human being. Initiates are told that God will never forgive them for what they have done. At one point, initiates are covered with a blanket so that God will not see them. Actually, God sees these people; it is they who choose not to see God. Prior to the initiation, initiates have absolutely no idea what they are getting into. Much fear is instilled in both the victim and initiates prior to, during and after the ceremony. Those who choose not to go through with the initiation are marked and meet their demise. From what I have seen removed from black magic initiates, death would have been the preferable option. During a black magic or demonic initiation ceremony, demons anchor implants into the etheric bodies of the initiates. Implants include devices to control the initiate, and they are all difficult to remove.

The clearing process may take one hour a day for a week. The healer must call in all the Higher Beings and help s/he has in his/her arsenal, and in order for this to work. It is also helpful to light three white candles. The healee must come in consciousness and with a contrite heart. The healer begins with the clearing for unstable fire energy (page 155). The rest of the clearing is Shamanic in nature because these clearings are accomplished with the power that Universal energy gives to the 3rd eye. While watching with the 3rd eye, Angels are asked to remove any shadows and bring in cobalt blue. Look to find implants, which are secured with chains, thick cords, anchors, screws, nails, locks, wedges, plugs and seals. Alligator and crocodile power animals may be called upon to unwind and unbind devices, and Angels of Exorcism to bring angelic dissolvent and angelic grease. Symbols, such as, Shanti and Release are helpful. Angels may take the object as is, or cut it up. Before removing it, ask the Angels to surround it in cobalt blue and gold. If the implant moves very slowly to 'behind the doors', look for attachments, and work with the Angels to remove them. Working with Archangels and the Assemblage Point Clearing (page 60), or with Pademo (page 69) is helpful. When aqua blue begins to come in, breathe a sigh of relief. Keep working until everything on this particular level is cleared. Demons are typically taken to a place of no escape, which Ramona Kirk calls, behind the doors. Puss or fluid is drained (pain drain on pages 33 & 34). When all has been removed for that day, ask the Angels to keep lubricating the devices.

Levels appear to be different lifetimes where the individual received demonic initiations. Black magicians who have gone through three initiations in one lifetime may have to be cleared everyday for six months. Before the second demonic initiation, the black magician knows exactly what s/he is getting into. The second initiation includes the torture of the victim. The third initiation involves the murder of the victim. Both the second and third initiations involve pacts with the devil. Lucifer is the father of lies! God's Forgiveness is available to every one. It is best to ask to be cleared, not out of fear, but seeking repentance. However, it is possible for fear to be a first step.

Buddha told me that **initiations into elemental rays** of healing begin at the crown, that they are given one-on-one, and once an initiation is started, the initiation should be given in its entirety. For example, when I was initiated into the first degree of Reiki, my teacher initiated the heart chakra in the morning and throat in the afternoon. We were warned to be careful driving home because we were out of balance. The third eye and crown were done the following day. This used to be a very common practice in Reiki I classes. As for group initiations, it is a possibility; however, if even one member of the group holds back, everyone is held back. As computers are portals through which anything is able to come through, using the Internet to give an initiation is not a great idea. Initiations may be given over the telephone, because the telephone establishes an earthly contact.

The **time period** between initiations is up to the individual. There are people who travel long distances to receive initiations. For their convenience, the initiations are given one after the other but the Angels stack additional initiations one on top of another above their crown. Many initiates feel as if they are wearing a hat. After the 21-day cleansing, the first stacked attunement comes in through the crown regardless of whether the initiate is meditating or shopping. Just as athletes prepare for a marathon, there is too much energy to process more than one level of Tera-Mai™ at a time.

Almost 200 years ago in colonial Pennsylvania, Joseph Smith found **golden tablets** inscribed in ancient Hebrew writing. According to these tablets, Jesus performed his greatest miracle by raising his physical body from the dead. Afterwards, he did not go to heaven; rather, he walked the earth. *(The Roman Church also changed the story of Adam and Eve. Lilith was Adam's first wife.)* Messiah means the chosen one, chosen to lead us out of unconsciousness and back to Wholeness. Jesus never claimed to be the only Son; he said that we are all sons and daughters of God. It was the Roman Catholic Church who voted by one ballot to make Jesus divine (Peter de Rosa, Vicars of Christ: The Dark Side of the Papacy). According to the tablets, Jesus left some of his disciples behind in Jerusalem, Jesus and other followers sailed for the Americas and landed in Cancun, Mexico. All Native American nations have a legend about a white man with reddish-brown hair, who could walk on water, raise the dead, and perform other miracles. It is no coincidence that 2,000 years ago, White Buffalo Calf Woman appeared to the nations to teach them the ways of the spirit. Could she have been one of Jesus' disciples? The original teachings of Jesus speaks of his women disciples. Joseph Smith established the Mormon Church, and the Mormons were gifted with the power and the knowledge of the **Order of Melchizedek**. One of the Gifts of the Spirit is healing others (Corinthians 12: 8-11). After Mormons altered the teachings on the Golden Tablets to fit their own patriarchal ideas, the Golden Tablets disappeared. The energy of the Order of Melchizedek disappeared as well, just as the Catholics and Jews had lost the energy before the Mormons.

I received the initiation into the Order of Melchizedek and the initiation process from one of my students, who had been initiated while in the clergy. One of us must have been carrying the energy of the Order of Melchizedek prior to the initiation, because the Catholic clergy no longer heals. In the last century, Catholic priests did exorcisms, but it was banned maybe 30 years ago.

The Order of Melchizedek connects the initiate to the Divine Plan for Earth and the Ancient Ones. It brings about a natural flow into life, grounds healing, and is a foundation for all healing. Not everyone who is initiated into the Order of Melchizedek receives the initiation. During the initiation, most people feel prickling in their feet and lower legs, and an expansion in their head. Most initiates begin at level 22. Those who have worked with this energy in prior lifetimes are initiated into level 33. The energy progresses in double-digit numbers (Master numbers) through meditation, right action and repeated initiations. When Jesus started his ministry, he was at level 77. As with other healing energy, the initiator has to have been initiated and also be channeling enough healing energy to be able to hold ceremony. The initiator calls upon the Priest Melchizedek and higher beings, who step into the aura of the initiator. Then using the initiator's energy field as a magnet, the initiation is draw in and grounded. Those who do not receive the initiation may be those who are stubbornly caught up in trying to make things happen their way, or who are trying to live somebody else's life. Thus, they are unable to surrender themselves to God's Divine Plan.

It is not just the crown chakra that connects an individual to the higher self. During the July 29, Wednesday Night 8:00 pm Clearing, Sharon King heard a humming sound and then realized that it was coming from within her. She said that it was like she had a piano string inside of her from the bottom of her heart chakra to her naval. The humming vibration moved up and down. She knew that she could direct the movement and that it was healing her. The solar plexus is the way that Edgar Cayce did his readings, which he did in an altered state. One day, a friend of Cayce's walked into the middle of a session. While Cayce's secretary transcribed what he said, Cayce's body laid unconscious, Cayce's astral lay above him and was connected to the physical body through the solar plexus. The friend apparently disturbed the session because Cayce stopped talking and the astral body turned and looked at the friend. Edgar Cayce's solar plexus was directly connected to God's Wisdom. This connection to God through the solar plexus is how prophets were able to look far into the future, great healers healed, and the Crow Indians shape-shifted. Before September 2009, I had begun to notice my own solar plexus heating up during healings or readings that I gave. When I met Edyta Ponikiewski, perhaps, the pieces we each had fit together perfectly to bring in the Tera Mai Reiki IV, V, VI & VII and Tera Mai Seichem IV, V, VI & VII energies and initiations? I would be a mad woman, but the fact is that these initiations exponentially increase healing and psychic abilities.

Cahokia initiations are a weaving of the complete expanse of the four elemental healing rays. Initiates oftentimes feel spinning and weaving within them. Some experience a cold beyond anything they have ever felt before. This same freezing aspect works in healing to isolate, numb and heal diseased tissue. With Cahokia, deeper healing and more instantaneous miracles are possible. When spontaneous healing occurs, the healer may be dissociated from the body. The healer is the silent observer, watching another aspect of him/herself working with Angels and Holy Spirits.

The three **Enochian Magic** initiations were taught to me by way of a former member of the clergy, and date back to the Old Testament. They cleanse the physical and astral body, and open psychic and healing channels. By widening these channels, more healing and information is able to flows through. Along with the etheric channels, the first initiation opens the third eye, etheric solar plexus and the soles of the feet. The second initiation opens the wingspread from the shoulder blades, the head, the second chakra, and the spine. The third Enochian Magic initiation concentrates on the spine and is also given in the palms. If the initiate is not channeling healing energy, the effects of the initiation may be likened to being invited to a formal dinner party where the table is beautifully set with fine china, but the silver serving dishes are empty.

There are several variations of the **3rd eye initiation**, which is actually a clearing, opening and energizing technique. I use one of the Wiccan methods. If the initiator is channeling Universal Energy from Source other things may occur. In its highest form, the crown is opened, and a connection is made for the initiate between the 3rd eye and the heart.

The **Violet Flame** initiation was also given to me; it is healing through transformation. An initiator who is channeling stable Universal fire energy passes on the initiation. The initiation helps the initiate adapt to changes, and may be helpful during these times. Anyone may use the Violet Flame. The initiation strengthens the connection to the Violet Flame and enhances the initiate's ability to work with this energy and the Angels of the Violet Fire; in the same way that proper initiation into specific Egyptian symbols enhances the ability to work with that energy (pages 135 & 136).

'Initiations' that are received in dreams, visions or meditation carry insufficient energy, which is necessary to ground the initiation into the physical body. In reality, these visions may be messages from the subconscious to the conscious mind that it is time to receive Universal initiations. Such visions have also been the basis for manmade initiations. People hear what they want to hear. The only way to **bring in Universal initiations** is through a consciousness-raising experience, like a near-death experience or the hoped-for results of a Native American Vision Quest. Braves deprived themselves of food and water. At the same time, they performed strenuous physical activities until they collapsed. At this point, there were three possibilities: Death, extreme over-exhaustion or fainting, or a heightened awareness of the physical body. From this super-awareness, the individual is able to go consciously into the Otherworlds. Yet, this is not the goal! The goal is to meet a higher being, who bestows a Gift of the Spirit upon the brave, which would be demonstrated later. If the Gift of the Spirit was healing, healings must actually take place. If the gift is prophecy, then what is foretold happens. Consciousness-raising experiences also tend to change the individual's whole life and perceptions. For example, a man unexplainably survived a horrible airplane crash. All around him people were burning and dying. He thought he was dead and burning himself. Somehow, he got to the back of the plane and exited safely. The experience changed his life; his emphasis no longer concerned how much money he could accumulate by whatever means possible.

When initiations are passed down exactly the way the higher being in the consciousness-raising experience has instructed, it works! All that said, initiations are not the only way to develop psychic and healing energy. Individuals who journey through life seeking truth or healing accumulate may find healing abilities. For example, the healing energy Hannah Kroeger channeled came from a life-long journey of searching for healing methods. Some people are given spiritual gifts after a near-death experience. Other people are born with healing and/or psychic abilities.

162

Wrapping it Up!

Ever since circumstances changed my life's course from being an artist represented by a Chicago art gallery to healer / author, God has continuously answered my initial prayer, that is, to know the Truth. For example, in 1990, the Zen monk, whom Takata had initiated, flew to California to attend Beth Sanders' Reiki Mastership class. The California man who sponsored Beth's class wanted to know if what I had taught Beth Sanders and what Beth would teach him were the same as what Takata had taught the Zen monk. He appealed to the monk's desire of knowing the Truth, emphasizing that fraud should not be a part of Reiki. After Beth's Reiki Mastership class, the monk said that Beth's class was identical to what Takata had taught him with the following differences: 1) Kathleen's class format was clearer. (I am a former first grade teacher and have had practice organizing and structuring class material.) 2) Takata taught the contractions and breathing but it was never emphasized. (I stress the breathing and the breath.) 3) Takata never allowed questions. (I welcome questions.) 4) Takata did not call attention to the order in which the chakras (energy centers) were to be initiated. (Margarette Shelton taught me to begin at the crown, because the healing energy is coming from a Higher Place, not within us.)

In 1996, I facilitated a healing session for Naomi White Bear (the widow of White Bear of Frank Water's <u>Book of the Hopi</u>). Naomi told those who were watching that the techniques I was using on her were the same as those used by Hopi Medicine Men. She also noted that I did some techniques 3 times (the number of creation), and that the Hopi Medicine Men did everything 4 times because of the power of 4 (4 directions, 4 elements, 4 races, 4 kingdoms, etc.) Either way works!

In the fall of 1995, I returned to Holland. Jane Rijgersberg said that a Dutch Sai Baba devotee had just returned from India. The devotee and others asked Sai Baba about me. Sai Baba's response was, "I have meditated on this matter, and it was not me who worked with Kathleen and Marcy but another higher being."

At that moment, the spirit dressed in orange and sprouting an Afro appeared in Jane's home. I asked, "In Divine Truth, in Divine Truth, in Divine Truth, you are Sai Baba?" In a twinkling the form changed to the image of a thinner man wearing gold, who told me that he was Buddha. He advised me to tell people what Sai Baba had said, and what had just happened, which I did. However, he asked me not to tell people just yet that it was he who had shown me what was missing from the original Reiki attunements. Buddha did not want the initiations he had given me referred to as Buddha Reiki. Several years ago, psychics who had taken my classes began asking me if it was Buddha who had come to me in Los Angeles. At that time, the word, Tera Mai, had come to stand for healing. After asking if it was time to reveal the whole truth, the go ahead was given to tell people that it was indeed Buddha.

In November 2005, I went to New York City and ended up in the Metropolitan Museum of Art. Wandering into a room with large, ancient statues, I looked up at a statue of Buddha. The eyes were represented by narrow rectangular slits, but behind the slits real brown eyes looked at me. Walking around the room, the eyes followed me. Then Buddha asked what I wanted. My response was that I wanted all my prayers for Tera Mai answered. Since then, the healing potentials of Tera Mai have escalated. When I went to Japan in 2008, I did check out the eyes of an enormous Buddha statue. No brown eyes behind the carved rectangular slits!

All of the above mentioned confirmations were important, and helped me to go ahead. However, the best affirmation has and continues to be the fact that real healings and miracles happen with Tera Mai. If healings did not occur, I'd be a mad woman. Yet, even with the healings happening, some people consider me to be over the top or around the bend. Oh well!

It was Buddha, who established the Tera Mai standards, not me! I don't look for ways to complicate my life! Buddha said that the Tera Mai standards are in place to maintain the integrity and purity of the energy of Tera Mai so that remarkable healings continue. When people change Tera Mai initiations, they inexorably alter and compromise the energy of the initiation. If they block their etheric channels with manmade attunements, the energies of Tera Mai are unable to flow.

Tera Mai is a Spiritual Gift from God. Whenever one is blessed with Spiritual Gifts, a sacrifice of the personal is required. Abiding by Buddha's standards is the sacrifice asked for. That is, a properly attuned Tera Mai master must pass down Tera Mai initiations in the standardized way, and that manmade attunements are NOT to be given or received. Buddha gave me initiations that worked. He did not give me healing energy. The extra-ordinary healing and psychic abilities in my natal astrology chart are too much for one person; they are seeds of possibility, a hope that the miraculous abilities demonstrated 2000 years ago, might once again help mankind and Earth.

There have been a few other extra-ordinary experiences, which are detailed in *Part II* of the novels, Between Two Worlds and Richard III: White Boar. Also included is how information came to me through psychic channels, research and going to sites. The riding instruction that allowed Christie and myself to win two blue ribbons in dressage at the Scottsdale Arab Show are in Richard III: White Boar. How the Celts did their healing is in Between Two Worlds. How to do Shamanic journeywork is found in Becoming a Shaman: It's Never Too Late To Be Who You Might Have Been.

Additional Books, and DVDs and CDs

Bookstore may order them from New Leaf or Baker & Taylor Books. DVDs are available from New Leaf. www.amazon.com carries books, DVDs and CDs.

DVDs: ($15 each) Reviews written by Jane Kuhn, which appeared in **Body Mind Spirit** magazine, are included on the following pages. **Tera-Mai™ Reiki Mastership** DVD and **Tera-Mai™ Seichem Mastership** DVD are available to those individuals who have taken these classes.

CDs: ($10 each) are as follows:
Candle Meditation: Meditator guided into the "gap" between thought and breath through spiritual techniques taught in ancient mystery schools. Some meditators are able to hear and experience the qualities of Angeliclight. Crystal Cave is the second meditation. It begins and ends in a crystal cave. In between, it is a space journey where the mediator discovers healing and self-empowerment.

Journey to Sacred Mountain: Incorporates the 4 directions, 4 elements, and Mother-Father God into our own heart centers, which is where sacred mountain lies. Ancient Symbology is the second meditation. It works with Universal archetypal energies found within Egyptian hieroglyphs. Mediator is guided into the Sphinx and Great Pyramid. These are basically the same meditations that I use in TM Reiki Mastership classes.

Past Life Regression: Begins with a healing meditation for the physical body and concludes with a healing for the past life that was experienced. Shaman's Drumbeat is the rapid, non-varying drumbeat used in Shamanic journeywork.

Other Books by Kathleen Milner

Tera, My Journey Home: Alternative Healing ISBN 1-886903-12-3, full-color illustrations by author, 308 pages, 8.5 X 11 inches, $21.95

Between Two Worlds: The Story of Henry VIII and Anne Boleyn – and Her Celtic Heritage ISBN 1-886903-21-2, 308 pages, 6 X 9 inches, $15.95

Richard III: White Boar Who Murdered the Princes in the White Tower? ISBN 1-886903-83-2, 263 pages, 6 X 9 inches, $15.95

Becoming a Shaman: It's Never Too Late To Be Who You Might Have Been ISBN 1-886903-29-8, 274 pages, 6 X 9 inches, $15.95

Reiki & Other Rays of Touch Healing is replaced by this book

Prints by Kathleen Milner

Babaji & Eight Ascension Symbols - full-color, 8 1/2 X 11 inch print - $11

La Voix - The Voice - Reproduction of a charcoal drawing of the head of the coming Christ. Individually signed, limited edition of 500, 21 X 30 inches - $150

Reviews & Comments

"She's the real deal!" Michael Harrison, *Talkers Magazine*

Symbols in Healing: Reiki II . . . August 1994 **Body Mind Spirit** magazine by Jane Kuhn: "In this video, Kathleen Milner draws and explains the symbols most people are given in Reiki II initiation and goes beyond to explore additional symbols that work to heal. The first symbols that Satya Sai Baba gave her for the purpose of releasing karma and past life issues is shown. Each symbol presented is for a different purpose and for healing a different part of the body. She encourages us to heal the past and create a beautiful life for ourselves in the present."

Healing Hands: **Reiki I** . . . August 1994 **Body Mind Spirit** magazine by Jane Kuhn: "Kathleen Milner works from the knowledge that all healing comes from God/Goddess and that we are all capable of channeling, healing and experiencing self-healing. She demonstrates working with touch points on the body to get to the root cause behind pain and disease. Angels and spirit guides are actively engaged in the healing process. She encourages participation of the healees as they share what they are experiencing in their minds and bodies as the healing occurs. Visualization and problem-solving techniques that have been used by great scientists and inventors including Thomas Edison and Albert Einstein are discussed. <u>The video and the healing experience are quite impactful. I experienced them first-hand.</u>"

Healing Animals . . . Native Americans say that the white man has only 3 directions; that is, sunrise, high noon and sunset. "Modern man" has also lost the knowledge of the power of animal medicine. Only by opening the heart to God's creatures and healing the wounds can mankind reconnect to the gifts that the animals bring. All animals (not just monkeys), be they 4-legged or winged, have the same bones and muscles that humans have; shortened or lengthened, combined or at a different angle. This video uses horses, a dog and the author to demonstrate some comparative anatomy, corresponding healing touch points and other healing techniques, dousing and moving color through the chakras, the effects of initiations on the crown chakra, emergency technique and a short riding lesson.

Tera, My Journey Home 2nd edition
Reviewed in March 2000 issue of **Magical Blend** by Kristian Rice

Kathleen Ann Milner is the author of the only two books that are available on Seichem and the aspects of the four elemental healing rays. In her newest edition (second edition) of *Tera, My Journey Home,* she deals with self-healing as a substitute for conventional medical treatment. Her focus is on symptoms, healing energies and the channeling of healing energy, which facilitates self-healing. She has combined Reiki with Buddhist beliefs to unlock this phenomenon. She educates and shares her insights on how to tune into healing and psychic abilities. Readers will find this gem of a book to be an insightful reference to the healing forces hidden within our universe.

Tera, My Journey Home: Alternative Healing
3rd edition
Summer 2004 issue of **Leading Edge Review**

Is your tongue white? Do you wake up tired? Do you have trouble losing or putting on weight? You will discover that the above symptoms are characteristics of secondary infections, which are unresponsive to antibiotics. Milner maps out the whys, hows and practical application of a variety of alternative therapies designed to restore homeostasis for this and other health issues.

Other chapters include a Shamanic & Divination system that may be used by anyone, retraining and therapeutics for abused horses, elemental healing, moving Qi, and healing past lives. Well-written, documented, witnessed accounts and stories of healings, and thought-out examples bestow credibility and meaning.

". . She educates and shares her insights on how to tune into healing and psychic abilities. Readers will find this gem of a book to be an insightful reference to the healing forces hidden within our universe." *2ⁿᵈ edition reviewed in Volume #68 Magical Blend Magazine*

Reiki & Other Rays of Touch Healing . . . November/December 1994 **The Inner Voice** by Nancy Rajala: "Cover art is a watercolor painted by the author. . . . A comprehensive manual on healing. The author gives concrete examples in both the use of symbols and a variety of healing techniques interwoven in her own healing process (following two automobile accidents) and her subsequent work on the inner planes with Sai Baba and other teachers. The book explains techniques that can be utilized to develop psychic abilities and how to achieve deeper levels of meditation, and then ties this in with the healing process and different mysticisms.

Kathleen offers her readers a fresh, meaningful understanding of the history of Reiki combined with Jesus' teachings and related aspects of other spiritualisms. There are chapters dealing with the use of healing energy in ceremonial work and Feng Shui, the Chinese art of altering life circumstances by altering one's environment. There's also a chapter devoted to healing animals, including a story of how a horse was healed of blindness in two weeks.

Kathleen believes that all healing energy comes from the Creative, Loving Force behind this universe, and the final chapter explains the dynamics of initiation into rays of healing. <u>If you are a healer, or you're involved in a healing process, it is a source you may find yourself often referring to.</u>"

Reiki & Other Rays of Touch Healing 5ᵗʰ Edition
Fall 2004 Issue of **Leading Edge Review**

Are you interested in developing your psychic or healing abilities? Going through a healing process? Do you want to understand the phenomenon of spontaneous healing? How do alterative healing methods and techniques work? If Shamanic Journeys and meditation operate in the field of possibilities described in quantum physics, are there specific procedures that aid or hinder the creative process? If so, this still original book may have the answers you seek.

Milner's writing style over the years has evolved into engaging texts that merit savoring as opposed to a quick read. She has an uncanny ability to perceive psychically, which impacts upon her writing, affording her readers the opportunity to observe in a fresh way. Stories and examples of healings are both touching and meaningful. We look forward to her take on Richard III in her soon to be released novel, *White Boar.*

Between Two Worlds; The Story of Henry VIII and Anne Boleyn – and Her Celtic Heritage
Reviewed in **Magical Blend** by Susan Dobra (issue dated June 2004)

Whenever a story is set in a distant time and place and dramatized, as this one is, we usually call it historical fiction. But Kathleen Ann Milner's story of Henry VIII and Anne Boleyn has an interesting claim on historical accuracy. Milner believes se was Boleyn in a past life. She details the evidence for her belief in the second half of this fascinating book, and makes a convincing enough case that the story presented in the first half appears in a whole new light.

We all know the story of King Henry's penchant for lopping off the heads of his wives – Anne Boleyn was the second of six. She is often treated unkindly by historians, as a usurper to the queen's throne. Milner sees it differently. She presents Boleyn as a sympathetic figure, and also weaves in the details of her skills in Celtic magic, taught to her by her grandmother. *Between Two Worlds* is a spellbinding book that brings to life Anne Boleyn's precarious place in one of the most treacherous social structures ever to exist. It deftly humanizes the key players and artfully engages the reader with its surprising revelations. If you're interested in what it was really like in the court of Henry VIII, you should read *Between Two Worlds.*

Index